THE TRAVELS OF A T-SHIRT IN THE GLOBAL ECONOMY

AN ECONOMIST EXAMINES THE MARKETS, POWER, AND POLITICS OF WORLD TRADE

Pietra Rivoli

WILEY

John Wiley & Sons, Inc.

Published by John Wiley & Sons, Inc., Hoboken, New Jersey.
Published simultaneously in Canada.

For general information on our other products and services please contact our Customer
Care Department within the United States at (800) 762-2974, outside the United States at
(317) 572-3993 or fax (317) 572-4002.

Wiley also publishes its books in a variety of electronic formats. Some content that appears in print
may not be available in electronic books. For more information about Wiley products, visit our web
site at www.Wiley.com.

Library of Congress Cataloging-in-Publication Data:

Rivoli, Pietra.
The travels of a t-shirt in the global economy : an economist examines the markets, power and
politics of world trade / Pietra Rivoli.
p. cm.
Includes bibliographical references.
ISBN 0-471-64849-3 (cloth)
1. T-shirt industry.   2. International trade.   3. Free trade.   4. International economic relations.
I. Title.
HD9969.S6R58 2005
382'.45687115—dc22
2004025910

Printed in the United States of America
10 9 8 7 6 5 4 3 2 1

For Dennis, Annalisa, and Denny

CONTENTS

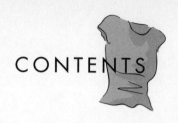

PREFACE

How Student Protests Sent a Business Professor around the World

On a cold day in February 1999 I watched a crowd of about 100 students gather on the steps of Healy Hall, the gothic centerpiece of the Georgetown University campus. The students were raucous and passionate, and campus police milled about on the edge of the crowd, just in case. As speaker after speaker took the microphone, the crowd cheered almost every sentence. The crowd had a moral certitude, a unity of purpose, and while looking at a maze of astonishing complexity, saw with perfect clarity only the black and white, the good and evil. Corporations, globalization, the International Monetary Fund (IMF), and the World Trade Organization (WTO) were the bad guys, ruthlessly crushing the dignity and livelihood of workers around the world. A short time later, more than 50,000 like-minded activists had joined the students at the annual meeting of the WTO in Seattle, and by the 2002 IMF-World Bank meeting, the crowd had swelled to 100,000. Anti-globalization activists stymied meetings of the bad guys in Quebec, Canada, and Genoa, Italy, as well. At the 2003 WTO meeting in Cancun, the activists were joined by representatives from a newly energized group of developing countries, and world trade talks broke down across a bitter rich-poor divide. Anti-globalization activists came from college campuses and labor unions, religious organizations and shuttered textile mills, human rights groups and African cotton farms. Lumped together, the activists were named the globalization "backlash."

At first, the backlash took the establishment by surprise. Even the left-leaning *Washington Post*, surveying the carnage in Seattle, seemed bewildered. "What Was *That* About?" they asked on the editorial page the next day. From the offices on the high floors of the IMF building, the crowd below was a ragtag bunch of well-intentioned but ill-informed obstructionists, squarely blocking the only path to prosperity. According to conventional economic wisdom, globalization and free trade offered salvation rather than destruction to the world's poor and oppressed. How could the backlash be so confused? By 2004, meaningful progress in world trade talks had been stalled for nearly five years.

At about the same time, however, the madness generated by the ill-informed and economically illiterate noisemakers began to quiet. "Phew," the business establishment seemed to say, "Glad that's over with." But a closer look reveals that nothing was really over with, and that, in fact, the reverse had happened. While some of the craziest slogans ("Capitalism is Death") had faded away, the backlash was not gone but had gone mainstream. Most of the issues that had been on the placards and in the chants were now being discussed in the halls of Congress, in global trade negotiations, and in the 2004 election debates: free trade versus fair trade, outsourcing, labor and environmental standards, trade agreements, and more broadly, rich countries versus poor countries and rich Americans versus poor Americans. While for much of American history, trade issues were of relatively little interest to the public, today these issues are central to political, economic, and moral discourse.

Back at Georgetown in 1999, I watched a young woman seize the microphone. "Who made your T-shirt?" she asked the crowd. "Was it a child in Vietnam, chained to a sewing machine without food or water? Or a young girl from India earning 18 cents per hour and allowed to visit the bathroom only twice per day? Did you know that she lives 12 to a room? That she shares her bed and has only gruel to eat? That she is forced to work 90 hours each week, without overtime pay? Did you know that she has no right to speak out, no right to unionize? That she lives not only in poverty, but also in filth and sickness, all in the name of Nike's profits?"

I did not know all this. And I wondered about the young woman at the microphone: How did she know?

During the next several years, I traveled the world to investigate. I not only found out who made my T-shirt, but I also followed its life over thousands of miles and across three continents. This book is the story of the people, politics, and markets that created my cotton T-shirt. It is a story about globalization.

It is fair to ask what the biography of a simple product can contribute to current debates over global trade. In general, stories are out of style today in business and economic research. Little of consequence can be learned from stories, the argument goes, because they offer us only "anecdotal" data. According to today's accepted methodological wisdom, what really happened at a place and time—the story, the anecdote—might be entertaining but it is intellectually empty: Stories do not allow us to formulate a theory, to test a theory, or to generalize. As a result, researchers today have more data, faster computers, and better statistical methods, but fewer and fewer personal observations.

The story, of course, has a more esteemed role in other disciplines. Richard Rhodes, in his Pulitzer Prize-winning book, *The Making of the Atomic Bomb*, peels back, layer by layer, the invention of the atomic bomb. In the process, he illuminates the intellectual progress of a community of geniuses at work. Laurel Ulrich, in *A Midwife's Tale*, uses the diary of a seemingly unremarkable woman to construct a story of a life in the woods of Maine 200 years ago, revealing the economy, social structure, and physical life of a place in a manner not otherwise possible. And in *Enterprising Elites*, historian Robert Dalzell gives us the stories of America's first industrialists and the world they built in nineteenth-century New England, thereby revealing the process of industrialization. So, the story, whether of a person or a thing, cannot only reveal a life but illuminate the bigger world that formed the life. This is my objective for the story of my T-shirt.

"Does the world really need another book about globalization?" Jagdish Bhagwati asks in the introduction to his recent book on the topic.[1] Well, certainly the world does not need another tome either defending or criticizing globalization and trade as abstract concepts, as the cases on both sides have been made eloquently and well.[2] I have written this book not to defend a position but, first of all, to tell a story. And though economic and political lessons emerge from my T-shirt's story, the lessons are not the starting point. In other words, I tell the T-shirt's story not to convey morals but to discover them, and simply to see where the story leads.

Of course I brought to this story my own biases and I no doubt harbor them still. As a classically trained financial and international economist, I share with my colleagues the somewhat off-putting tendency to believe that if everyone understood what we understood—if they "got it"—they wouldn't argue so much. More than 200 years after Adam Smith advanced his case for free trade in *The Wealth of Nations*, we are still trying to make sure that our students, fellow citizens, and colleagues in the English department "get it" because we are sure that once they understand, everyone will agree with us. When I happened by the protests at Georgetown and listened to the T-shirt diatribe, my first thought was that the young woman, however well-intentioned and impassioned, just didn't "get it." She needed a book—maybe this book—to explain things. But after following my T-shirt around the world, my biases aren't quite so biased anymore.

Trade and globalization debates have long been polarized on the virtues versus evils of global markets. Economists in general argue that international market competition creates a tide of wealth that (at least eventually) will lift all boats, while critics worry about the effects of unrelenting market forces, especially upon workers. Free trade in apparel, in particular, critics worry, leads only to a downward spiral of wages and working conditions that ends somewhere in the depths of a Charles Dickens novel.

My T-shirt's life suggests, however, that the importance of markets might be overstated by both globalizers and critics. While my T-shirt's life story is certainly influenced by competitive economic markets, the key events in the T-shirt's life are less about competitive markets than they are about politics, history, and creative maneuvers to avoid markets. Even those who laud the effects of highly competitive markets are loathe to experience them personally, so the winners at various stages of my T-shirt's life are adept not so much at competing in markets but at avoiding them. The effects of these avoidance maneuvers can have more damaging effects on the poor and powerless than market competition itself. In short, my T-shirt's story has turned out to be less about markets than I would have predicted, and more about the historical and political webs of intrigue in which the markets are embedded. In peeling the onion of my T-shirt's life—especially as it relates to current debates—I kept being led back to history and politics.

Many once-poor countries (e.g., Taiwan or Japan) have become rich due to globalization, and many still poor countries (e.g., China or India) are nowhere near as poor as they once were. The poorest countries in the world, however, largely in Africa, have yet to benefit from globalization in any sustained way, and even in rapidly growing countries such as China many are left behind. My T-shirt's life is a story of the wealth-enhancing possibilities of globalization in some settings but a "can't win" trap in others, a trap where power imbalances and poorly functioning politics and markets seem to doom the economic future.

My T-shirt's story also reveals that the opposing sides of the globalization debate are co-conspirators, however unwitting, in improving the human condition. Economist Karl Polanyi observed, in an earlier version of today's debate, his famed "double movement," in which market forces on the one hand were met by demands for social protection on the other.[3] Polanyi was pessimistic about the prospects for reconciling the opposite sides. Later writers—perhaps most artfully Peter Dougherty—have argued instead that "Economics is part of a larger civilizing project," in which markets depend for their very survival on various forms of the backlash.[4] My T-shirt's story comes down on Dougherty's side: Neither the market nor the backlash alone presents much hope for the poor the world over who farm cotton or stitch T-shirts together, but in the unintentional conspiracy between the two sides there is promise. The trade skeptics need the corporations, the corporations need the skeptics, but most of all, the Asian sweatshop worker and African cotton farmer need them both.

I could not have predicted when I began this book that my T-shirt's story would be relevant for some of the most significant economic events of our time. The 40-year-old regime governing textile and apparel trade—first put in place following a John F. Kennedy election promise—would expire as this book was finished to leave a brave new world of many losers, a few big winners, and an uncertain future. At about the same time, in a stunning David-Goliath maneuver, the poorest countries of the world held global trade talks hostage over U.S. agricultural subsidies, particularly those on cotton, the main (or indeed really only) ingredient in my T-shirt. And in the days following September 11—below the public's radar screen—T-shirt sales and military support were bundled up in a bizarre negotiation between the Bush administration and Pakistan, a negotiation that revealed the surprising power still held by the U.S. textile industry.

China, where my T-shirt spent much of its life, assumed center stage as the world's second largest economy. As I wrote this book, China's strange capitalist police state swelled up like a balloon and flooded the United States with low-cost imports, forcing virtually every American company of any size to devise a "China strategy," meet the "China price," or manage the "China threat," while both Democrats and Republicans struggled to explain their position on the "China issue."

Finally, since I first encountered the protests at Georgetown University, students peacefully occupied the university president's office and refused to budge until the university and its apparel suppliers agreed to address the alleged "sweatshop" conditions under which Georgetown T-shirts and other licensed apparel were produced. Similar protests went on at dozens of universities across the country. During the past five years, the students and their compatriots around the globe have made remarkable progress in changing the rules in the race to the bottom, and in changing the way some of the world's largest companies do business. Thanks to the backlash, the life story of a T-shirt made today is a different and better story than that of a T-shirt made just a few years ago. I thought, when I started this book, that I would in the end have a story that would help the students to see things my way, to understand the virtues of markets in improving the lives of the poor. I do have such a story, I hope, but it is not the whole story. To the students, I also say, I (now) see where you're coming from.

I also now know the characters in my T-shirt's life story: Their names are Nelson, Ruth, Gary, Yuan Zhi, Ed, Gulam, Qin, Mohammed, Yong Fang, Auggie, and Patrick. They are great people, every one, and I am honored to have met them. I wish that everyone who has an interest in globalization and international trade could meet them. This book is the next best thing.

PROLOGUE

Finding My T-Shirt's Likely Birthplace

Walgreen's Drugstore
Ft. Lauderdale, Florida
Spring 1999

The civic leaders of Fort Lauderdale have laid new paint over much of the city in recent years. The stoned surfers and rowdy college students are less visible now, pushed away from the beach with its new cafes and high-end hotels. The college students of the 1970s are parents now, and they have money to spend. The city bends toward the money like a palm tree, polishing, sweeping, painting. Yet, like tourist destinations everywhere, a scratch on the shiny paint reveals a bit of the tawdry underneath. Though the city fathers might prefer art galleries, it is T-shirt shops that line the beach because that is what people want to buy.

A large bin of T-shirts sat near the exit of a Walgreen's drugstore near the beach. The bin was positioned to catch shoppers on the way out, and it worked: Nearly everyone who walked by pawed through the bin, if only for a minute. The bin was full of hundreds of T-shirts, each priced at $5.99, or 2 for $10. All were printed with some Floridian theme, seashells, bright fish, or palm trees.

I reached in and pulled out a shirt. It was white and printed with a flamboyantly colored parrot, with the word "Florida" scripted beneath. I went to the checkout line, and then stepped out into the sun and looked at the shirt through the wrapper.

"You're it," I thought.

Back in Washington, I took the T-shirt out of the poly bag and looked at the label. "Sherry Manufacturing," it said, and underneath, "Made in

China." I typed "Sherry Manufacturing" into my search engine. A few minutes later I had reached Gary Sandler, Sherry's president, on the telephone. "Sure," he said. "Come on down. We don't get many visitors from Washington."

Sherry Manufacturing Company
Miami, Florida
Summer 1999

Sherry Manufacturing Company is located in Miami's original industrial district, a bleak landscape of factories and warehouses not far from the airport. Gary Sandler is Florida-tanned and friendly, with a healthy skepticism about college professors. He is completely without pretension, but clearly proud of what he and his family have built. On the wall of his office are pictures of his children and his sales force.

Gary's father, Quentin, formed Sherry Fashions just after World War II, naming the company for his only daughter. Quentin started out as an independent wholesaler, going shop to shop along the beachfront, selling souvenir trinkets to the store owners. He would travel to New York to buy and return to Miami to peddle his wares during the tourist season. Then, as now, people liked to shop while on vacation, especially for souvenirs. Quentin found that trinkets with a tropical theme were especially popular with the visiting Northerners.

In the 1950s, options for "wearable" souvenirs were limited, and vacationers typically brought home trinkets rather than clothing. However, Quentin found that one of his most popular items was a souvenir scarf, a small cotton square printed with a Floridian motif. The scarf, like much of the tourist kitsch of the era, was made and printed in Japan. Before long, Sherry found itself in a classic wholesaler's predicament, with margins being squeezed between the suppliers and the retailers. In 1955, Quentin Sandler dispensed with his New York suppliers and opened his own cloth printing shop in Miami. Sherry Fashions became Sherry Manufacturing Company.

In the mid-1970s Gary Sandler quit college to join his father's company, and in 1986 was named president. Today, Sherry is one of the largest screen printers of T-shirts in the United States. It remains a business focused on the tourist trade. In Key West, Florida, and Mount Denali, Alaska, and many tourist spots in between, as well as in Europe, Sherry has T-shirts for sale. Sherry's artists design motifs for each tourist market, and the designs and locations are printed or embroidered on shirts in the Miami plant.

Sherry's inventory of blank T-shirts (as well as beach towels and baseball caps) fills a two-story warehouse. The blank goods go from the warehouse to the printing machine, which resembles a Ferris wheel lying on its side. Workers slide each shirt on the flat end of a wheel spoke, which then turns and stops briefly up to 14 times. Each time the wheel stops, a different color is shot through the tiny holes in the screen. When the shirt returns to the starting point on the wheel, a worker slides it off and passes it to another worker, who lays it flat on a drying conveyor belt. The next worker picks it up from the end of the drying belt and lays it flat on a second conveyor belt, which swallows it into a tunnel and shoots it out, neatly folded, from the other end. It's no longer underwear, it's a souvenir.

A walk through Sherry's printing facility is a travelogue. The shirts piled up in rolling carts tempt with scenes of beaches, mountains, skyscrapers, and glaciers. Each shirt will allow someone to take a bit of a place, and to wear it home. A walk through the warehouse adjoining the plant is a travelogue, too, but for the more adventurous. Where the shirts are headed you need sun lotion, but where they come from you need shots.

Gary Sandler buys T-shirts from Mexico, El Salvador, the Dominican Republic, Costa Rica, Bangladesh, Honduras, China, Pakistan, Botswana, India, Hong Kong, and South Korea.

My T-shirt is from China. It likely departed Shanghai in late 1998 and arrived in the port at Miami a few weeks later. All told, the shirt cost Sandler $1.42, including 24 cents in tariffs. The shirt was 1 of about 25 million cotton T-shirts allowed into the United States from China under the U.S. apparel import quota system in 1998. The shirt's journey, we shall see, is a testament to the power of economic forces to overcome obstacles. To arrive here, the shirt fought off the U.S. textile and apparel industries, Southern Congressmen, and a system of tariffs and quotas so labyrinthine that it is hard to imagine why anyone would take the trouble. But Gary Sandler takes the trouble. Despite the best efforts of Congress, industry leaders, and lobbyists; despite the quotas, and tariffs, and Chinese bureaucracy, China has the best shirts at the best price.

But China is a big place. Where, exactly, I asked Sandler, did the shirt come from? Sandler ruffled through his Rolodex and pulled out a card. "Mr. Xu Zhao Min," the card read, "Shanghai Knitwear."

"Call him up," said Sandler. "He's a great guy. He'll tell you everything."

"Xu Zhao Min," I tried to read aloud.

"No, no," said Sandler. "Patrick. His American customers call him Patrick."

Patrick Xu and his wife accepted my invitation to visit Washington during their next trip to the United States.

Georgetown University
Washington, D.C.
Summer 1999

Patrick Xu straddles East and West, rich and poor, communism and capitalism with almost cat-like balance. He travels to the United States two or more times each year, visiting old customers and scouring for new ones, watching the Western fashions and bringing ideas back to the factories. While Patrick is happy to sell white T-shirts to established customers like Gary Sandler, he does not see much of a future in white T-shirts for Shanghai Knitwear. There is too much competition from lower-wage countries and other parts of China, and soon, he believes, his hard-won customers will be sourcing T-shirts far from Shanghai. Patrick is trying to move up the value chain into fancier goods such as sweaters.

"Come to China," Patrick said. "I'll show you everything."

I wanted the whole story, I explained. Could he show me where the shirts were sewn? No problem. What about where the fabric is knit? Yes, of course. I pushed my luck: What about the yarn the fabric is made of? The spinning factory? Yes, he could arrange it. But this wasn't quite the beginning. What about the cotton? To tell the life story of my shirt, I had to start at its birthplace. I knew that China was one of the world's largest cotton producers. Could I go to the farm and see how the cotton is produced?

Patrick looked at the T-shirt. "Well, that might be difficult. I think the cotton is grown very far from Shanghai. Probably in Teksa."

"Teksa? Where is Teksa? How far away?" I asked. There was a globe on my desk and I spun it around to China. Could he show me Teksa on the globe?

Patrick laughed. He took the globe and spun it back around the other way. "Here, I think it is grown here." I followed his finger.

Patrick was pointing at Texas.

PART I

KING COTTON

HOW AMERICA HAS DOMINATED
THE GLOBAL COTTON INDUSTRY
FOR 200 YEARS

Nelson and Ruth Reinsch at Their Farm in Smyer, Texas. (Photo courtesy of Dwade Reinsch and Colleen Phillips.)

REINSCH COTTON FARM, SMYER, TEXAS

U nlike French wine or Florida oranges, Texas cotton doesn't brag about where it was born and raised. Desolate, hardscrabble, and alternately baked to death, shredded by windstorms, or pummeled by rocky hail, West Texas will never have much of a tourist trade. Flying into the cotton country near Lubbock on a clear fall day, I had a view of almost lunar nothingness: no hills, no trees. No grass, no cars. No people, no houses. The huge and flat emptiness is jarring and intimidating at first, since one can't help but feel small and exposed in this landscape. Though I have traveled to dozens of countries and to almost every continent, Lubbock, Texas, was one of the most foreign places I had ever been. There is a very good chance that my T-shirt—and yours—was born near Lubbock, the self-proclaimed "cottonest city" in the world.

The people of this forbidding yet harshly beautiful place are well suited to the landscape. Indeed, they are the product of it. The land has humbled them with its unpredictable temperament and its sheer scale, yet made them proud of each small success in taming and coaxing from it the fluffy white gold of the cotton plant. According to local legend, when God created West Texas, He made a mistake and forgot to fashion hills, valleys, rivers, and trees. Looking at His desolate and barren mistake, He considered starting over, but then had another idea. "I know what I'll do," He said. "I'll just create some people who like it this way."

And so He did.

Nelson Reinsch, cotton farmer, stands tall and handsome at the age of 81. He laughs easily but speaks carefully. He calls his wife, Ruth, "Sugar" and every other woman "ma'am." Nelson is a gentleman in the older sense of the word, well mannered and considerate from the inside. In his 81 years, Nelson has missed four cotton harvests, all of them during his Navy service in World War II. Nelson and Ruth are happy enough (or perhaps just polite enough) to talk about the past if that is what their guests want to hear about. But they wallow not one bit in "the good old days," and their minds are opening rather than closing as they approach the ends of their lives. The world is still very interesting to Nelson and Ruth Reinsch.

Producing cotton is no longer the backbreaking physical process it once was, but every year Nelson and Ruth still battle both the whims of nature and the vagaries of markets. Each summer they take on the wind, sand, heat, and insects; and each fall, at harvest, they take on the world markets, in which they compete with cotton farmers from over 70 countries. The Reinsches' 1,000 acres can produce about 500,000 pounds of cotton lint if fully planted, enough for about 1.3 million T-shirts. That Nelson is ending his life in the same occupation in which he began tells us much about him. It also tells us much about the U.S. cotton industry.

History shows that almost all dominance in world markets is temporary and that even the most impressive stories of national industrial victories typically end with sobering postscripts of shifting comparative advantage. Within the baby boomers' lifetime, preeminence in consumer electronics has shifted from the United States to Japan to Hong Kong to Taiwan to China. Apparel production has moved from the American South to Southeast Asia to the Caribbean and back to Asia. Advantages in steel have moved from the U.S. Rust Belt to Japan to South Korea. But for over 200 years, the United States has been the undisputed leader in the global cotton industry in almost any way that can be measured, and other countries, particularly poor ones, have little chance of catching up. The United States has historically occupied first place in cotton production (though recently second to China), cotton exports (though occasionally second to Uzbekistan), farm size, and yields per acre.[1]

On the surface, cotton is an unlikely candidate for economic success in the United States. Typically, American industries compete with those in "like" countries. American firms compete with Japanese automakers, German chemical companies, and Swiss pharmaceuticals. But for climatic reasons, few advanced industrial economies produce cotton. Instead, American cotton growers compete with producers in some of the world's poorest and least developed regions. If our labor costs—among the world's highest—have toppled or relocated industries as diverse as apparel, steel, and shipbuilding, how has U.S. cotton maintained its world dominance?

More broadly, how can an industry so basic and "downstream" as cotton production continue to thrive in an advanced, service-oriented economy? There would appear to be little sustainable advantage in an industry such as cotton. Models of business strategy would predict that dominance in such an industry can only be fleeting and stressful: The lack of product differentiation, the intense price competition, and the low barriers to entry make it scarcely worth the trouble. Business professor and strategist Michael Porter notes that

> advantages [are] often exceedingly fleeting [in these industries]. . . . Those industries in which labor costs or natural resources are important to competitive advantage also often have . . . only low average returns on investment. Since such industries are accessible to many nations . . . because of relatively low barriers to entry, they are prone to too many competitors. . . . Rapidly shifting factor advantage continually attracts new entrants who bid down profits and hold down wages. . . . Developing nations are frequently trapped in such industries. . . . Nations in this situation will face a continual threat of losing competitive position. . . .[2]

While this description of life on the economic precipice rings true for poor cotton farmers in South Asia and Africa, it does not describe the cotton industry around Lubbock. Year in and year out, American cotton farmers, as a group, are on top. What explains American cotton's success as an export commodity in a country that has experienced a merchandise trade deficit in each year since 1975? And what explains U.S. cotton producers' ability to export such a basic commodity to much poorer countries? Why here? Why was my Chinese T-shirt born in Texas?

Oxfam, the British charity, believes it has the answer. According to *Cultivating Poverty*, a scathing report released in 2002, the comparative advantage enjoyed by U.S. cotton farmers lies in their skill at collecting government subsidies. In the fall of 2003, bolstered by Oxfam's research and resources, the poorest countries in the world cried foul against the richest at the opening of the World Trade Organization (WTO) trade talks in Cancun, Mexico. Tiny, desperately poor countries such as Benin and Burkina Faso stood firm and stared down U.S. negotiators: They charged that U.S. cotton subsidies were blocking their route out of poverty, and that it was impossible to compete with Uncle Sam's largesse to U.S. cotton farmers. In a sound bite that carried considerable punch, the poor countries pointed out that U.S. cotton subsidies exceeded the entire GDP of a number of poor cotton-producing countries in Africa. If the United States was going to champion the case for free trade, Americans needed to walk the walk as well as talk the talk. The stare-down continued for several tortured days until the talks collapsed and both rich and poor gave up and went home.[3] The point, however, had been made, and several months later the WTO ruled that U.S. cotton subsidies violated global trade rules and unfairly tilted the playing field toward American producers. In the summer of 2004, with the huge subsidies in the public spotlight, U.S. trade negotiators agreed not only to put cotton subsidies on the table, but to tackle the cotton issue "ambitiously, expeditiously and specifically" during the Doha Round of trade negotiations.[4]

There is no doubt that the subsidies are big, and little doubt that they are unfair to poor countries. But anyone who believes that America's competitive power in the global cotton industry reduces to government subsidies should spend some time near Lubbock, Texas. While the subsidies are, of course, a boon to U.S. producers, the success of cotton growers such as Nelson Reinsch is a much more complex phenomenon.

First, the dominance of the U.S. industry predates by well over a century the implementation of national farm subsidies. As Chapter 2 describes, the U.S. cotton industry passed its competitors over 200 years ago. Therefore, while subsidies may account for some cost advantages today, they cannot be the longer-run explanation for the industry's dominance.

Second, the subsidy explanation for America's dominance gives short shrift to the astounding entrepreneurial creativity of the American growers. In many ways, the American cotton farmers are MBA case studies in adaptability and entrepreneurship. American cotton growers have adapted their production methods, their marketing, their technology, and their organizational forms to respond to shifts in supply and demand in the global marketplace. The shifts in demand and supply that reveal cotton's story as a business were sometimes gentle and predictable trends of ascendancy and decline, and the farmers could see what was ahead; but times also came when changes were sudden and cataclysmic, reshaping the world in front of them. In each case, the cotton farmers responded with a creative maneuver—a new idea, a new technology, a new policy. Whether it occurs by design or necessity, the open-mindedness and forward orientation that struck me within minutes of meeting Nelson and Ruth Reinsch is a regional trait as well as a comparative advantage, because farmers in poor countries who are tradition bound—for whatever reason—rather than innovation bound, lose. The American growers' remarkable adaptability and entrepreneurial resourcefulness have their roots in character but also in the institutions and governance mechanisms taken for granted in the United States, which are lacking in many poor countries. In the United States, the farms work, the market works, the government works, the science works, and the universities work; and all of these elements work together in a type of virtuous circle that is decades away for the poorest countries in the world. In much of West Africa, with or without U.S. cotton subsidies, these institutional foundations for global competitiveness are weak. In addition, the institutions that are in place in many poor countries serve to funnel resources and power away from farmers rather than toward them.

While subsidies alone cannot explain U.S. dominance in this industry, the subsidies are but one example of a much broader phenomenon that has contributed to the U.S. farmers' seemingly immutable spot at the top. For 200 years, U.S. farmers have had in place an evolving set of public policies that allow them to mitigate the important competitive risks inherent in the business of growing and selling cotton. They have figured out how to compete in markets but also—and at least as important—how to avoid competing when the risks are too high. Put another way, U.S. cotton growers have since the beginning been embedded in a set of institutions that insulate them from the full strength of a variety of market forces.

When we consider the risks that a cotton boll faces on its way to becoming a T-shirt, it is a wonder we have clothes at all. The cotton can't be too hot, and it can't be too cold; it is susceptible to both too much water and too little; and it is too delicate to survive hail or even heavy wind and rain. Cotton plants are easily overtaken by weeds; there are dozens of varieties of pests that can take out a cotton crop; and crop prices are highly volatile. There is labor market risk as well, as workers must be available at a reasonable price when the cotton is ready to be picked. Every cotton farmer in the world faces these risks. And of course there are the normal business risks associated with falling prices and rising costs, foreign competition, and access to financing. As explained in Chapters 2 and 3, however, American cotton's story, and its success, have been about excellence in avoiding—or at least cushioning the impact of—these risks.

Today's proponents of markets and globalization can find much to like in the story of American cotton's victory, but the backlash can find support as well. For every noble victory in this industry, and for every case in which the Americans were smarter, faster, and better than the competition, there is a shameful victory as well. The most shameful of all was the cotton slave plantation, where the U.S. cotton industry was born, and where the Americans first trounced their foreign competition. Less shameful but still embarrassing are today's high subsidies. But to understand American cotton's long-run dominance, we should begin by agreeing to neither demonize nor romanticize American cotton farmers. During the 200 years in which the United States has dominated this industry, sometimes it was possible to win on the high road and sometimes it wasn't. My T-shirt's parentage in the fields of the American South has many things to be proud of, but some things to hide.

THE HISTORY OF AMERICAN COTTON

WINNING BY DUCKING THE LABOR MARKETS

Demand Pull: The Humble Class's Taste for "Gaiety of Dress"

The world's first factories were cotton textile factories, and it was entrepreneurial developments in production of cotton cloth and yarns that launched the Industrial Revolution in eighteenth-century Britain. A rapid-fire series of technical improvements in both the spinning and weaving of yarns made large-scale production possible and opened the way for the manufacture of textiles to move from the home and workshop into the factory. The exploding productivity of the English cotton industry dramatically lowered prices, so that for the first time, the poor could dress attractively. A consumer class was born. Edward Baines, a nineteenth-century historian, described the consumer pull of cheap cotton clothing:

> It is impossible to estimate the advantage to the bulk of the people, from the wonderful cheapness of cotton goods . . . the humble classes now have the means of as great neatness, and even gaiety of dress, as the middle and upper classes of the last age. A country-wake in the nineteenth century may display as much finery as a drawing room of the eighteenth.[1]

As technological innovation increased productivity, productivity, in turn, lowered prices. The lower prices spurred demand for textiles, which then left England starving for raw cotton. Once the British masses had a taste of "gaiety of dress," there was no turning back. The cheap cotton clothing available to the masses was the historical equivalent of today's $5.99 cotton T-shirt. Then, as now, consumer demand was behind the push and pull of world trade flows.

Of course, British demand for cotton does not fully explain American success in meeting that demand. Indeed, at the takeoff of the Industrial Revolution, the United States did not seem like a promising source of cotton at all. As Figure 2.1 shows, in 1791, the U.S. share of world cotton production was almost too small to be counted. The American South produced barely 2 million pounds of cotton in 1791, a minuscule amount compared to the output of producers elsewhere. It is doubtful that producers in Asia (primarily India), with production of nearly 400 million pounds, perceived much of a competitive threat from the American South.

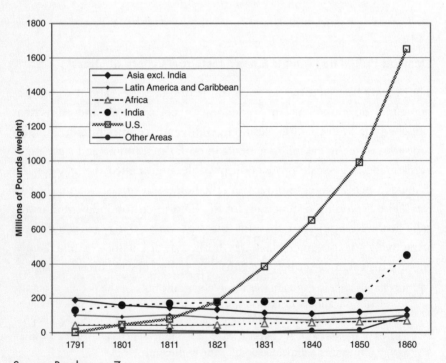

Source: Bruchey, p. 7.

FIGURE 2.1   *World Cotton Production by Region and Time*

The boom in American cotton production that happened next was astounding. In 10 years, U.S. production increased by 25 times. And by the outbreak of the Civil War, the South was producing more than a billion pounds per year, approximately two-thirds of the total world production. Cotton production was overwhelmingly export oriented. From 1815 to 1860, cotton constituted approximately half of the value of *all* U.S. exports, and more than 70 percent of all American cotton produced was exported, primarily to England.[2] In a relatively short period of time, American cotton farmers had trounced their foreign competition.

The victory did not come cheaply. First, the single-minded concentration of capital, labor, and entrepreneurial energies into cotton production left the American South far behind the North in broader industrial development, a gap that has narrowed decisively only during the past 25 years. Second, early American cotton production took place mostly, though not entirely, on slave plantations, and there is little doubt this system of human captivity contributed significantly to the "productivity" of the American cotton grower. And while plantation slavery was undoubtedly the most horrible of the many labor systems in American economic history, as we will see, slavery is not the only instance in which a horrific—or at least objectionable—labor system played a role in the production and trade of cotton clothing such as T-shirts. On this issue, today's trade skeptics have a point.

Slavery was the first significant American "public policy" that served to protect cotton growers from the perils of operating in a competitive market. For a number of reasons, relying on a competitive labor market—rather than on captive slaves—was a risk that growers were loath to assume, and it was also a risk that would have likely precluded the explosive growth in American cotton production.

Growing cotton in the slave South was mind-numbing, backbreaking physical labor. Beginning in mid-spring, the ground would be prepared for planting with hoes, and later, mule-drawn plows. Following planting, the battle of the weeds began. The tender cotton plant was not able to hold its own against the rapacious weeds, and so required the constant help of workers who guarded the young plants against their encroachment. Indeed, numerous journals and diaries reveal that keeping cotton "out of the grass" was perhaps the planters' biggest worry and the most physically demanding work.[3] Weeding and thinning continued, although at a slower pace, almost until the four-month harvest season began in late summer. On a large plantation, one worker could prepare, plant, weed, and harvest about 18 acres of cotton.

Critically, the timing and intensity of each of these tasks was dictated by the weather, so the growers were unable to predict their labor requirements beyond the weather forecast. During a very rainy spring, each field had to be weeded up to six times, which doubled the typical labor requirement during that season. The harvesting of cotton was perhaps the most unpredictable task. (Even today, Nelson and Ruth Reinsch cannot plan for Thanksgiving travel.) Cotton cannot be picked either in the rain or while still wet, and it typically takes 3 to 4 days to dry. A few days of rain, then, might leave pickers idle for a week. But once the cotton was open and dry, it needed to be picked as soon as possible, so that the tender fluffs did not blow away or fall to the ground. Cotton that had been rained on became spotted and weaker, so often planters tried to hurriedly get the cotton picked as rain clouds approached.

These exacting and unpredictable labor requirements were impossible to meet while relying on the market. As Gavin Wright has argued, farm labor markets in the American South barely functioned, if in fact they existed at all.[4] Farms were geographically dispersed, which made communication and transportation difficult. The very low population density, combined with uneven labor requirements throughout the year, as well as poor information flows, meant that a farmer who relied on the "market" to meet his labor needs might not be able to harvest his crop at any price. The problem of farm labor, then, was not limited to a shortage of workers or high wages. Rather, the problem was the absence of a well-functioning market where farm workers and growers could transact with any degree of effectiveness. Relying on the market to supply the right number of workers at the right time was a business gamble that cotton farmers preferred to avoid.

Even with a functioning labor market, however, it is doubtful that workers would have been attracted to opportunities as wage hands in cotton production. As a very early student of the cotton economy noted, "the difficulty or impossibility of inducing the whites to become wage earners

while they were in contact with cheap land is undoubtedly the chief reason why the cotton industry in the country was developed by slave instead
of by free labor."[5] Of course, the same could be said of blacks. In the
absence of slavery, blacks as well as whites would prefer a farm of their
own to work as wage hands. And, in the early years of the American South,
land was available to all comers.

In summary, free labor—black or white—was unlikely to be attracted
to wage work on Southern cotton farms, because of both the poor functioning of labor markets and the superior alternative available to these
workers—the family farm. Slavery, then, allowed cotton farmers both a
way to avoid the risks associated with transacting in the labor market and
a way around the family labor constraint. Slavery also enabled the growers
to cultivate greater acreage. The greater acreage, in turn, allowed cotton
production to increase. The average farm size in the cotton South was
nearly twice that of the free states of the North, and there was a strong
positive relationship between farm size and relative cotton production, at
least for farms below 600 acres.[6] Put simply, large farms were slave plantations, not family farms, and it was the slave plantations that produced most
of the world's cotton by 1860.

Keep the Fiddler Well-Supplied with Catgut

Slave ownership alone did not guarantee successful large-scale cotton production. Effective systems of control, monitoring, and incentives were also
required. These systems accounted for both the economic success of the
slave plantation for the planters, and for the inhumanity of slavery. The
profitability of the plantation depended not on slave ownership per se, but
on the planter's ability to induce his slaves to perform repetitive and
exhaustive physical labor at unpredictable times. Large volumes of cotton
production required that the planter devise a "factory" system wherein a
large number of workers performed repetitive tasks, and the factory "shift"
could be activated at the whim of the weather. The planters were able to
induce this repetitive labor on demand with a complex blend of positive
incentives (e.g., prizes), negative incentives (e.g., whipping), and paternalism.[7] A common theme in slaveholder journals is that the planters had

a moral duty to protect those "in dependent status," and that slaves who were well-cared-for and happy would be more productive. A large plantation owner in Georgia offered his own practices as exemplary:

> My first care has been to select a proper place for my "Quarter" well protected by the shade . . . and to erect comfortable houses for my negroes. . . . A large house is provided as a nursery for the children where all are taken at daylight, and placed under the care of a careful and experienced woman, whose sole occupation is to . . . see that they are properly fed and attended to. . . . I have a large and comfortable hospital provided for my negroes when they are sick . . . [and] I must not omit to mention that I have a good fiddler, and keep him well-supplied with catgut, and I make it his duty to play for the negroes every Saturday night until twelve o'clock.[8]

Lest we be tempted to sign up, the writer later notes that his solicitous human resource policies reduced, but did not eliminate, the need for whipping. Whatever its motivation, paternalism clearly strengthened the control of the planter over his slaves and served as a governance mechanism. And when combined with constant monitoring, and the positive and negative incentives that ruled the workday, the planter's domination was complete.

To summarize, slavery was the first in a set of evolving public policies that served to insulate farmers from the perils of the market. American success in producing large volumes of cotton for world markets required a reliable supply of farm labor, but this labor was likely both unwilling and unavailable through a market mechanism in the pre-Civil War South. But slave ownership alone did not assure productivity. To induce slaves to perform the repetitive and exhausting tasks associated with cotton production, planters used a complex blend of governance mechanisms, including positive and negative incentives, paternalism, and monitoring. Many elements of the command and control factory system, of course, survive today in many industries. And complicated blends of incentive and monitoring mechanisms survive as well.

The lessons of the early American cotton industry are relevant for modern debates. America's early dominance of the cotton industry illustrates that commercial success can be achieved through moral failure, an observation especially relevant for T-shirts, which critics allege are produced under sweatshop conditions not far removed from slavery. But the early story of American cotton also reveals a critical lesson for the market-phobic: It was not the perils of the labor market but the suppression of the market that doomed the lives of the slaves. More generally, the tactic of suppressing and avoiding markets rather than competing in them continues today to be a viable business strategy, particularly in agriculture but also in other industries. This ability to suppress and avoid competition, as we will see, is often the result of a power imbalance between rich and poor, an imbalance that persists in world cotton agriculture today.

With the labor problem "solved" by slavery, unlimited land to the West, and unlimited demand from the East, the pieces were still not quite in place for American cotton's victory. In their westward expansion, cotton growers encountered perhaps the greatest production bottleneck in American economic history. Once they had pushed farther than 30 miles from the Atlantic coast, the cotton growers found that the lustrous and strong Sea Island cotton demanded by British mills would not bloom. Only Upland cotton, with a shorter fiber and stickier seed, would grow further west. However, while Sea Island cotton could be separated from the seeds with a simple roller gin modeled on an ancient device from India (the *Churkka* gin), this device was unable to separate the sticky seeds in Upland cotton from the lint.

The severity of this supply bottleneck is difficult to overestimate. A young and healthy slave could pick up to 300 pounds of cotton each day. Even children could typically pick 100 pounds per day. With the seeds, however, the cotton had no market. Since the roller gins would not remove the seed from Upland cotton, slaves were required to pick the seeds out by hand. So sticky and stubborn were the seeds, however, that a slave could clean no more than 1 pound per day. England's mills would die of cotton starvation at this pace.

So if it hadn't been Eli Whitney, it likely would have been someone else, and soon. In the fall of 1792, the necessary ingredients for entrepreneurial success converged: a production bottleneck, an idea, a source of capital, and a way to make a profit. For developing countries today, the important part of the story is not Eli—poor countries have plenty of smart and inventive people—it is the convergence of all the ingredients necessary for forward leaps.

Eli Meets a Venture Capitalist

From his childhood in Massachusetts until his graduation from Yale, Eli Whitney was known to friends and family as a talented and inventive tinkerer. Following his graduation he traveled South to assume a position as a private tutor. What happened next is perhaps best related by Whitney himself, in a letter to his father dated September 11, 1793. Whitney's letter conveys his technical brilliance and entrepreneurial energy, but more touchingly, also the guilt and excitement of a young man who in pursuing his entrepreneurial dream has somewhat neglected his familial duties. He starts by admitting he should have written sooner to let his parents know what he was up to:[9]

> Dear Parent:
>   I received your letter of the 16th of August with peculiar satisfaction and delight. It gave me no small pleasure to hear of your health and was very happy to be informed that your health and that of the family has been so good since I saw you. . . . I expected to have been able to come [home to] Westboro' sooner than I fear will be in my power. I presume, sir, you are desirous to hear how I have spent my time since I have left College. This I conceive you have a right to know and that it is my duty to inform you and should have done it before this time. . . .

On the way to Savannah, Whitney had met the widow and family of Major General Greene of Revolutionary War fame. Mrs. Greene took a liking to the polite young man and invited him to spend a few days on the family's plantation before continuing his journey. When a group of Revolutionary War officers who had served under General Greene came to the plantation to pay their respects to his widow, the conversation soon turned to the pressing need for a mechanism to separate Upland cotton from its seeds so as to meet the British demand. The seeds, the planters were sure, were the only obstacle to their fortunes. "Gentlemen," Mrs. Greene remarked, "apply to my young friend, Mr. Whitney,—he can make anything."

Whitney quickly protested that he had never seen either cotton or cottonseed. Yet he was immediately intrigued, as is evident from the next paragraph of his letter:

> I went from N. York with the family of the late Major General Greene to Georgia. I went immediately with the family to their plantation . . . with an

expectation of spending four or five days. . . . During this time I heard much said of the difficulty of ginning Cotton, that is, separating it from its seeds. There were a number of very respectable gentlemen at Mrs. Greene's who all agreed that if a machine could be invented which would clean the cotton with all expedition, it would be a great thing for both the Country and the inventor.

Critically, there was a venture capitalist at the Greene plantation, as Whitney explains later in his letter:

I involuntarily happened to be thinking on the subject and struck out a plan of a machine in my mind, which I communicated to Miller (who . . . resides in the family, a man of respectability and property). He was pleased with the Plan and said that if I would pursue it and try an experiment to see if it would answer, he would be at the whole expense, I should lose nothing but my time, and if I succeeded we would share the profits. . . .

The machine worked, of course. Whitney's simple and elegant model was quickly duplicated throughout the South. The good news was that in the next eight years, cotton production rose 25-fold, and by 1820, more than 90-fold. The bad news was that more than any other single factor, Eli Whitney's cotton gin solidified the slave plantation in the cotton South. For the growers, it was good while it lasted. For the men and women who had been bought and sold and bred and whipped and captured and fiddled to, it was good when it ended.

Where Was the Competition?

Where, we have to ask, was the competition? What of India and China, especially? Why were these countries, world leaders in cotton production in the late 1700s, left in the dust by the Americans?

At the beginning, as Figure 2.1 shows, other countries continued to produce cotton in relatively stable quantities while American production soared. It was not a matter, then, of American producers squashing the competition with low-cost and efficient production. Instead, for the older cotton producers, it was business as usual. But business as usual was not good enough.

British demand for cotton had exploded with the new textile machinery and the burgeoning consumer class. It was not a matter of steady growth in demand, not a curve that the old cotton producers could ride profitably on into retirement. The British Industrial Revolution was a lightening bolt in cotton's story, like the cotton gin or the boll weevil or emancipation, which changed everything ahead. By 1860, Britain was consuming over a billion pounds of cotton per year, which was considerably more than the entire production of the world, excluding the United States.[10]

An explosion in demand required an explosion in supply. The question, then, becomes why the supply exploded in the United States rather than in the countries that had been the world's major producers since the beginning of the cotton trade. The question of American success becomes more intriguing when we note the remarkable lengths to which the British went—quite unsuccessfully—to reduce their risky dependence on American cotton.

Put simply, modern markets did not yet work in India or China, in cotton or in anything else. As economic historian David Landes advises, a useful way to understand why something in economic history did or did not happen at a certain place and time is to ask, who would have benefited?[11] If cotton growers in India or China could have benefited by increasing their productivity, improving quality, and selling cotton to British mills, they would have done so. It appears, though, that they would not have benefited; the risks were too great, the rewards likely minimal. Capitalism of the type that rewards an idea, an improvement, an initiative, had not yet taken hold in Asia. The foundations were lacking.

First, there were no property rights, or as Francois Bernier, a Frenchman who lived in India during the seventeenth century, wrote, no *mien et tien* (no mine and yours).[12] There were no incentives to improve age-old methods, to learn, to grow more, to do better. The agricultural workers were at the mercy of rulers who were often absent, and who changed and moved frequently. And even if wealth had been created, Bernier wrote, it had to be hidden lest it be extorted or seized.[13]

In China, too, cotton growers would not have benefited. Under the tyranny of the emperor, there was little reason to take a business risk in the modern sense of the term. As a Christian missionary remarked in the late 1700s, "Any man of genius is paralyzed immediately by the thought that his efforts will win him punishment rather than rewards."[14] As Landes notes, too directly for most tastes, China's "cultural triumphalism and petty downward tyranny made [the country] a reluctant improver and a bad learner."[15] Culturally, the Qing dynasty, which ruled China from the 1600s until the early 1900s, displayed an aversion to all things Western, and to change in general. A Jesuit passing through commented that the Chinese were "more fond of the most defective piece of antiquity than of the most perfect of the modern. . . ."[16] In other words, all of the Elis in China had no reason to try.

On the surface, of course, the American cotton victory over India and China appeared to be due to slavery. An 1853 observer confidently noted that American cotton growers' "superiority" was due to the "cheap, and reliable labor they derive from that patriarchal system of domestic servitude."[17] While certainly it was slavery that allowed the cotton factories on the plantations to produce such enormous volumes of cotton, India and China, too, had millions of people who were made to work for nothing by tyrannical rulers, millions of people who could not say no. Why these people were never organized to produce large volumes of cotton for export is another matter entirely.

Thus, while slavery allowed farmers to evade the risks of the labor market, it does not explain why other countries failed to seize the opportunities presented by the Industrial Revolution. The institutions necessary to support factory-style cotton production—property rights, incentive structures, what is today called "governance"—also had an important role to play. Governance still has an important role to play, which will remain the challenge for many poor cotton-producing countries. As we will see, all of the Eli Whitneys in Mali, Burkina Faso, and Benin still have little reason to try.

All God's Dangers Ain't a White Man

Shortly before the beginning of the Civil War, James Henry Hammond of South Carolina—senator, former governor, plantation owner, cotton farmer—stood to address the U.S. Senate. In one of the most famous pieces of Southern political oratory of the era, Hammond thundered on about the destruction of the world that would surely accompany the demise of the cotton slave plantation. It was not just the Southern gentleman's way of life that Hammond sought to preserve, it was civilization itself:

> Would any sane nation make war on cotton? Without firing a gun, without drawing a sword, should they make war on us, we could bring the world to our feet. . . . What would happen if no cotton was furnished for three years? . . . this is certain: England would topple headlong and carry the whole civilized world with her, save the South.[18]

This dire prediction about the demise of civilization rested on the importance of cotton to the industrial centers of the Northern states and Europe. The giant textile mills that lined the rivers of the new industrial centers depended upon the South to supply cotton. This bit of fluff, the boll as big as a fist yet lighter than a breath, reigned supremely, if not benevolently, over the world's new economic order. Southern cotton had a God-given monopoly. Because it could not be grown either in the Northern states or in England, Hammond reasoned, the industrial world would bow to cotton, and the South had nothing to fear:

> No, you dare not make war on cotton. No power on earth dares make war on cotton. Cotton is king.[19]

It is clear from his words that Hammond did not believe that the cotton kingdom could thrive under the rules of the North. To destroy the slave plantation was to destroy the cotton economy, or so he thought.

But while the Civil War eliminated slavery, the cotton economy of the South survived because public policy evolved to continue to protect the growers from the perils of the labor markets. Labor requirements in cotton production remained highly seasonal, and the challenge was still to have sufficient labor available at critical but unpredictable times in the cotton cycle. However, transacting in a labor market was fraught with risk as the market still offered no guarantees about either the price or availability of labor at these critical times. Without the tight control of slavery, landowners needed an alternative system to bind labor to their land upon demand. The labor system that emerged—tenant farming, or "sharecropping"—fit the bill.

In exchange for their labor, the landowner provided the sharecropper with housing and food (known as the "furnish") as well as the right to hunt and to fish. By providing housing and food, rather than cash, the landowner bound the worker to the property and assured himself of labor at critical times. The worker was contractually bound as well, since he was indebted to the landlord through the harvesting of the crop.

A wide variety of public policies were instituted to bind the sharecroppers to the land and insulate the cotton growers from the risks of transacting in the labor market.[20] Gradually, the legal definition of "sharecropper" shifted in favor of the landowners, especially through the passage of crop lien laws.[21] These laws changed the status of the sharecropper in the courts to a laborer who was paid wages in crops rather than a tenant with ownership of a share of the crop. The difference was critical. As a laborer, the sharecropper could not offer his crop for lien because it technically belonged to the landowner. The crop lien laws, then, shut the sharecropper out of the capital markets while widening access to capital for the landowners. Other laws, such as vagrancy laws and "alienation of labor" laws (which protected the landowner from having his labor hired away) also served to bind the sharecropper to the land. At the same time, planters opposed public schooling for blacks and poor whites, so illiteracy and lack of education kept the balance of power in the sharecropping arrangement heavily in favor of the planter, and limited the alternatives of the workers.

Moreover, the contractual arrangement between sharecropper and landowner left the sharecropper little hope of climbing out of subsistence. The sharecropper's dream—to own land—was thwarted by a cycle of perpetual debt whereby the sharecropper's share of each harvest was barely enough to settle the year's debts, and by exclusion from external capital markets. A remark reportedly made by Louis XIV of France is apt: "Credit supports agriculture as a cord supports the hanged."[22]

Ned Cobb, an Alabama cotton farmer, recalled the standstill that trapped him as a sharecropper. While he made six bales of cotton in 1908, a respectable crop:

> It took all them six bales to pay Mr. Curtis. In the place of prosperin', I was on a standstill. . . . I had not a dollar left out of the cotton. . . . Mr. Curtis had Mr.

> Buck Thompson furnish me groceries . . . kept a book on me. . . . [Mr. Curtis] paid Mr. Thompson and I paid him—the deal worked that way—out of my crop. So he made somethin off my grocery bill besides gettin half my crop when the time came.[23]

Cobb's biography repeats this theme year after year. Some years, there was a little cotton left after paying the landlord; in other years, there was not enough to settle the debts and Cobb had to start the next year in the hole. Thanks to creative accounting, it was typical to come out even. In Macon County, Alabama, researchers uncovered a remarkable coincidence: 62 percent of black sharecroppers had come out even for the year in 1932.[24]

Ironically, the success that the planters had in devising public policies to keep the workforce docile and uneducated soon began to backfire. When the boll weevil began to ravage the Southern cotton crop in the early 1900s, government extension programs were mobilized to spread advice to farmers on how to combat the weevil and save their crops. The news and advice reached the large farms and the educated farmers, but often passed by the poor and illiterate sharecroppers, black and white, who had to fend for themselves.[25] In 1921, approximately 30 percent of the cotton crop—predominantly that produced by small sharecroppers—was lost to the weevil.[26] Many were pushed off the land. Ned Cobb remembered the time well:

> That was boll weevil time. . . . these white folks told the colored people if you don't pick them cotton squares off the ground and destroy them boll weevils we'll quit furnishin' you. Told em that—puttin the blame on the colored man for the boll weevil. Couldn't nobody pay his debts when the weevil et up his crop.[27]

"Yes," he added later, in reference to the weevil, "all God's dangers ain't a white man."[28]

For Deep South sharecroppers, not much changed from the end of the Civil War until the late 1920s: a few acres of tired soil, a few mules, a few bales at the end of the year, and a perpetual crushing debt.

But while this rhythm played on in the Deep South, a new type of cotton factory was rising in the West. By the early 1900s, Texas would be the country's largest cotton producer. By the 1920s, Texas would be selling cotton to China.

Cotton Factories Arrive in Texas

Texas and Oklahoma were the new cotton frontier, wide-open, blue-sky places with no crumbling plantation houses, no old ways of doing things, and plenty of room to build cotton factories. Between 1900 and 1920, the area around Corpus Christi was divvied up into huge landholdings on a scale never seen before, and rarely since, for the purpose of growing cotton. Henrietta King of Corpus Christi owned 1.4 million acres, Charles Taft owned over 150,000 acres, and C.W. Post—the man behind the cereal—owned 200,000 acres.[29]

The requirements for successful large-scale cotton farming had changed little from the pre-Civil War South. The landowners still required large numbers of workers to be available on demand to plant, weed, and harvest the crop at the whim of the weather. Relying on a labor market in the modern sense of the term was still fraught with risk and expense. How would the planter be assured that the market would provide for labor requirements when the weeds bloomed or the cotton opened? And what if the market wage went up or help was hired away by competitors?

Creative solutions abounded.[30] Planters imported monkeys from Brazil and tried to teach them to pick cotton, but the animals in the end were uncooperative. And geese, it turned out, will weed a cotton field when fenced in, and the farmers discovered that only two geese could weed an acre of cotton. They also discovered, however, that geese could not be trained not to trample cotton plants, and that insecticide is also goosicide. For a time, farmers also used flamethrowers to weed cotton fields, but taking fire down the rows of their livelihood proved too difficult for most. In the end, neither monkeys nor geese nor fire could accomplish the tasks as well as a captive labor force.

This time, to tie the labor to the land and to avoid the market, the cotton growers borrowed an idea from the North: the company town.

The Taft cotton ranch, near Corpus Christi, occupied 39 percent of the land of San Patricio County.[31] The ranch was organized as a corporation, but in reality it was a community in which people's lives—not just their work—were hierarchically managed for the purpose of cotton production. The ranch had company housing, schools, and churches segregated along ethnic lines for whites, Mexicans, and blacks. Like the "furnish" provided to old South sharecroppers, workers were paid partly in scrip, which could be redeemed only at company stores. Finally, like the plantation owner who kept his "fiddler well-supplied with catgut," the Taft Ranch provided holidays, music, and festivities as well, again designed for the three different ethnic groups. This entire system, of course, served to ensure that workers were around when the cotton needed to be planted, weeded, and harvested. The new cotton factories not so much influenced public policy, they *were* public policy over vast stretches of Texas.

These large and tightly controlled production systems were hailed as models of the farms of the future, models of productivity, efficiency, and profitability. Once again, successful large-scale cotton production depended on a factory system in which large numbers of workers were available on demand to complete the repetitive chores associated with weeding, planting, and picking. Once again, success depended upon avoiding—not competing in—the labor market.

Of course, observers of the day also acknowledged that the economic success of these large Texas cotton "factories" also meant the demise of the smaller family cotton farms. It was sad but inevitable, the way of the future.

Well, maybe.

Perhaps someone forgot to tell Nelson and Ruth Reinsch.

BACK AT THE REINSCH FARM

ALL GOD'S DANGERS AIN'T THE SUBSIDIES

Today, Lubbock, Texas, is indeed the "cottonest city in the world," and the surrounding farmland is the leading birthplace of the world's T-shirts. Lubbock has the world's largest cotton cooperative and the world's largest cottonseed oil mill. More than 25 percent of American-grown cotton passes through Lubbock, and the surrounding region produces most of the cotton in the country's largest cotton-producing state. Texas Tech University, on the west side of town, performs some of the most advanced cotton research in the world. And Lubbock is an international cotton center. A majority of the region's cotton is exported, loaded onto trucks and trains in Lubbock, bound for ports on every U.S. coast. And at the bottom of this successful chain are neither plantations nor sharecroppers nor company towns nor even family farms, but people like Nelson and Ruth Reinsch.[1]

No single factor explains the success that cotton farmers in West Texas have had in competing in international markets. The growers are embedded in a web of institutions that help them to continue their tradition of shifting market risks away from themselves, and they continue to win by limiting competition rather than competing. Texas cotton farmers have solved, once and for all, the age-old labor market risk problem associated

with cotton production, creatively applying both mechanization and public policy to the challenge. These producers were also leaders in the development of the modern agricultural cooperative, a brilliantly simple
organizational form that allows cotton farmers such as Nelson and Ruth
Reinsch to capture every shred of value from the cotton plant, backward
into the oilseed and forward into blue denim. Texas cotton farmers are also
masters of political influence, leading the American government to assume
the business risks—including price and nonpayment risks—that the farmers would rather not. Remarkably, the Reinsches and their West Texas
neighbors have even taken control of the wild Texas climate. They can
make it rain, they can stop the sand from blowing, and they can even
freeze the cotton plant on a warm and sunny day.

Perhaps most significant, Lubbock is the center of the "Silicon Valley"
of cotton production. The Lubbock area benefits from a highly symbiotic
and virtuous circle relationship between farmers, private companies, universities, and the U.S. government. The farmers, well-educated and entrepreneurial, both contribute to and benefit from the research that takes
place in the universities and firms, while the United States Department of
Agriculture (USDA) supports both the research and the farmers with fund-
ing, technical, and business assistance. Cotton growers in poor countries
are challenged not so much by the prospect of competing with Nelson
Reinsch, but by competing with the much larger and permanent advantages of this interlocking virtuous circle. Competing with Nelson is hard
enough, but competing with Nelson as he is teamed up with Texas Tech
and the USDA is another matter entirely.

Today, it looks as though Nelson and Ruth have arrived at something
of a comfortable place. They are still here, bringing in the cotton each
year, more than 50 years after they arrived. It all works pretty well on the
Reinsch farm: the machines and the science and the cooperatives and the
government programs. They can relax now, as Ruth keeps saying.

Nelson's trying. He really is.

C.F. and Hattie Move West (and Bring a Tractor)

As cotton continued its westward push in the 1920s and 1930s, the Reinsches
moved, too. Although Texas had already become the nation's biggest cotton

producer by 1890, at this time virtually all of Texas cotton was produced in the eastern part of the state, bordering on the plantation South. By the 1930s, however, cotton began to take hold of the West Texas region surrounding Lubbock. It was during this period that C.F. and Hattie Reinsch arrived here with young Nelson, then a teenager.

The Reinsches come from a long line of early adopters and innovators. Cotton farmers near Lubbock were starting from scratch. There was no dismantling of the old ways to be accomplished, no old habits to break, no traditions to hold back progress. This freedom to start from scratch undoubtedly explains why most innovations in cotton production spread from west to east rather than from east to west. They still do.

In the old South, mule farming in cotton production persisted into the 1960s. In West Texas cotton country, it never started. When cotton farmers began to settle near Lubbock—the mid-1920s—the gasoline tractor arrived with them. While the old South cotton farmers gradually sold their mules and replaced them with tractors, cotton farming in West Texas used tractors from the beginning. This led to drastically different labor patterns in the two regions, differences that would have lasting implications.

Richard Day has divided the mechanization of cotton production to 1960 into four stages (see Figure 3.1).[2] In Stage 1, all land preparation and planting is mule powered, and weeding is done by hoe. Cotton is handpicked. In Stage 2, some cultivation and weeding is also mule-powered, but land preparation is done by tractor. Cotton is handpicked. In Stage 3, the use of fertilizer increases cotton yields, and more cultivation and weeding is done by tractor implements, but cotton is still handpicked. Finally, in Stage 4, cotton is mechanically harvested and only a small amount of hand weeding remains in the spring and summer seasons.

Early tractor technology was only capable of the brute strength chore of breaking the land in winter and so did little to solve the ancient labor problem of cotton production. There was little reason to buy a tractor for land breaking, since this chore required the least labor. Therefore, there was little incentive for Deep South cotton farmers to move from Stage 1 to Stage 2, since the labor force was still needed on demand for the rest of the year for weeding, cultivating, and harvesting, and the mules would be needed as well. Gradually, tractor implements became capable of the finer tasks of weeding between rows, though weeds close to the cotton plant

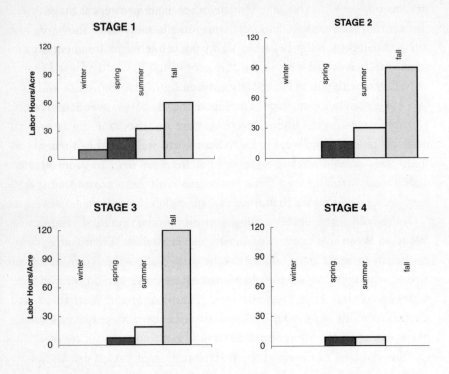

STAGE 1: Mule-powered landbreaking and cultivation. Extensive hand weeding and hand picking.

STAGE 2: Tractor land preparation in winter. Mule powered cultivation. Some hand weeding. Hand picking.

STAGE 3: Tractor-powered land preparation and cultivation. Some hand weeding. Hand picking.

STAGE 4: Complete mechanization with a small amount of hand weeding.

COTTON LABOR CYCLE:

Winter: land-breaking
Spring: planting, cultivation, weeding
Summer: weeding
Fall: harvest

Source: Adapted from Day, p. 440.

FIGURE 3.1 *Manual Labor Requirements in Cotton Production at Alternative Stages of Mechanization*

still had to be pulled by hoe. On the other hand, growers at Stage 3 who had started with tractors had every incentive to mechanize the harvest, or move to Stage 4, because of the highly uneven labor requirements associated with harvesting.

The remarkable mechanical leapfrogging of the Reinsches and their West Texas neighbors is shown in Figure 3.2. By 1946, over 80 percent of Texas cotton production—including that on the Reinsch farm—had reached Stage 3, while in the Deep South, this stage had been reached by only 14 percent of cotton farmers. In 1946, more than 20 years after the widespread introduction of the tractor into West Texas cotton country, 67 percent of Deep South cotton farms were still exclusively mule powered.

The reluctance of Deep South cotton farmers to trade in their mules for tractors in the move to Stage 3 was due largely to a faithful attachment to tradition (and even to the animals themselves) and reluctance to change, as well as to the economics of small holdings. To give up mule farming was to relinquish a way of life, and many were loathe to do so, even as they clearly saw the future in front of them. Here is Ned Cobb of Alabama, speaking in the early 1970s:

> I was a mule farmin' man to the last; never did make a crop with a tractor. I've owned some of the prettiest mules that ever walked the roads. Now there ain't none of my children, nary one by name, got a mule.[3]

But while the Reinsches had nary a mule, either, there still was not a satisfactory mechanical way to pull the fluffy white lint from the cotton plant. From the settling of West Texas cotton country, this was done as it

Percentage of Work Done with Tractors

STATE	LANDBREAKING		PLANTING		CULTIVATING	
	1939	1946	1939	1946	1939	1946
ALABAMA	10	33	3	15	5	14
TEXAS	49	85	45	80	43	83

Source: Adapted from Street, p. 164.

FIGURE 3.2   *Use of Tractor Power in Cotton Production, Alabama vs. Texas*

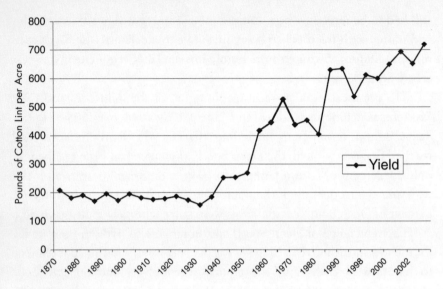

Source: USDA.

FIGURE 3.3   *Cotton Yields Per Acre*

always had been, by men, women, and children pulling heavy sacks between the rows. And there was more to pick. Thanks to the introduction of advanced fertilizers, cotton yields were increasing (see Figure 3.3). While a traditional Deep South plantation might hope for 120 pounds per acre, by the 1950s the Reinsches were coaxing nearly a bale (480 pounds) out of each acre planted in cotton. As Day's estimates show then, the labor necessary to harvest the crop from an acre of cotton had approximately doubled from the pre-Civil War South. At the same time, labor require-ments during the rest of the year were dropping dramatically. Rather than solving the labor problem, the mechanization made the labor problem at harvest even worse.

White Guys Get All Draggy-Like

Though public policies had ameliorated growers' labor market risks since the beginning, on the eve of World War II the federal government entered the labor market directly to assume these risks on behalf of farmers. With the December attack on Pearl Harbor and the resulting drain of agricultural labor to the military, Congress charged the USDA with mobilizing women and children to bring in the crop. Farmers across the country insisted, however, that additional workers were needed, not just to harvest the crop, but even to win the war. Once again, it seemed, civilization teetered on the ability to get the cotton picked. Governor Olson of California wrote to Washington in 1942:

> Without a substantial number of Mexicans the situation is certain to be disastrous to the entire victory program, despite our united efforts in the mobilization of youth and city dwellers for emergency farm work.[4]

Congress responded in 1942 by authorizing the Bracero program, which allowed Mexican labor to enter the United States for short periods to work in agriculture. And Mexican farm labor, according to the growers, was much better than white labor, which was "lazy and draggy-like," or black labor, which exhibited "too much independence."[5] So, as Nelson went off to war at the age of 20, Mexicans flowed across the border to pick the Reinsches' cotton. Though the Bracero program was authorized as an emergency wartime measure, farm interests succeeded in extending the program until 1964, 19 years after the war had ended. By that time, 90 percent of cotton was mechanically harvested. Most cotton was in Stage 4 of mechanization, and the workers were no longer needed.

The Bracero program—and its long-term extension—illustrates again the political influence that enabled cotton farmers to avoid competitive markets. The program went much further than simply easing immigration restrictions into U.S. farm work. Had the program stopped there, cotton producers still would have had to contend with the dreaded labor market. Even with the influx of Mexican labor, how would they know that workers would be there when the cotton needed to be picked? Further, wage uncertainty in this volatile market posed an economic risk as well. Because all of a region's cotton had to be picked at the same time, "the market" might allow wages to be bid up to uneconomic levels to meet peak demand. Though there were a number of attempts by growers to collectively fix the price of Mexican farm labor, none of these attempts had any lasting effect. Attempts to restrict worker mobility to keep laborers from seeking higher wages on the next farm were also largely unsuccessful.[6] In brief, simply lifting the floodgates to allow Mexican labor onto U.S. farms still left the growers at the peril of a competitive labor market. They didn't like it then any more than they had before.

What the growers wanted was three-fold. First, they wanted the labor they needed to be available on demand. Second, they wanted to know in advance what the labor would cost, and they did not want to compete with one another on the basis of price. Third, they wanted a guarantee that the labor would be productive. In other words, the growers wanted to assume none of the labor market risks that are normally associated not just with agriculture, but with business in general.

Congress gave the growers everything they asked for. Under the Bracero program, which was administered by the Department of Labor, the growers ordered a certain number of workers to be picked up on a certain day. The government guaranteed that the growers' order would be filled at a certain price. The laborers imported could only work for a single employer, so growers no longer had to worry about workers leaving in search of higher wages. Government workers also assumed the role of screening workers for health, likely productivity, and political ideology.[7]

Nelson and Ruth remember well the days of the Bracero program, the hundreds of Mexicans crawling through the cotton fields plucking the low Texas cotton. Whatever its effect on liberal sensibilities, they believe the program was a good one. How else could the cotton have been picked? How else could these workers have supported their families? Nelson and Ruth treated the workers fairly, and required their two sons to perform the same chores as the Bracero workers. Their older son, Lamar, remembers it this way, too.

Bureaucrats Push Out Sharecroppers

By the early 1930s, cotton prices had dropped to the lowest level ever observed (see Figure 3.4). While public policies had cushioned farmers' labor market risks since the beginning, with the federal price support programs of the early 1930s, the government also began to assume the risks of falling commodity prices. As the economic situation on Southern cotton farms became increasingly desperate, attention turned to Washington. For cotton farmers, the critical element of the New Deal's agricultural policy

was the Agricultural Adjustment Act (AAA), which, for the first time, introduced government price supports for agricultural products, and also introduced the concept of paying farmers to take land out of production. The
objective was for the government payments to put a safety net under rural
poverty while at the same time helping commodity prices to stabilize.

A look at the winners and losers from farm price support programs,
however, suggests a lesson about the beneficiaries of government policy. In
practice, while growers such as the Reinsches benefited, landowners in the
Deep South typically chose to take the government check and then take
their sharecroppers' acreage out of production, pushing farmers into the
ranks of migrants who gradually went west into the pages of *The Grapes of
Wrath*. Rarely did the sharecropper have the means to fight the landlord for
his share of the government's payment.[8] In a cruel irony, it was the government programs designed to alleviate the sharecroppers' poverty that
intimidated Ned Cobb out of cotton farming. Cobb had never intended to

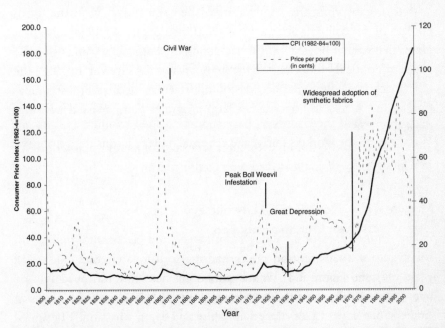

Sources: Cotton prices from USDA. CPI 1800 to 1912 from Mitchell (1998). CPI
1913 to 2003 from Bureau of Labor Statistics.

FIGURE 3.4   *Cotton Prices and Consumer Prices*

give up cotton farming. He had wanted to die growing cotton, and certainly was not about to be pushed aside by whites:

> I was born an raised here and I have sowed my labor into the earth and lived to reap only a part of it, not all that was mine by human right . . . I stays on if it gives 'em satisfaction for me to leave, and I stays on because its mine.[9]

A short time later, Ned Cobb gave up. And he gave up because of, not in spite of, the government's efforts to help:

> the government took over this cotton business to a greater extent than ever before; I jumped out right there. Didn't want to fill out them papers every year, and a whole lot of red tape to it. I can't read and write; Josie can't either. And if I couldn't conduct my business myself, I weren't going to have nobody do it for me.[10]

And the final cruel joke: Many large farmers used their AAA payments to buy tractors, so many small sharecroppers were "tractored out" by World War II.

The cause of Ned Cobb's demise as a cotton farmer bears an important lesson for explaining the winners, both then and today. With the introduction of government price supports and the dozens of federal farm programs that soon followed, skill at navigating the bureaucracy and using the levers of political influence became prerequisites for survival. In 1999, the USDA acknowledged that decades of indifference and blatant discrimination against blacks in government farm programs had persisted well into the 1990s.[11]

For Ned Cobb, dealing with bureaucrats meant a brave new world: All of a sudden, if you couldn't read, you couldn't farm.

Machines That Don't Get All Discouraged

In the center pages of a catalog from Lands' End, a beautiful young girl beams into the camera from the center of a cotton patch. She is 17 or 18 years old, with long and shiny beauty shop hair. She has peaceful and happy deep-pool eyes that say all is well in this place with the blue sky. And she has perfect teeth, lined up white and evenly, in a smile designed to bring forth your credit card. We are supposed to buy the polo shirt: It comes in many colors of the softest cotton. In the highlands of Peru, Maria picked the cotton by hand, fluff by fluff. It's better, says the catalog, than the machine-picked cotton.

Better for whom? In researching this book I met many people who had grown up handpicking cotton, but I didn't meet anyone who was nostalgic for it. Cotton farmers in almost all countries outside the United States still handpick their cotton; indeed, Terry Townsend of the International Cotton Advisory Committee (ICAC) told me that he did not believe that there was a mechanical picker in all of Africa. While handpicking cotton may be a job, it is not a job of choice. The Marias of the world don't get their hair done, and their teeth haven't been fixed. Surely they smile now and again, out there in the field, but it's not because they are picking cotton. In 1999, Adrian Gwin still harbors a memory of picking cotton. It was only one day, long ago, but it was enough:

> There just ain't enough money in the world for me to do that again. I was a full-fledged, on-the-payroll cotton picker for one whole day about 70 years ago, and it cured me. . . . I've been there. It was about 1925 or 1926 that I got my cotton picking baptism, right out in a mile wide cotton field. . . . I'd seen other little boys making fortunes picking cotton, and I wanted some of that easy money. Cotton picking paid a dime a hundred. Ten cents for picking only a hundred pounds of cotton in the fields. I'd seen black boys and girls make 2 dimes a day. . . . To make that dime you had to loop a strap of mattress ticking around a shoulder, and drag behind you a six-foot ticking bag that would hold 30 or so pound of cotton. You went down the cotton row and grabbed the fluffy white cotton off the bolls and flipped it into the mouth of the bag. Before the sun was half up in the sky, I was convinced my bag had a hole in the bottom. My shoulders ached. My legs ached. My arms ached. My fingers ached. I was plumb sore all over before I got to the end of that first row. . . . I was ready to call it a day—but the day was hardly half-spent. And I wasn't yet halfway to that shiny bright dime I wanted. When Stentius blew his horn and twilight hovered over the cotton field, I looked back at my 100-pound bag diggin its feet into the ground as I dragged it—and it wasn't full yet.
>
> I remember so well. I didn't get a dime. I got a nickel. Five cents. The weighmaster at the gin was generous. I hadn't quite picked 50 pounds of cotton in my 14-hour day. Long years later, I remembered that day of cotton picking. . . . Never again would I drag a bag down a cotton row. Never again that cotton pickin' cotton picking. Today, they have machines to do it. Great big super-efficient machines that don't get tired all over and discouraged.
>
> Boy, I'm glad.[12]

Nelson and Ruth are glad, too. With a cotton-picking machine, they could drastically reduce once and for all their risky association with farm labor. While inventive farmers had tried various ways to mechanize the harvest before, it was not until the 1920s and early 1930s that researchers based in Lubbock, only a few miles from the Reinsch farm, began to perfect the tractor-mounted cotton stripper in one of many applications of the fruitful relationship among USDA cotton researchers, universities, and farmers. The basic stripper technology, which survives today, consists of a set of brushes that are pulled around the cotton plant, knocking the bolls onto a belt and blowing them into a trailer. Though this essential technology was developed in the 1920s and 1930s, widespread adoption of mechanical strippers did not take place in West Texas until shortly after World War II, and in the Deep South, much later.

The mechanical march forward was halted first by the Depression, and second by the necessity to adapt other phases in the production chain, especially ginning, to mechanically picked cotton. And mechanical cotton picking required farms of a certain size as well. It was difficult to justify an investment in cotton-picking machinery on a farm of under 150 or so acres. While most Texas farms were easily large enough to benefit, the small cotton patches across the Deep South were not. Today, the millions of farmers across Africa and Southeast Asia also find it difficult to make the leap to mechanical harvesting. Even if the farmers banded together to share the machines, because of the whims of nature, everyone would likely need the machine at the same time.

It was 1953, Nelson believes, when the two-row International Harvester cotton stripper arrived at the farm and changed everything. The machine could pick 10 bales a day, the work of 25 men in the field, and, like Adrian Gwin said, it didn't get all tired and discouraged.

But while the machine solved the picking problem, it created new bottlenecks. The cotton picking weather windows in West Texas had always posed a problem: a race to get to the cotton before the Texas elements. The cotton needed water, yet it couldn't be picked wet. The hail would come down and knock the fluff right off the plant, or the gusty wind would blow it away, or the sand would make it dirty and lower its price. In the three-month picking season, Nelson needed windows where he could get to the cotton after it had bloomed and dried but before the wind or hail or sand or rain. Unfortunately, the new stripper made this already random challenge trickier yet.

With the mechanical harvester, Nelson had to wait for a hard freeze as well. The machine could not strip the cotton from live green plants. In order to work properly, the cotton stripper required that the plant be brown and brittle, as happened after a freeze, so that the cotton bolls could snap off easily. And worse yet, the picking day was shorter, because the stripper also did not do well in the morning dew. So into the already impossible climate constraints on cotton picking came more things to wait for, while hoping the Texas weather monsters wouldn't get there first.

The result, for C.F., Hattie, and Nelson, and by now, for Nelson's young sons, too, was that when the stars were finally lined up right for picking, the crew worked frantically. Harvesting the cotton required three to four workers: one to drive the tractor, the rest to ride in the trailer mounted behind the stripper. The riders' job was to move the cotton evenly around the trailer as it blew in, using pitchforks, and to tramp the cotton down to get better use out of the trailers. There was a definite hierarchy: Driving the tractor was better than riding the trailer. Nelson would drive the trailer and his sons Lamar and Dwade would ride in back, often with a hired hand. Because they couldn't strip the cotton until mid-morning, they went until darkness was complete, until they had to stop because of the pitchforks.

Lamar's memory of riding the cotton trailer is permanently engraved, like Gwin's memory of cotton picking. It was hard, noisy, dirty work. Hard was okay, he was young and strong. Even though his hearing is still damaged, noisy was okay, too. But, dirty, well, you just can't imagine.

This is what he remembers: as darkness fell, being splattered with bloody rabbit pieces, from the ones that didn't jump quickly enough.

Lamar decided to go to college.

Of course, in a given region, the hard freeze came at the same time for everybody, so while Nelson and his sons worked frantically, all of his neighbors were working frantically, too. This created a major bottleneck in getting the cotton to market. First, there were never enough trailers, and never enough time to tow them to the gin. In the middle of the harvest, Nelson needed empty trailers to catch the cotton, but to get them empty he had to stop work and tow them to the gin. And once he arrived there, his cotton trailer had to get in line with everyone else's, and wait its turn to get emptied into the gin. In those very brief West Texas weather windows, the cotton poured into the gins at a much faster rate than the system could handle.

Just as the mechanical stripper had been the result of symbiotic research among farmers, the USDA, and the universities, the challenge created by the stripper also began to be addressed by the virtuous circle. As the mechanical stripper had closed the weather window, researchers turned to opening it. The idea was to let Nelson decide when the hard freeze would come. And, indeed, to let him decide which part of his field would freeze today, and which tomorrow. Scientists soon created chemical compounds that could make the cotton plant brown and crunchy, no matter what the temperature. Today, Nelson doesn't wait for the hard freeze. When the cotton is open and the weather stars are lined up, he freezes the cotton himself, with chemicals sprayed from behind his tractor, or he hires an airplane to spray at $2.25 per acre. The plants turn as dead and crunchy as can be, whenever he wants them to. In fact, there isn't much that looks deader than a defoliated cotton field in West Texas. When I stood in the middle of the Reinsches' chemically frozen field, I felt like the earth itself was rusting away around me.

Even with the stripper and the defoliants, there was still plenty of human labor involved in Nelson's cotton production in the late 1960s. Though the huge number of seasonal factory workers was no longer needed, Nelson, Lamar, and Dwade had plenty to do. The Reinsches described to me a system of team production, a real family farm where each member of the family had a job to do in getting the cotton to market. Nelson and his sons were busy in the field, and Ruth and daughter Colleen kept the books, tended the garden and canned, kept the family fed, and sold eggs in town. The next chapter in cotton's story, though, beginning in the early 1970s, would change all this. The next chapter would let the children go off to the city and let Nelson do it all, hundreds of thousands of pounds, pretty much by himself.

The Reinsch Children Leave the Farm

Until the late 1960s, Nelson needed his sons, or at least reliable hired help, in every season except winter. In the fall, the cotton trailer needed two to three riders while Nelson drove the tractor and ferried cotton to the gin. In the spring and summer, irrigation was almost a full-time job for Lamar, as keeping the right amount of water going to the right places, through a system of wells and pumps and pipes, required pretty much constant attention. And in the spring, there were the weeds that threatened to overtake the young cotton plants, and somebody needed to drive up and down the rows, carefully chopping and burying them, for most of the season.

One by one, the USDA and university scientists invented these jobs away. First, in the early 1970s, new methods were devised that eliminated the need for riders during the harvest (no more rabbit pieces or pitchforks) and also did away with the need for Nelson to ferry his cotton to the gin. Nelson replaced his trailers with large baskets that caught the cotton but didn't carry riders. When the basket is full, Nelson simply tips it into a "module builder," a metal box with an open top, about the size of a large moving van. As the module builder fills, Nelson doesn't need his sons to tramp down the cotton. He has a hydraulic press, powered by the tractor, that turns the cotton into a gigantic snowy brick. When the brick is the right size, up to the top of the box with about 22,000 pounds of raw cotton, Nelson slides the box away, leaving the white brick in the field and the box empty and ready for more cotton. Workers from the gin drive a module truck over to pick up the cotton: A giant spatula slides under the cotton and lifts it up onto the truck. The cotton arrives at the gin only minutes later.

The irrigation man's job was the next to go. Though some of Nelson's cotton is still irrigated by pipes, most is watered by a giant computerized sprinkler that moves back and forth across the field like a big windshield wiper. It doesn't actually spray or sprinkle—West Texas is much too dry for Nelson to spray his water into the sky—instead it drags hundreds of tiny dripping hoses gently across the field.

Finally, keeping cotton "out of the grass" has gone from hoe to mule to machine and now to chemicals. Nelson no longer pulls up weeds behind his tractor. In addition to the hours of labor, pulling up the weeds stirred up the soil and increased water loss to evaporation. Now, Nelson goes out over the field twice per season to apply chemical herbicides. There is a little bit of labor left in this activity. Maybe once or twice he needs help with the most stubborn of the weeds. Then he hooks up his spot spray rig to the tractor and pulls five high school kids, each with a little seat under a sun umbrella. Each kid has a squirt gun in each hand, and they take aim and squirt mean chemicals directly at the weeds that have the audacity to still be coming up. The kids like it fine: They drink sodas, chat outside in the fresh air, and get $5.50 an hour.

In telling me about their lifetimes farming cotton, Nelson and Ruth Reinsch did not set out to tell me a story about forward progress. But forward progress is the story, a narrative of discovery after discovery, advance after advance in a region of the country where the gears continue to engage among the government, the scientists, and the farmers. The virtuous circle of scientific discovery and application in American cotton farming has not only done away with many risks, it has almost done away with farmers. Today, growing cotton in America is almost a one-man show. Most days, Nelson even takes a nap after lunch.

Alone on the Farm but Together in Town

The remarkable improvements in cotton production that Nelson has witnessed—the machines, the chemicals, the technology—have occurred alongside equally remarkable advances in business practices. Just as Nelson gradually overcame his powerlessness against the Texas elements, he has overcome his powerlessness against the world markets as well. And, ironically, while advances in production methods have left Nelson out in the field by himself, advances in business organization, marketing, risk sharing, and political influence have led West Texas cotton farmers to band together as a united front against the markets that once dominated them. Little by little, as they became more alone on the farm, they banded together in town.[13]

The journey of the Reinsches' cotton to China begins with a trip just a few miles down the road, to the Citizen's Shallowater Cooperative Cotton

Gin. Though the number of cotton gins in the United States has been falling steadily since observers began to count, they are still located next to the cotton fields. It was not so long ago that growers were at the mercy of the local gin, which stood like a roadblock between farmers and their cash. Only a few gins served hundreds of farmers, so the economic power was with the gins rather than the farmers, and farmers desperate for cash lined up at the gin and waited and waited for a turn to pay whatever the ginner wanted.

On the surface, the power structure looks even more lopsided today. The market for cotton ginning is even more concentrated: From 1900 to 1990, the number of gins in operation in the United States fell by over 90 percent, from 20,214 to 1,513, and the capacity of the typical gin has risen by a factor of 30.[14] Cotton gins are big and profitable businesses now, driven to be larger and more productive by advances in gin technology and economies of scale. But as the gins became bigger and more profitable businesses, something else changed, too. Today, Nelson and Ruth are no longer at the mercy of the gin; instead, they own it. The Reinsches, along with about 300 other farmers, own the Shallowater gin, and their income from selling cotton is augmented by dividend checks from the cooperatively owned gins.

Backward to Seed and Forward to Denim: Farmer Profits at Every Step

Cotton growers have also shown an astounding ability to coax value out of cotton production by throwing nothing away and finding somebody, anybody, to eat it or buy it. Out of the 22,000 pounds of raw cotton that leave Nelson's farm in the module truck, only about 5,300 pounds is the white lint that will be turned into T-shirts. Everything else on the truck looks like garbage, and it was once garbage, but not anymore. Even the garbage produced by the garbage is now sold. The reusing, recycling, and repackaging that take place in Lubbock's cotton industry today would shame the thriftiest Depression-era housewives. And often, for Texas cotton farmers, the garbage is the difference between red and black at the end of the year. As with virtually all other aspects of cotton farming, substantial assistance has been provided by the government. While much agricultural research has been devoted to increasing the quality and quantity of cotton production, the USDA at the same time has been actively involved in research to find creative and profitable uses for everything else that arrives in the module.[15]

In addition to the 5,300 pounds of the module's contents that are destined to be spun into cotton yarn (which in turn could produce about 13,500 T-shirts), the module also contains 9,000 pounds of bolls, stems, leaves, and dirt that have been sucked in along with cotton by Nelson's stripper (see Figure 3.5). Once a little molasses is stirred in, much of this trash becomes cattle feed, trucked just a short distance to the feedlots dotted among the cotton fields. This trivial recycling practice doesn't add much to Nelson's dividend check, of course. It does, however, turn a cost—trash disposal—into a revenue, however small, for Texas cotton farmers, and it is typical of the hundreds of small ways that the farmers have figured out to waste nothing and use everything.

Eight thousand pounds of the snowy white module is cottonseed. The cottonseed, like the bolls and leaves, once had an unprofitable fate as trash, dumped into gullies and streams, or burned in gigantic piles. The volume of cottonseed garbage during the 1800s became so problematic that a number of states passed laws to regulate its disposal.[16] But while the bolls and leaves were still trash, in the early 1900s the seed began to move up the value chain to be used as fertilizer and animal feed. The cattle loved it, just raw. After their cotton had been ginned, farmers would keep some

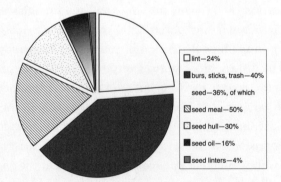

lint—24%
burs, sticks, trash—40%
seed—36%, of which
  seed meal—50%
  seed hull—30%
  seed oil—16%
  seed linters—4%

Source: USDA, National Cottonseed Products Association.

FIGURE 3.5   *Contents of Seed Cotton*

of the seed for next year's planting, plow some into the ground as fertilizer, and use the rest to feed their cows. Now, however, the bolls and leaves are used as feed but the seed is off to bigger and better things. Nelson still sometimes keeps some of his seed, but not usually, and not much. Today, the Reinsch cottonseed has much better things to do than stay on the farm, and thanks to the farmers' marketing efforts, it is much too valuable to use as animal feed.

Nelson's cottonseed is trucked from the Shallowater gin to the Plains Cooperative Oil Mill (PCOM), on the east side of Lubbock. The PCOM was born in the late 1930s as a desperate act of self-defense by West Texas cotton farmers, who at the time could hardly give their seed away. The West Texas seed had a reputation for poor by-products, and therefore brought low prices. Furthermore, the marketing of the seed was fragmented, with individual gins trying to negotiate with the likes of Palmolive, Wesson Oil, and Ralston-Purina. PCOM gradually proved to customers that West Texas seed by-products were in fact superior, not inferior, to those of its competitors, and also gradually consolidated the marketing efforts of the region's gins.[17]

The oil from the seed, about 16 percent of the seed's weight, is sold to buyers in Lubbock. It comes back into the Reinsch house in Snickers bars, Ragout spaghetti sauce, Peter Pan peanut butter, Girl Scout cookies, Certs breath mints, and almost any kind of crispy snack food. The biggest buyer of cottonseed oil in the world is Frito-Lay. Connoisseurs agree that when it comes to frying chips, cottonseed oil is best. In fact, gourmet chefs increasingly tout the benefits of cooking with cottonseed oil. The National Cottonseed Products Association (NCPA) offers recipes such as "Chocolate Banana Bread Pudding with Mascarpone Caramel Cream and Banana Beignets" to anyone who might be interested. Cottonseed oil is also the primary input in the production of Olestra, a frying fat that glides through humans without leaving a trace of fat or calories, and is also an important source of vitamin E for pharmaceutical producers. And finally, the oil is also processed into "soap stock" that turns up in soaps and detergents of all kinds. Colgate-Palmolive is also a major customer.

The meal of the cottonseed constitutes almost half of the seed's weight. It contains high-quality protein and is now used to feed not just cattle, but as Dave Kinard of the NCPA told me, "just about any critter at all," including horses, hogs, chickens, turkeys, sheep, and mules. Ralston-Purina is another major customer for cottonseed meal. And recently, researchers in aquaculture (fish farming) have discovered that cottonseed meal makes a high-quality fish food.[18] Catfish, in particular, appear to love cottonseed meal, and will eat it even when offered fish meal instead. Because fish stocks throughout the world are falling, driving up the prices of fish meal, and cotton production is rising, driving down the price of cottonseed, feeding cottonseed to catfish works for farmers of both cotton and catfish. And it's convenient, too, as the catfish farms in the South are close to the cotton fields. Dr. Lance Forster, a scientist at the NCPA, predicts that fish farms may soon consume 10 percent of the production of U.S. cottonseed meal.[19]

And humans are critters, too. If current research in genetic engineering pays off, cottonseed flour will turn up in the bakery aisle in breads, cakes, and cookies. Even today, it is possible to produce a baking flour for human consumption from cottonseed meal. The problem, however, is that the cottonseed varieties that produce high-quality flour do not produce high-quality lint. As a result, farmers are unwilling to plant the flour varieties. As plant genetics research advances, however, industry scientists hope that it will be possible to breed cottonseed that produces superior flour, high-quality lint, and oil, so that almost every ingredient in a birthday cake can be produced with the leftovers from Nelson's cotton production.

Approximately 30 percent of the cottonseed's weight is in the hull, or outer covering. Like the cottonseed meal, the hulls show up in animal feed. But they are also used in the production of fertilizer, garden mulch, and soil conditioner. And in some regions, cottonseed hulls are processed into oil-drilling mud, a sticky, industrial-strength type of Play-Doh that is used to plug leaks in oil wells.

And finally, a ton of cottonseed will contain about 150 pounds of "linters," which are tiny bits of cotton fuzz that are stuck to the seed after ginning. The oil mill scrapes off the tiny fuzzy bits with microscopic saws and turns them into big bundles of fuzz to be sold. The fuzz turns up again in throw pillows, automobile upholstery, mops, candlewicks, blankets, mattresses, twine, rugs, and medical supplies. Linters are also used in the production of cellulose and viscose, which turns up in toothbrushes, ballpoint pens, picnic cups, and almost any item made of hard plastic. The cellulose from the linters is also found in cheaper brands of ice cream, where it is used to improve texture and reduce ice crystals. Linters are also used in hot dog and sausage casings, as well as writing paper, and in most countries, paper currency. And for those with sensitive skin, an environmental conscience, or both, "tree free" toilet paper made from cotton linters is now available. The toilet paper, according to entrepreneur Willy Paterson-Brown, is "reassuringly expensive."[20]

In October 1999, PCOM merged with the Yazoo Cotton Oil Mill and the new entity, the Plains Yazoo Cotton Oil Mill (PYCO), markets about one-third of the cotton oil produced in the United States.[21] The Plains Cooperative Mill in Lubbock is the world's largest cottonseed oil mill, receiving about 1,200 tons of seed per day from the region's gins, and churning out the makings for peanut butter, soap, and throw pillows.

The PYCO oil mills have quite a monopoly on acquiring seed from the region's gins, which would appear to give the farmers little power in marketing their seed. But the Shallowater gin, along with about 175 other gins across the South, own PYCO, and the Reinsches, of course, own a piece of the gin. The income from the world's largest oil mill, then, is paid to the region's gins, which in turn pass it through in dividends to growers like Nelson and Ruth.

So, Nelson doesn't throw away his cottonseed anymore. Instead, he gets a tiny dividend every time city folk spread peanut butter on their toast.

While his seed is trucked to the oil mill, Nelson's baled cotton lint is trucked to the Farmer's Cooperative Compress (FCC) not far from the cottonseed mill. In earlier times, cotton was compressed here, to reduce the space the cotton occupied in the ships bound for export markets. Now, however, most cotton is compressed at the gin, yet the FCC retains its name. The FCC is the distribution and warehouse point for Nelson's cotton. The FCC stores and insures cotton until it is sold, and then ships it by rail or truck, and for exports, by ship, to its destination. Cotton bound for Chinese mills typically leaves the FCC by truck for Long Beach, California, where it is loaded onto ships bound for Shanghai or Guangzhou. The FCC handles over 10 percent of the Upland cotton grown in the United

States each year, and it paid out more than $150 million in dividends during the five years ending in 2002.[22]

Surprise: Nelson owns a piece of the Compress, too.

And there is one more thing. In Littlefield, a short drive through the emptiness from the Reinsch farm, smack in the middle of the cotton fields, the farmers have built a denim mill.[23] The farmers made a deal: They promised to grow the cotton and Levi-Strauss promised to buy the denim. The established textile industry scoffed, called the mill "the farmer plant," and refused to help. And the things that went wrong—from rattlesnakes burrowing in the denim, to denim of such poor quality it couldn't even be sold as "thirds," to month after month of returns from the meticulous Levi-Strauss inspectors, to trying to find a workforce in the Texas emptiness—did not bode well for the farmers' foray into the textile industry. But by 1998, the Littlefield denim plant was winning Levi-Strauss quality awards, and a short time later the growers had purchased another textile mill in New Braunsfels, Texas.

Today, then, the Plains Cotton Cooperative Association (PCCA) owns two textile mills with approximately $100 million in sales and $20 million in profits. The organization as a whole markets more than 3 billion bales of cotton annually and distributed more than $140 million to its members in the five-year period ending in 2002.[24]

To Market, to Market

Once all of the cotton is in from the fields, it would seem, the farmer deserves a rest. The next step, however, marketing the cotton, takes the farmer out of his element and subjects him to vagaries every bit as cruel and unpredictable as the weather. Nelson remembers well the days of trying to sell his own cotton. He would take his neatly tied bales down to Avenue A in Lubbock, where the cotton buyers all had storefronts. The buyer would poke his hand right into the bale and pull out a big fistful, look it over and name a price, take it or leave it. Usually the farmers had to take it. The season's bills had to be paid, and it was risky for the farmer to hang onto his cotton in the hope that the price would go up. It was the fistfuls that bothered Nelson, still do, thinking back. At the end of the season, Nelson suspects, the cotton buyers down on Avenue A had their own bales to sell.

Ned Cobb remembered selling cotton, too, hitching up the mules and taking a bale into town. But he tried not to take his cotton right to the buyer. He let a white friend do that as he found that this made a big difference in the price:

[C]olored man's cotton weren't worth as much as white man's cotton less'n it come to the buyer in a white man's hands.[25]

If cotton farmers everywhere had a tough time marketing their cotton each fall, nowhere was it tougher than in West Texas, where the cotton had a reputation, mostly but not entirely deserved, for poor quality. For one thing, the West Texas cotton was short fibered, averaging less than one inch; and for another, the fiber was weak. The cotton that was best suited to surviving the West Texas wind, hail, and sand was not, to discerning buyers from the textile mills, very good cotton. Many domestic mills wouldn't touch West Texas cotton, which meant that most had to go for export. And when the cotton did compete, it was only because of its steeply discounted price. It was possible for the West Texas farmers to grow better cotton, but they had no incentive to do so because West Texas cotton was priced by its origin and not by its quality. Buyers simply assumed that the cotton was shorter and weaker than its competition.[26]

The virtuous circle was as effective in advancing cotton marketing as it was in advancing science. Clearly, banding together to improve the quality and reputation of the region's cotton made sense. The Plains Cotton Cooperative Association was formed in 1953 with a $12,000 loan from the PCOM. In 1958 a media blitz on 2,100 radio programs and 50 area newspapers was directed at the West Texas farmers. The farmers were bombarded with the whys and hows of producing better, stronger, longer cotton. As the quality of the cotton improved, the PCCA took on the task of proving it to the textile world.

Most important, the "grab a handful" method of classing cotton gave way, under USDA leadership, to high volume instrumentation (HVI) testing, in which samples from each bale were graded by computer for color, leaf content, fineness (or micronaire), strength, and length at the USDA classing office in Lubbock. An electronic scanner measures the percent-age of the lint's surface that is covered with extraneous matter and grades the cotton on a 1 to 7 scale. Fiber length is measured in hundredths of an inch by passing fibers through a sensing point and estimating the mean length of the fibers in the longest half of the fibers. The sensors also mea-sure length uniformity as the ratio of the upper half mean length to the mean length. Next, fiber strength is measured by the force in grams needed to break a 1,000-gram bundle of fibers; and fiber fineness is mea-sured by forcing compressed air through the cotton fibers. Finally, both color grade (30 possibilities) and leaf content are judged by computer. There is almost no human judgment involved today in classing cotton; the computer does it all, so it is no longer possible to discriminate against West Texas cotton just because of where it was born, and buyers the world over know exactly what they are getting.[27]

Cotton buyers I spoke to in China loved doing business with the PCCA in Lubbock. They loved the West Texans as people, and found them, as I did, to be ideal business partners, as well as unfailingly gracious and brimming with hospitality. They especially loved the cotton classed at the USDA lab in Lubbock, which they told me was the best facility of its kind in the world.

The PCCA also took on the task of selling cotton. In the mid-1970s, the PCCA launched TELCOT, an electronic cotton exchange linking buyers and sellers. Today, electronic marketing takes place through a sys-tem called TheSeam, an internet-based system that provides buyers from all over the world access to West Texas cotton, and allows textile mills to examine on the computer screen the classing results for millions of bales. This all beats hitching up the mule, or driving downtown to Avenue A.

PCCA also gives the farmers the option of not worrying about selling cotton at all. Many farmers, including Nelson, put their cotton into the PCCA's marketing pool. The pool advances some cash as soon as the cot-ton is ginned, and then pools the cotton with that of other growers to sell throughout the year. Farmers receive periodic payments as cotton is sold from the pools. It is a risk-sharing arrangement that leaves no big winners or losers, as all of the farmers in the pool are assured of receiving "average" prices. Today, all Nelson has to do to sell his cotton is to tell Barbara

Burleson at the Shallowater gin to "put it in the pool." The next day, he gets his first check, and three more will come along as the cotton is sold. All told, the PCCA markets about 18 percent of the American cotton crop, about half of that through pools.

All This and Subsidies, Too

As we have seen, throughout American history U.S. cotton farmers have solidified their political influence to manage virtually every business risk to shape the world in front of them. This political influence is striking both in its repetitive pattern of protection from market risks and in the evolution of the relationships among researchers, government programs, and farmer resourcefulness. While farmers have long wielded significant political power in the United States, it seems that recently their power has grown even as the number of farmers has dwindled, especially in the case of cotton farmers. Texas cotton farmers have both a kindred spirit and a staunch ally in George W. Bush, who spends long weekends on his ranch in Crawford, Texas. Crawford lies 300 miles southeast of the Reinsch farm, an interminable drive but only a brief psychic distance from Texas cotton country. According to at least some observers, the definitive source of U.S. cotton farmers' comparative advantage is their ability to get help from friends in high places.[28] On a per acre basis, subsidies paid to cotton farmers are 5 to 10 times as high as those for corn, soybeans, and wheat, and subsidies to cotton are also 3 to 6 times higher relative to production than are subsidies to soybeans and corn.[29] Even by the normally generous standards of U.S. farm policy, the 2002 Farm Bill went "over the top" for cotton.

Under the 2002 Farm Bill, cotton farmers receive a direct payment of 6.66 cents per pound of cotton. In addition, under the commodity loan program, farmers are guaranteed minimum payment at the "loan rate" that was fixed in the Farm Bill legislation at 52 cents per pound. Finally, growers are also entitled to "counter-cyclical payments," which kick in when the farmer's income per pound from the direct payment plus the loan rate (or market price, if it is higher) is less than the target price of 72.24 cents per pound.[30] In total, the 2002 Farm Bill therefore brings the cotton farmer's income up to a minimum of 72.24 cents per pound. The average world price of cotton in mid-2004 was 38 cents per pound, so the effect of the provisions was to guarantee that U.S. cotton farmers could receive almost double the world market price for their cotton. For the 22-year period ending in 2002, the average U.S. farm price of cotton was 59 cents per pound, and the average direct subsidy was 19 cents per pound. As a result, direct subsidies amounted to one-third of the market value of production during this period.[31]

So-called "Step 2" subsidies are to many observers the most egregious of America's cotton support programs, especially from the perspective of producers in poor countries. These subsidies are an attempt to simultaneously manage the irreconcilable demands of the ailing U.S. textile industry for cheaper cotton with the demands of American cotton producers for higher prices. Or, put more directly, the Step 2 program is designed to reconcile the diametrically opposed interests of voters in the Carolinas and voters in Texas. As a support for U.S. cotton producers, the U.S. textile industry is limited in its ability to import cotton, even when the price of foreign cotton is significantly lower than the U.S. price. The effect of this limitation is to increase the raw materials cost for textile mills, by, for example, about 30 percent in 2004.[32] Under the Step 2 program, however, the U.S. government pays American textile mills to purchase U.S. cotton, thereby simultaneously excluding foreign cotton producers from the U.S. market while protecting both the textile and cotton producers. Step 2 payments are also available to exporters of American cotton: The subsidy roughly offsets the difference between world market prices and U.S. prices and therefore guarantees that U.S. cotton is priced competitively in world markets. In mid-2003, Step 2 payments to U.S. textile mills or exporters were approximately 9 cents per pound. For the 8-year period ending in 2003, Step 2 payments to cotton buyers totaled $2.16 billion.[33]

The 2002 Farm Act and its antecedents protect cotton farmers from a wide variety of other business risks that most other industries must bear on their own, including bad weather, bad credit, bad luck, and tough competition. The Crop Disaster Program reimburses farmers for losses due to unusual weather or related conditions, while Farm Loan Programs provide financing to farmers who are unable to get credit from private sources. In addition to the Step 2 programs, the government offers a variety of "Agricultural Trade and Aid" assistance programs to help farmers export cotton, including guarantees against customer default. The government also offers a variety of crop insurance schemes, and subsidizes the purchase of most types of insurance.

The Reinsch farm is located in Hockley County, Texas, which has a population of just 22,000. During the 1995 to 2003 period, direct subsidies to Hockley County cotton farmers totaled more than $86 million. This figure includes only direct price support, and so it excludes conservation program payments of more than $34 million, Step 2 payments to textile mills, and other forms of indirect assistance.[34]

Of course, all this—especially the 2002 Farm Bill—seems like a cruel joke to cotton farmers in the poorest countries of the world, where such sums are fantastic enough to lose meaning. In West Africa, cotton is a principal cash crop and export, and provides more than one-quarter of export earnings for 11 countries.[35] While decades behind the United States in technology, productivity, and yields, because of low-priced or even free family labor, West African cotton farmers can produce cotton at a far lower cost than Texas growers.[36] Though West Africa has many more players— 18 million cotton farmers to America's 25,000—the American government's deep pockets virtually assure the continued dominance of the United States. Remarkably, U.S. government subsidies under the cotton program—approximately $4 billion in 2000—exceed the entire GNP of a number of the world's poorest cotton-producing countries, as well as the United States' entire USAID budget for the continent of Africa.[37] American agricultural subsidies—much like American military might—are simply a force too big for small countries to reckon with.

The primary effect of U.S. government subsidies is to increase the supply of cotton grown in the United States and therefore to decrease the world market price of cotton.[38] Declines in world cotton prices, in turn, lower the income of farmers outside of the United States. Virtually all studies on the topic have found that U.S. subsidies do indeed affect the world price of cotton, and that the removal of direct subsidies would increase the market price of cotton by anywhere from 3 to 15 percent. The removal of subsidies would also weaken U.S. cotton exports, to the advantage of producers elsewhere.[39]

In the summer of 2004, the United States agreed to put agricultural subsidies generally, and cotton subsidies in particular, "on the table" for the current round of trade negotiations. It is far too soon to tell what will ultimately become of this gesture, though it is clearly a step in the right direction. But even if U.S. subsidies to U.S. cotton growers are cut dramatically, it is not at all clear that substantial benefits will then accrue to farmers in the poorest countries of the world, where the subsidies may be the least of farmers' challenges.

Where Is the Competition?

So 200 years after the story began, American cotton farmers still have the comparative advantage they seized in 1792. This dominance jumps out from any list, any table of data, any pie chart on the topic. In 200 years, the United States has rarely dropped below second place in production and export of cotton, and is the clear leader in yields, technology, farm income, and farm size.

Yet in trying to understand this comparative advantage, the pie charts only tease us, giving us nothing at all about the "how." And even the textbooks cannot help, as they explain the idea, but not the reality, of comparative advantage in a global industry. And the idea, as far as the international business textbooks can take it, is almost circular (a country exports what it has a comparative advantage in; look at all those exports—must be comparative advantage). Even when the idea is amplified, we are still in a circle, as it helps not at all to say that the American growers produce more cheaply, or that they are more productive. The "how" is not in the data, it is embedded in the story.

How did they do it? And what can American cotton's story reveal about today's globalization debate?

In *The Lexus and the Olive Tree,* author Thomas Friedman speaks about the winners in globalization as both lions and gazelles. The gazelles win by running faster and smarter than the competition, but the lions win by catching and eating their prey. American cotton growers are both gazelles and lions, and sometimes have taken the high road but other times have not. We see the gazelles in the farmers' entrepreneurial spirit and creativity. And we see them as gazelles by how they squeeze income out of every step in the production chain, and feed cattle, fish, and finally people with their leftovers. This is a complex recycling and value creation that other cotton-producing countries can only dream about. We see the gazelles in the research and scientific progress that freed Nelson Reinsch's children from the farm, that allows him to take a nap after lunch. We see the gazelles in the cotton farmers' business practices in which the growers' ownership of the gin, the oil mill, the textile factories, and the Compress gives the farmers power in their battle against world markets, and ensures that all of the extra pennies so creatively squeezed out of the cotton business flow into the farmers' pockets. And finally, we see the gazelles in the relationships among farmers, universities, and the U.S. government.

But many see lions rather than gazelles in the political power of the cotton farmers, which has shifted risks from weather to prices onto the American taxpayer. We also see lions in the long practice of dominating in one market in order to suppress another. Since the beginning, the American growers have been avoiding the labor market. Yet at least for the first 150 years, cotton production was among the most labor-intensive industries in the country. Most of American cotton's history—from plantation slavery to sharecropping to company towns to Bracero workers—is about yet another creative way of avoiding having to find workers and pay the market wage. Suppressing the labor market has been a central "how" of American dominance in the global cotton industry. And in suppressing the labor market, basic freedoms were denied to generations of people—slaves, sharecroppers, and migrant workers. It was not the perils of the labor market but the absence of the market that doomed these generations of workers.

The subsidies to cotton farmers that have in recent years attracted so much attention are everything recent critics have charged: way too big, way too unfair, and embarrassingly hypocritical when practiced by the world's self-proclaimed free trade champion. But they are also not the whole picture.

Competing with Nelson Reinsch requires a systematized method of factory cotton production. But cotton factories require capital, and profitable factories of any kind require functioning markets and both technical and basic literacy, as well as at least a semblance of the virtuous circle of institutions that support not just agriculture but broader development. At the close of the twentieth century, many poor cotton producers lacked capital, working markets, literacy, or all three. And in spite of our intuition, it is far from clear that cheap labor is an advantage at all. Labor costs are low when people have no choices, and people who cannot read have few choices indeed. It is worth remembering that Ned Cobb stuck it out through sharecropping and boll weevils and all God's dangers and even the arrival of tractors. Cobb ultimately gave up only when the government introduced programs that required that he be able to read. Labor costs are low for people who cannot read, but people who cannot read can only do hand-to-hand combat with cotton's enemies: weather and insects and picking and weeding—all of the enemies against which Nelson Reinsch has sophisticated weapons with complicated instructions. While critics of U.S. agricultural policy are quick to point the finger at U.S. cotton subsidies as the source of America's advantage, the removal of the subsidies would do little—at least in the short term—to develop the literacy, property rights, commercial infrastructure, and scientific progress required to take on Nelson Reinsch in world markets. Activists at Oxfam would do well to take on these causes as well.

If Nelson Reinsch is embedded in a system that protects and enriches him, cotton farmers in West Africa are embedded in a system that exposes and impoverishes them. According to Terry Townsend of ICAC, the state still controls the distribution of inputs to these farmers, and sometimes seeds and fertilizer come to the village and sometimes they do not. Virtually all of the farmers are illiterate, and when they are blessed with pesticides or fertilizers, they often send their children barefoot down the rows with the toxic chemicals, or prepare food with the same implements that are used to spread poison. Even scientists cannot avoid value-laden descriptors of the African cotton farmers' battle. According to agricultural specialists, the cotton farms in the poorest countries have a four-stage life cycle: subsistence, exploitation, crisis, and disaster.[40] According to Townsend, each cotton-producing village has a leader to deal with the cotton buyers: The leader can typically add and subtract, but not read, write, or multiply.

The concept of percentages, then, critical to a range of activities in selling and growing cotton, is as foreign as a mechanical cotton stripper.

There are only two prices paid to farmers for their cotton in West Africa: the A price and the B price, and buyers decide which to pay by the "grab a handful" method that Nelson Reinsch remembers well but has not experienced in decades. A prices and B prices are set once a year by the government and, in recent years, according to Townsend, have averaged about half of the price for which the cotton is sold in the export market. In rough figures, then, if the international price of cotton is 50 cents per pound, West African farmers will receive 25 cents while American farmers receive 72 cents per pound. Not only does this steep discounting impoverish the farmers and enrich the state, but the exclusion from the market created by the A/B system gives the farmers no incentives to improve quality; all of the Eli Whitneys with better ideas have no reason to try.

While the PCCA (which is owned by the Texas farmers) is at work marketing the Reinsch cotton crop, most West African cotton is marketed by a firm named COPACO. COPACO, in turn, is a subsidiary of the DAGRIS corporation. Seventy percent of DAGRIS, according to Townsend, is owned by African governments, while 30 percent is owned by the government of France. This state of affairs is an improvement over the structure of the mid-1990s, when—decades after independence—DAGRIS was 70 percent owned by the government of France.

For West African cotton farmers, then, the political and economic power balance between the farmers and the government has been and remains almost symmetrically inverted from that in the United States.

The Worms Win

The low labor costs that might give the poor farmers an advantage are in fact their undoing. For while there may be worse ways to make a living than to bend in the blistering sun all day, pinching worm eggs between your fingers, it is hard to imagine what they are. Yet if labor costs are low enough, it makes sense to hire worm egg squishers rather than to battle the insects with more sophisticated methods. Or, as experts from the World Bank point out, apparently with a straight face: "Hand collection of pests is feasible only in countries with a plentiful supply of cheap labor."[41] Yet no matter how cheap and plentiful the egg squishers, it is difficult to imagine how they can have an advantage over Nelson's Texas Tech entomologists, his pesticides, his chemicals, and his machines. And if they cannot, then in the end the cheap and plentiful labor is the downfall, not the advantage, of Nelson's competition.

In China, where the textile factories suck in more cotton than any country in the world, cotton production is much closer to Ned Cobb's world than to Nelson Reinsch's. In the year 2002 China was the world's largest cotton producer as well as consumer, but since the dismantling of the communes, virtually all of this production is at the level of the family, usually with an ox or maybe two, and about 10 acres, and typically no machines at all.

Though India and Pakistan are also large cotton producers, Nelson and Ruth Reinsch would also find very little that seems familiar on a South Asian cotton farm. Ned Cobb, again, would recognize almost everything: the vise of the moneylender at 120 percent interest, the tiny number of acres, the illiteracy, the lack of government support or extension, the collapsed rural banking system, the backbreaking physical labor, and especially, life alone on the economic precipice, where little puffs of wind blow farmers right over the edge.

In 2001, for the first time in his life, Nelson Reinsch lost his entire cotton crop. It was June, the plants still young and tender, when a freak hailstorm showered icy bullets over the cotton fields around Lubbock. Nelson, ever the optimist, looked on the bright side. ("It melted. That'll be water for next year.") Nelson planted milo grain in the ravaged fields, which brought in some income to augment the government crop insurance and the disaster subsidy. In American cotton farming, because of the variety of protections in place, disasters happen to cotton but not to people. Nelson Reinsch wasn't happy to lose his cotton, but he did not lose sleep and he did not miss a meal.

Disasters happen to people in other cotton-producing countries. A short time before Nelson Reinsch lost his cotton crop, more than 500 cotton farmers in the Andra Pradesh region of India committed suicide as worms ate the last of their cotton.[42] The farmers could hear the worms chomping, with a sickening *click click* sound that kept the villagers awake all night. Dealers had "furnished" the farmers with pesticides at 36 percent interest, but it was the wrong pesticide with the wrong directions, and the farmers couldn't read anyway. There was no government extension service to give the right advice, no federal financing to replace the moneylender, no public school to learn to read, and, in the end, no way out. The pesticides so useless on the worms worked quickly as poison, and hundreds of farmers dropped twitching to the ground in the middle of the cotton fields. All of these cheap and plentiful people, working all day in the Andra Pradesh sun, just couldn't squish the worms quickly enough. They never had a chance against Nelson Reinsch, Texas Tech, and George W. Bush.

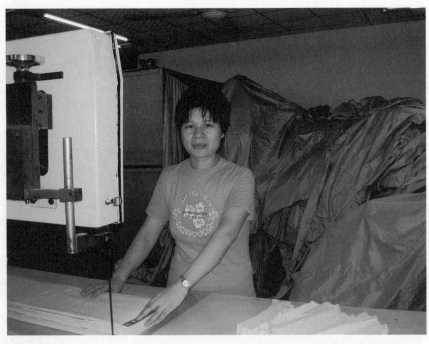

He Yuan Zhi at Her Cutting Machine at the Shanghai Brightness Factory.
(Author's photo)

PART II

MADE IN CHINA

The Author with Tao Yong Fang, Manager of the Shanghai Number 36 Mill. (Author's photo)

Cotton Comes to China

Nelson Reinsch's cotton leaves the Compress in Lubbock and turns left toward China. Usually by truck, but sometimes by train, the cotton heads through the blank space of West Texas, New Mexico, and Nevada, stopping finally at the Pacific Ocean in Long Beach, California. The cotton boards a ship and keeps going west, arriving a few days later at the port in Shanghai, and into the deafening pulse of China's weird new capitalism. Here, the Reinsch cotton is spun into yarn, knitted into cloth, cut into pieces, and finally sewn into a T-shirt. A "Made in China" label will be tacked to the collar. Thus transformed, the Texas cotton will return to America.[1]

Nelson and Ruth's son, Lamar, thinks it is funny that he never thought about the Reinsch cotton actually *going* to China. In fact, even as a professor in a business school, Lamar's cotton consciousness ended at the gin in Shallowater. He never thought about what happened next, where the cotton went, or how it got there. But there is a low buzz about China in Lamar's childhood memories. At the gin, or at church, or at the dinner table, China was one of the things grownups talked about, one of the topics that would make his parents sigh and shake their heads. To a child, the China conversations were like the weather conversations, or the cotton price conversations. China, cotton prices, weather: the wild cards in the life of a Texas cotton farmer. Lamar remembers only that China mattered.

China matters even more today. During the past several years, I found that it was impossible to get more than one or two minutes into a cotton conversation anywhere in the world before someone mentioned China and heads began to shake. Today, China is not only (usually) the largest buyer of American cotton, it also consumes nearly one-third of the world's cotton production.[2] Cotton was America's ninth largest export to China in 2003, and cotton exports increased by nearly 400 percent from 2002 to 2003.[3] In a circular linkage that ebbs and flows (but mostly grows), demand by Americans for cheap clothing from China leads to demand from China for cotton from America.

As the Texas cotton is hoisted from the ship in Shanghai, it enters not just a new country but a new global industry. The production of textiles and apparel is almost as old as agriculture, and, since the beginning, agriculture and textiles have been linked: Whether wool, silk, flax, or cotton, whatever humans have spun or woven had to first be grown. Today, however, the agricultural and industrial chapters in a T-shirt's life often take place on different continents. It takes a little over a third of a pound of cotton lint to produce a T-shirt, maybe 15 cents' worth, so an acre of West Texas farmland can produce about 1,200 T-shirts each year. In a good season, then, Nelson could produce enough cotton for over a million T-shirts, and, as we have seen, he does this by supervising not people but land, capital, and technology. But to become a T-shirt, the cotton requires workers: cutters, spinners, knitters, and stitchers. While the labor component of American cotton production is almost too small to be measured, labor still accounts for more than half of the value added in the production of apparel. So Nelson's cotton travels to China, to where the people are.

Travelers who wistfully bemoan the homogenization of the world today will feel better if they travel between Lubbock and Shanghai. The cities seem to occupy different planets, so different that it is not even possible to discuss their differences because they have nothing in common as a place to start, not even a Starbucks, which Shanghai has but Lubbock does not. Although cultures may be converging in Paris and New York, or L.A. and Hong Kong, it will likely be a while before one can buy ostrich leather boots in Shanghai or ground rhino horn in Lubbock. Yet the cotton textile industry is as important to Shanghai as the cotton agricultural industry is to Lubbock, so the cities, planets apart in every way, are bound together by soft cotton fiber, and each city keeps a constant watch on the other.

The cities have been linked together by cotton fiber for nearly a century, but evolution in Lubbock has taken place alongside revolution in Shanghai. In July 1921, when the Texas cotton stood broiling in the first summer of Nelson Reinsch's life, before there really was a Lubbock, the Chinese Communist Party (CCP) was founded in a Shanghai schoolhouse. At this point, nearly half of the factory workers in Shanghai were employed in the cotton mills, and whatever labor tensions simmered in China boiled over in the Shanghai mills.[4] Throughout the 1920s, igniting events in the textile mills—beatings, wage cuts, murders—spilled up and down China's coast, mobilizing workers and paralyzing industry.[5] Labor activism in 1920s China was not for the weak of heart: As the workers stood up, the army squashed them, and many strike leaders in the textile industry were publicly beheaded as a lesson to others.

But as Shanghai's cotton textile industry bred the labor revolutionaries, it also generated the lavish wealth that transformed Shanghai into an X-rated Disneyland for the new industrialists. As cotton agriculture took hold in West Texas, Shanghai became known for its glittering and seamy decadence. The city offered the new industrialists opium dens, "singsong houses," and amusements for any appetite. And though it is not at all clear who counted or how, Shanghai in the 1930s reportedly had more prostitutes per capita than any city in the world.[6] Perhaps most illustrative of Shanghai during this period were the "pleasure palaces" to be found lining the mains roads of the International Settlement. A wide-eyed American visitor remembers the Great World Pleasure Palace this way:

> On the first floor were gaming tables, singsong girls, magicians, pick-pockets, slot machines, fireworks, bird cages, fans, stick incense, acrobats and ginger. One flight up were . . . actors, crickets and cages, pimps, midwives, barbers, and earwax extractors. The third floor had jugglers, herb medicines, ice cream parlors, photographers, a new bevy of girls, their high collared gowns slit to reveal their hips, and (as a) novelty, several rows of exposed (Western) toilets. The fourth floor had shooting galleries, fan-tan tables, . . . massage benches, . . . dried fish and intestines, and dance platforms . . . the fifth floor featured girls with dresses slit to the armpits, a stuffed whale, story tellers,

balloons, peep shows, masks, a mirror maze, two love letter booths with scribes who guaranteed results . . . and a temple filled with ferocious gods. On the top floor and roof of that house of multiple joys a jumble of tightrope walkers slithered back and forth, and there were seesaws, Chinese checkers, mahjongg, . . . firecrackers, lottery tickets, and marriage brokers.[7]

With a 12-hour workday and often just two holidays per year, the cotton mill workers lacked both the price of admission and the time to visit this multistoried wonder. So as the divide between labor and capital yawned wider, the Communists gradually and secretly infiltrated the cotton mills, where thousands of workers were locked in a steamy hell, ripening for revolution. In 1949, when Nelson's children were young and the Mexican migrants were still crawling through his fields, the Communists drove the mill owners from Shanghai, closed the pleasure palaces, and seized the factories for the people. Women cotton mill workers alone comprised more than one-third of the infamous Shanghai proletariat.[8]

And in the 1960s, as Nelson's sons rode the cotton trailer with their pitchforks, Mao Zedong and his Red Guards went mad in the Cultural Revolution, terrorizing the management of the spinning and weaving factories, forcing the lucky managers to confess to capitalist crimes, the less lucky to be jailed, and the least lucky to be executed or face starvation in the countryside. And finally, in the late 1970s, as Nelson's module builder freed his children from the farm, China opened its door to the world. Shanghai grandparents, after a 30-year break, tasted chocolate and coffee again, and Shanghai parents tasted them for the first time. The blinding neon lights came back on down Nanjing Road, the Great World Pleasure Palace was turned into a G-rated shopping mall, and China began to sell T-shirts to Americans.

Through all of the revolutions—Nationalist, Communist, Cultural, and now Capitalist—the cotton spindles have clattered on, an unbroken thread through the tumultuous times.

Comparatively speaking, things have been very quiet in Lubbock.

Shanghai Number 36 Cotton Yarn Factory

"Come to China," Patrick Xu told me when we met in Washington. "I'll show you everything." In the spring of 2000, a few months after leaving Lubbock, I took Patrick up on his offer.

The Shanghai Number 36 Cotton Yarn Factory is on the far east out-
skirts of the city, reached by a one-hour drive through a crowded landscape that manages to be colorfully bleak. While the drive to the Reinsch
farm is a journey through nothingness, the drive to the cotton yarn factory
is a journey through an impossibly crowded jumble of alleys and high-
rises, shacks and workshops, bakeries and tea shops, bicycles and push-
carts, water buffaloes and chickens. Mostly, however, southeastern China
is a giant factory floor. Though some factories are new and gleaming,
many are ramshackle and dusty workshops making things like hose fit-
tings, engine parts, shoes, umbrellas, bicycles, toys, and socks.

Down a bumpy unpaved road where people cook on the sidewalks and
the buildings look close to collapsing, a quick left turn leads to a jumble of
buildings. To the visitor who cannot read Chinese there is no hint at all
about the purpose of the buildings until one arrives at a loading dock.
There, in stacks perhaps 30 feet high, sit bales of Texas cotton.

Stepping into the Number 36 Cotton Yarn Factory was more than a sensory assault. The noise is a metal blanket, a deafening clatter of real
machines, rather than the electronic buzzing or beeping emitted by factories in America. The metal noise blanket smothers not only conversation
but thinking as well. Everyone and everything in the factory wears a light
dusting of cotton flurries. For breathing, there is not air, but dusty steam,
as the factory is kept moist to reduce the incidents of broken thread. Perhaps the worst sensory assault, because there is no reason for it, is the color
inside this factory. It might be titled Communist Green, and it is everywhere. I kept looking back at the walls to make sure that the color was
really there: It was ugly enough to be astonishing. But to compensate for
the awful color and deafening noise there is the feel and smell of the cotton itself. As the cotton is transformed from plant into yarn, it becomes
softer and softer—impossible not to touch—and the musty-sweet smell of
the cotton and yarn is comforting and mildly addictive. Coming from
Texas, Shanghai smells foreign: green tea, frying dumplings, hairy crabs.
But here in the factory, Shanghai smells like Shallowater, Texas.

The word "factory" conjures up an image of linear assembly, one thing
attaching to another and another until an end product, a collection of parts

made into a whole, appears at the end of the line. But nothing is assembled in the production of cotton yarn, and nothing is linear, either. The process is a transformation rather than an assembly, and almost every stage of the process is circular rather than linear: winding, twisting, spinning, coiling.

The cotton bales, still speckled with Texas leaf bits and rabbit fur, are hacked open, and the contents are sucked into a French-made vacuum cleaner. The vacuum cleaner's tubes are clear Plexiglas, and the clumps break up and whoosh through the tubes to clean whatever bits of Texas dirt and rabbit were left behind by the gin in Shallowater. While the cotton had to be compressed to a brick for shipping, now it must be blown apart into a cloud in preparation for spinning. After it is blown apart, it is smoothed into a soft flat blanket. The blanket is a sheet of fluff, with soft tufts pointing in every direction. Next, the cotton is carded, tiny wire teeth forcing the fluff to lie down flat and face its fibers in the same direction. The now-flat blanket is drawn into a snowy rope perhaps an inch in diameter, called a sliver (pronounced with a long "i").

The slivers are but a brief moment in the transformation from Texas plant to Chinese yarn, but for me they were the best part of the factory. The slivers are so transparent and gossamer that they are almost not there, like ghosts in a children's cartoon, and they are impossibly soft. My sensory extreme experience in the factory was complete: I could not wait to escape the metal noise blanket and the appalling Communist Green walls, but I wanted to take the smell and the slivers back home with me to Washington.

The slivers are coiled around and around into tall metal cans, until they mound over the top like ropes of cotton candy. The ropes are then fed into the spindles and are twisted into yarn. In the final circular process, the yarn is wound onto bobbins, leaving a spool of yarn the size and shape of a motel ice bucket.

Supervising all of this circular motion is Tao Yong Fang, manager of the Number 36 factory. Tao stands not much taller than Nelson Reinsch's belt buckle, and she is so slight that she looks as if she could be picked up by a West Texas windstorm. But Tao walks and talks at double speed while seeing everything and knowing everyone in the factory.

The Number 36 Cotton Yarn Factory was built in 1944, five years before all factories were seized in the Communist Revolution. While much of China's textile industry has been privatized to some degree since the 1980s, the Number 36 factory remains a classic Chinese state-owned enterprise, or SOE, though it has recently put toes in the capitalist waters by entering into a joint venture with a Hong Kong firm. When Tao was assigned to the Number 36 mill in 1983 she did not move so quickly. Tao, the workers, and the factory itself were cogs in the wheel of China's central economic planning machine, with no room at all for initiative, no reason to be in a hurry. Well into the 1980s, the central planners delivered set quantities of cotton bales, machinery, and factory workers to the doorstep, and came back later to collect the production quota of cotton yarn.

Americans, and now Russians and Slovaks and Chinese, disdain such central planning for its inefficiencies. A system that ignores market signals, that provides no incentives, that subsidizes losers cannot be efficient in producing goods and services. Central planners will produce the wrong goods, use the wrong inputs, set the wrong prices, hire the wrong people, and ultimately produce shoddy products, and not enough of them, anyway. But to meet Tao in the Number 36 factory is to realize that the real tragedy of central planning lies not in its inefficiency but in its crushing of the intellect, of 20 years of Tao's energy and intelligence laid to waste. For 35 years the spindles in the Number 36 mill clattered, and no one working in the mill had to *decide* anything. So today there is determination but bewilderment as Tao faces the basic questions of running a business rather than turning a cog: what to produce, where to sell, whom to hire, what to pay?

There are experts in each phase of a T-shirt's life: experts whose job it is to know about things that the consumer never thinks about as they pull on the shirt. To the consumer, the T-shirt is made of cotton, but to the cotton expert, "cotton" is like "snow" to an Eskimo: Because of its infinite varieties, the general term conveys very little. So as the consumer thinks "cotton," the expert thinks fiber length and fiber color, sugar content, trash particles, moisture, and fiber strength. And so it is at the Chinese yarn factory. Tao Yong Fang can answer few questions about yarn, or even T-shirt yarn. It all depends. And the complexity of even this most simple industrial process means that Tao must be an expert as well as a businessperson, in order to make the dozens of decisions that never reach the consumer's consciousness. Which types of cotton should be blended and in what mix? What is the best tradeoff between strength and fineness? Should the cotton fiber be combed or not? Should the cotton be twisted to the right or the left? How much twist should be put into the yarn? And finally, because a pound of cotton can be transformed into anywhere between 800 and 2,500 yards of yarn, what yarn "count" should be produced, and with which grades of cotton? And most important, who will buy?

The Shanghai Brightness Number 3 Garment Factory

On the opposite side of Shanghai's sprawl is another clump of buildings surrounded by farms. From the outside, the factory looks like a rural schoolhouse. On the inside, the Reinsch cotton is again transformed, this time from yarn into clothing.

The bucket-shaped spools of yarn are unloaded from a truck and placed on a knitting machine. As draping folds of fabric slowly and rhythmically fall from the machine, a lone inspector facing a large mirror simultaneously eyes both sides of the fabric for defects. On the second floor of the factory, the fabric is cut into pieces: sleeves, fronts, backs, and collars. In the United States, T-shirt pieces are cut largely without human interference, in a process that involves lasers, software, and a great deal of capital. At Shanghai Brightness, however, cutting is a peopled process, a bustle of workers manning big saws, little saws, and just plain scissors. The cut fabric pieces are piled into plastic laundry baskets and ferried to the sewing room.

In the production of T-shirts and other apparel, it is the sewing stage that has been most difficult to mechanize. Almost every other stage of apparel production has gradually replaced labor with capital, in a trend that mirrors cotton production in the United States. But despite millions of dollars in research in mechanization, people are still required to piece together fabric and feed it into sewing machines. The sewing stage of a T-shirt's life is also unique because it is sewing—not cotton farming, yarn spinning, or fabric knitting—that is most often associated with the evils of the sweatshop.

While both the Lubbock cotton farm and the Chinese textile mill had been completely foreign experiences for me, when I walked into the sewing room at Shanghai Brightness I found an oddly familiar sight. Approximately 70 women were lined up in rows, each sitting at a sewing machine. It was relatively quiet, and on this sunny spring day the room was bright. Each woman performed just one operation, over and over again: sleeves, side seams, collars, or hems. At each worker's side is a plastic laundry basket, which the worker gradually fills as she completes her designated operations. When the basket is full, it is passed to the worker behind for the next operation. It only took a minute for me to realize what the setting reminded me of: Our Lady of Bethlehem Academy, La Grange, Illinois, 1969, 7th grade. We were all girls, lined up neatly in rows. We were doing what we were told, over and over again, and we were quiet. It is not that the experience was awful, far from it. But we watched the clock obsessively, waiting for recess. When we looked up, we saw a large crucifix and Sister Mary Karen's stern glare, so we usually looked back down. When the women at Shanghai Brightness look up, they see a sign on the wall:

Quality Has 3 Enemies: Broken Thread, Dirt, Needle Pieces

Then they look back down and continue working, waiting for recess, too.

Shanghai Brightness was founded in the mid-1980s as a Town and Village Enterprise collective owned by the local government. Like Tao Yong Fang, Su Qin, the company's director, gained his early experience as a cog in the central planning wheel, assigned right out of school in 1976 to work in a state-owned garment factory. Also like Tao, he is gradually coming to terms with markets. Today, he has no guaranteed customers; instead he competes with over 40,000 garment factories in China alone, each trying to meet the relentlessly high standards of quality, delivery, service, and price in the international markets. Su does not remember any of these issues from his days in the state-owned garment factory, where he supervised the production of the utilitarian Mao-style jackets and trousers. He remembers no discussions at all about broken thread, dirt, or needle pieces. But today the T-shirts are commodities, and such details mean everything. Su remembers how surprised he was when he first heard a customer complain about needle pieces. But now Su has a metal detector, and every article of clothing passes through the detector on its way to the truck to minimize the risk. Su's efforts are paying off. During the past several years he has expanded from one factory to seven and has more than tripled the number of employees. When I went back to visit Shanghai Brightness in 2003, Su had left T-shirts behind and moved up the value chain into high-end cotton knit children's wear.

Shanghai Brightness is but 1 of approximately 60 apparel manufacturers that funnel knitted apparel to Shanghai Knitwear, the mammoth state-owned apparel export-import company that occupies the middleman's place between Chinese producers and American importers. Shanghai Knitwear maintains a secure spot as one of China's top 100 exporters, and is the largest exporter of knit clothing in the country. In the year 2000, Shanghai Knitwear shipped about 2.5 million T-shirts to the United States, at a price of approximately $13 per dozen.

Today, China dominates the global textile and apparel industries as the United States dominates the world cotton markets. In 1993 China became the world's largest exporter of apparel, a position it has held every year since.[9] Chinese apparel has significant markets in North America, Europe, and Japan, and Americans purchase approximately 1 billion garments made in China each year, four for every U.S. citizen.[10] Since 1980, Chinese apparel exports have grown at an average annual rate of 30 percent, more than six times the rate of growth in merchandise trade.[11] By 2003, China's share of world apparel exports was approximately 30 percent. By most measures—production, exports, employment, or growth—China's textile and apparel complex leads this global industry today (see Figure 4.1).

Yet as Americans snap up the cheap T-shirts along the beach, there is uneasiness in the United States about China's dominance in the labor-intensive textile and apparel industries. Could it be that China's victory is a failure? A failure for American trade policy, a failure for American workers, a failure for American consumers, and a failure especially for Chinese workers, who toil in poor conditions for pitiful wages in a quest to produce the cheapest shirts? In *The Race to the Bottom*, Alan Tonelson argues that the enormous "surplus" of labor in China imperils workers worldwide as international competition puts incessant downward pressure on wages and working conditions, leading the apparel and textile industries to favor the cheapest and most Draconian producers. If the means to victory in this

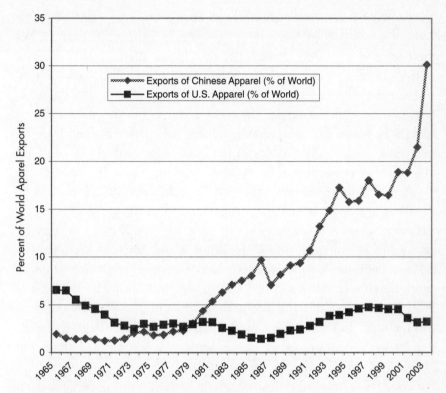

Source: United Nations COMTRADE database.

FIGURE 4.1 *China's Share of World Apparel Exports*

industry are to provide the lowest wages, the poorest conditions, and the most restrictive regimes to apparel producers, then is not the victory hollow at best? And does the race to the bottom have a bottom, or will the seemingly infinite surplus of unskilled workers in China lead to an incessant downward spiral into the depths of a Charles Dickens novel?

The "sweatshop" stories pour out of China almost as fast as the T-shirts, each more wrenching than the last. For example, the National Labor Committee found that apparel workers in China were:

> young women forced to work seven days a week, 12 hours a day, earning as little as 12 to 18 cents an hour with no benefits, housed in cramped, dirty rooms, fed on thin rice gruel, stripped of their legal rights, under constant surveillance and intimidation—really just one step from indentured servitude . . . [12]

Globalization's critics continue to charge that the price of cheap T-shirts is high indeed. Sweatshops spawned by global capitalism exploit the poor and powerless, forcing people without alternatives to work in prison-like conditions for pennies a day. The factory villages also destroy traditional family structures and cultures, and weaken indigenous agriculture. In short, the critics claim, the cheap T-shirts from China are a victory for U.S. consumers and for corporate profits, but a failure for humanity. To free trade advocates, the swells of cheap Chinese clothing flowing into U.S. ports are evidence that the system is working, but to critics the swells illustrate what is wrong rather than what is right with global capitalism.

But whether we view China's dominance in textiles and apparel as a failure or victory, China's position at the top is strikingly different from the dominance of American cotton producers. While American cotton growers have held their position for 200 years, experience suggests that dominance in the textile and apparel industries has historically been a fleeting moment, a brief stop in the race to the bottom in this intensely competitive industry. To understand China's victory in the race today, to understand why American cotton travels so far to become a T-shirt, and ultimately to decide whether the race to the bottom (or perhaps the top) is a good thing or a bad thing, something to be stopped or facilitated, let us examine the course of the race itself: Where did it start? Where does it end? What happens to the winners and losers? And what about the young women eating thin rice gruel?

THE LONG RACE TO THE BOTTOM

Inventive Brits versus Thrifty Chinamen

The gaping divide between the poor sweatshop workers of the East and the rich consumers of the West is a relatively recent phenomenon. Kenneth Pomeranz has convincingly shown that until at least 1750, China rivaled Europe in virtually all measures of well-being and development.[1] Meticulously examining data ranging from life expectancy to technological development, to consumption of sugar and cloth, to the sophistication of markets, Pomeranz finds that China, if anything, was more favorably positioned for industrial development than even the most advanced regions of Europe until the middle of the eighteenth century. Early travelers to China agreed, finding the country superior to Europe in prosperity, politics, and art.[2] But though they may have been evenly matched at the starting line, Europe took a great leap forward in the late 1700s. Though scholars continue to debate the underlying causes of what Pomeranz has called "The Great Divergence" that occurred at this time, there is no debate that Europe's leap forward began with the Industrial Revolution, and the Industrial Revolution, in turn, was ignited by cotton textile factories that clothed much of the world in cheap, serviceable cotton garments that were similar in function though not in form to today's cotton T-shirts.

In China most early textile production took place at the level of the family. Families were generally self-sufficient in textiles and clothing, and each phase of the process—spinning, weaving, cutting, and sewing—took place at home. In contrast, particularly in England, textile production by the 1700s had become at least somewhat specialized. While cotton and wool spinning remained auxiliary home industries, weaving in Britain gradually became a cottage industry. The "putting-out" system evolved wherein families would "put out" the yarn they had spun to professionals for weaving. A British visitor to China in the 1850s marveled at the self-sufficiency of the "thrifty Chinamen" and the ability of the household to engage in all phases of production:

> [A]ll hands in the farmhouse, young and old together, turn to carding, spin-ning and weaving this cotton; and out of homespun stuff, a heavy and durable material . . . they clothe themselves, and the surplus they carry to the nearest town. . . . It is, perhaps, characteristic of China alone, of all countries in the world, that the loom is to be found in every well-conditioned homestead. The people of all other nations at that point stop short, sending the yarn to the professional weaver to be made into cloth. It was reserved for the thrifty Chinamen to carry the thing out to perfection. He not only cards and spins his cotton, but he weaves it himself, with the help of his wives and daughters.[3]

The writer, marveling at the self-sufficiency of the Chinese household, went on to extol the virtues of the system. By engaging the wives and daughters in all phases of production, the system was innately more flexi-ble and less prone to bottlenecks than the British putting-out system. The family production system meant that at almost all times of the year all members of the household could be productive in one way or another.

But what the writer had not appreciated was the value of bottlenecks. As Eli Whitney had shown, bottlenecks create a force behind them, attracting geniuses trying to go over, under, around, or through. Some-times bottlenecks blow the future apart. This is what happened in the late 1770s when a choking bottleneck in the production of cotton cloth launched the modern world.

In traditional methods, the spinning of cotton was far more labor intensive than weaving, as it generally required between four and eight spinners to keep one weaver supplied with yarn.[4] Edward Baines noted in 1845 that it was no uncommon thing for a weaver to walk three or four miles and call on five or six spinners, before he could collect (enough yarn) to serve him for the remainder of the day.[5]

The problem was exacerbated by the fact that spinning was a home-based industry, engaged in only to the extent that agricultural tasks had been completed. During the harvest season, it became difficult for British weavers to get any yarn at all. The bottleneck was made still worse by the technological progress that had occurred in weaving: The flying shuttle, widely adopted by the 1760s, multiplied further the number of spinners required to supply a weaver with yarn. In desperation, the British government began to sponsor competitions and award prizes to those offering solutions to the spinning bottlenecks.

James Hargreaves rose to the challenge and patented his spinning jenny in 1770. The first jenny contained eight spindles, immediately multiplying by eight the yarn that could be produced by a single worker. But by 1784 the jennies held 80 spindles and by the end of the century more than 100. Yet Hargreaves' was but one of many imaginative inventions to revolutionize the production of cotton cloth during the next 50 years, and they came with dizzying speed: the water frame, the mule, the steam engine. By 1832, the price of cotton yarn in Britain had fallen to one-twentieth the price it had sold for in the 1780s.[6] The race to the bottom had begun.

The spinning jennies gave rise to the factory system and to an entirely new economic order. Factory employment meant not only that workers gave up their domestic textile activities, but also that they gave up their agricultural activities and moved from farms to the new urban areas. The necessary business infrastructure, from finance and insurance to transportation and communications, soon developed to meet the needs of the new industrialists. And ancillary industries, from textile machinery to chemicals, steam, iron, and mechanical engineering, emerged as well. The new urban population, in turn, stimulated the development of the retail trade: the food, drink, and medicine trades, as well as the clothing and housewares industries. Cotton spinning was also the first manufacturing industry to utilize the publicly subscribed limited liability company as a legal structure, which in turn formed the basis for the publicly held corporation as a form of ownership.

More broadly, innovation in cotton textile production was the ignition switch for the modern economy, leading to what economic historian W.W. Rostow has called "the takeoff," in which economic growth and continual improvement in the human condition came to be the normal and expected state of affairs. Indeed, prior to the revolution in Britain's textile industry, world economic growth had been barely perceptible. The importance of cotton textiles to Britain's economic development was such that Joseph Shumpteter has argued that the industrial history of Britain from 1787 until 1842 "can be resolved into the history of this single industry."[7]

Help Wanted: Docile and Desperate Preferred

Early cotton mill workers were pushed into the mills not by preference but by desperation and a lack of alternatives. Little skill was required for most jobs in the textile factories, so many workers were children from the "poorhouses" who were sent by the parishes to earn their keep. Work in the cotton mills meant that children could be economically self-sufficient from the age of five. The factories also drew labor, particularly women, from the agricultural sector. The enclosure movement of the 1700s had left much of the rural population without land, and increasing agricultural productivity meant that there was less wage work for rural laborers. Whether children without parents or farmers without land, an abundant and cheap labor force of desperate people powered the development of the factory system as surely as the steam engine.[8]

Children and rural women were recruited by early mill owners not only because of their abundance and low price, but also because owners found them temperamentally well-suited to the mind-numbing drudgery of early textile work. Manufacturers found men to be more difficult while women and children were just as productive and a lot less trouble. An observer wrote that the master:

> finding that the child or women was a more obedient servant to himself and an equally efficient slave to his machinery—was disposed to displace the male adult labor.[9]

Not only was women's labor cheaper than men's, women were "more easily induced to undergo severe bodily fatigue."[10] Married women with hungry children were best of all, as one mill owner explained that he:

> employs females exclusively at his power looms . . . [and] gives a decided preference to married females, especially those who have families at home dependent on them for support; they are attentive, docile, more so than unmarried females and are compelled to use their ultimate exertions to procure the necessities of life. . . .[11]

Another factory owner concurred, noting that he too preferred females for their docility:

> Their labor is cheaper, and they are more easily induced to undergo severe bodily fatigue than men, either from the praiseworthy motive of gaining additional support for their families, or from the folly of satisfying a love of dress.[12]

The British cotton industry from the beginning developed an export bias, and by 1800 was shipping cotton cloth to Asia, Continental Europe, and the Americas. As a result, while the development of the industry fostered the growth of ancillary industries and broader economic development at home, it also fueled the engine of export-led growth. During the first half of the nineteenth century, cotton goods comprised nearly half of Britain's exports, and at the industry's peak Britain supplied nearly half of the world's consumption of cotton cloth.[13] And while the British monopoly of the world cotton trade began to decline in the later 1800s, Britain nonetheless remained the world's largest exporter of cotton textiles until the 1930s.

Yet the British recognized the precarious economic logic of an industry that imported cotton from the United States and India, only to sell cloth back to the poor of these countries. British dominance was assured only as long as they alone had the new textile technology. As a result, the British textile technology assumed the characteristics of smuggler's contraband. Britain forbade not only the export of textile machinery, but also the export of plans or drawings. To tighten the seal further, Britain also forbade skilled textile operatives, who might carry ideas abroad, from leaving the country.

Today, China's defenders are quick to point out that America's industrial might began with intellectual property violations, and especially with a "stunning act of industrial piracy" committed by Francis Cabot Lowell, a blue-blooded Bostonian.[14]

In 1810, Lowell traveled with his wife and young sons to England. No one would have any reason to suspect him of industrial espionage. Instead, as historian Robert Dalzell writes, Lowell "must have struck the people he met as very much what he was: a well-connected, mild-mannered American merchant traveling in Europe . . . for reasons of health."[15] Only a few close friends knew his true purpose: a seemingly foolhardy scheme of industrial espionage that would bring textile factories to America.[16] Using his significant mathematical aptitude, Lowell memorized the critical details of Edmund Cartright's power loom and returned home to Massachusetts. While Lowell's act was exceptional in securing for America the crown jewel technology of the power loom, complementary technology also leaked into the United States during this period, most often in the minds of skilled artisans from Britain who had managed to evade emigration restrictions. By 1812, virtually all of the important technology related to cotton textile production had been transferred to New England.[17]

So as it had in England, the production of cotton textiles led the Industrial Revolution in America, once again igniting parallel developments in urbanization, business infrastructure, and supporting industries. Enormous textile mills, the scale of which had not been seen before or since, soon lined the banks of the rivers throughout Massachusetts and New Hampshire. The U.S. mills produced a standardized and cheap cotton cloth, well-suited to clothing slaves in the South, farmers in the Mid-Atlantic, and settlers on the western frontier. The New England mills took the growing and profitable American mass market from England, leaving only the smaller market for fancy goods for the British. By the late 1800s the world's largest textile mills were in New England. The biggest of all, the Amoskeag Mills on the Merrimack River, had 650,000 spindles and 17,000 employees, and produced 500 miles of cotton cloth per day.[18] By the early 1900s the United States had surpassed Britain in cloth production, and British dominance of the international trade faded rapidly (see Figure 5.1).[19]

New England had emerged as the leader in the race to the bottom, and the golden era of British cotton manufacture came to a close. While the United States and Europe had absorbed nearly 70 percent of Britain's cloth exports in 1820, by 1896 they accounted for only 8 percent of these exports.

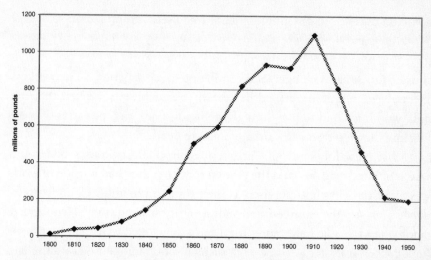

Source: Robson 1957, pp 332–333. Data reported for the initial year of each decade.

FIGURE 5.1   *British Cotton Piece Goods Exports, 1800 to 1950*

Fortunately for the British, Asia would not mechanize textile production until much later, so much of the loss in American and European markets was made up in exports to India and China. But while Britain would maintain its preeminence as an exporter into the 1900s, its singular position at the top of the industry had come to an end. The profitability of cotton textile production in England fell steadily throughout the 1800s, and by 1912 exports of British cloth had peaked. Today, Britain is not a significant exporter of cotton textiles and clothing.

Like their British predecessors, the labor force of the New England mills was drawn from the ranks of "surplus" labor with no alternatives. Most of the early New England mill workers were young single women from the farms of rural New England and Canada who could contribute to their family's livelihood only by leaving the rocky farms and joining the swelling ranks of "mill girls." Working conditions were better than in Dickens' famed "Satanic mills," but not by much. The mill girls worked more than 70 hours per week in the steamy and suffocating heat with a bell to wake them at 4:30 A.M. and only short breaks for meals. Mills offering a 12-hour workday were lauded as humane, because such lenience "gave an opportunity for the girls to wash, mend, or read."[20] Even so, it was common practice to obtain more labor by falsely setting factory clocks.[21] Working conditions were compared unfavorably to life in jail, with a physician who had visited the mills noting that in prison work hours were shorter, lunch breaks longer, and ventilation much superior.[22] The workers themselves, in a petition filed in Lowell, Massachusetts, argued that the mill working conditions, through pain, disease, and privations, were hurtling the employees toward a premature death.[23]

Most New England mill girls resided in boardinghouses under the watch of hired matrons, and the limited time that they had outside of work was almost as closely supervised as their time in the mills. Church attendance was strictly enforced and moral purity a condition of continued employment. In one mill, causes for dismissal included levity, captiousness, impudence, or hysteria, and even a suspicion of immorality was sufficient for blacklisting by both fellow workers and management alike.[24]

Like their British predecessors, the mill owners had clear conceptions of the type of worker who was most desirable. Francis Cabot Lowell believed that young women, since they were "useless" on the farms, would be especially "docile and tractable," with the added benefit that keeping young women busy in the factory would reduce their chances of being tempted into impurity or other bad habits.[25] The New England mills later preferred the French Canadians, whom the owners found to be "docile, industrious, and stable" with the added advantage of their strict Catholicism and resulting large families.[26]

So while the British mills had drawn upon pauper children and landless laborers, the New England spindles were powered by rural "mill girls"—also often children—and later, immigrants. In both cases the growth of the cotton textile industry was dependent upon a multitude of poor people with few alternatives, and in both cases the "ideal" laborer was hardy, docile, and uncomplaining. Early textile work and apparel work required neither creativity nor intelligence, but physical stamina and mental fortitude in the face of repetitive drudgery.

In the race to the bottom, New England's golden age in textile manufacture would be much briefer than Britain's. Between 1880 and 1930, cotton textile production gradually withered in New England and took root in the southern Piedmont region.[27] The main draw to the South was lower wages: Wages in the North Carolina textile industry during this period were generally 30 to 50 percent lower than those paid to textile operatives in Massachusetts.[28] While the Southern mill workers had slightly lower labor productivity, significant cost advantages remained for the Southern producers. The Southern labor cost advantages stemmed not only from differences in wage levels, but also from poorer working conditions. In addition, regulatory and cultural restraints on child labor and hours of work were significantly weaker in the South than in the New England mills. Child labor was more prevalent in textiles than in any other industry, and reliance on child labor was four times greater in the South than in the North.[29] Indeed, more than 60 percent of the females working in Southern cotton mills in the early 1900s were 13 years old or younger.[30] Finally, the Southern mill workers were more "docile and tractable," traits at least as important as wage levels in the comparative advantage of the industry.[31] In a precursor to today's call for global labor standards, the New England industrialists argued that their industry's only hope lay in convincing lawmakers to legislate working conditions and hours in Southern factories so that the lack of worker protections in the South could not be used to its competitive advantage.[32]

Like the New England mills of the early 1800s, the Southern mill workers and managers lacked the skills to compete at the higher end of the cloth market. As the more experienced New England and Mid-Atlantic mills increasingly specialized in fancier goods, the Southern mills seized the advantage in providing heavy and coarse cotton cloth to the U.S. market. But perhaps the South's most remarkable victory was in toppling British preeminence in Asia.

Southern mills from the beginning adopted a strong export orientation and by the late 1800s were systematically eliminating their British competition in Asia. Indeed, the Chinese export market was perhaps the single most important engine of growth for the Southern textile industry before 1900. Because the Asian textile industry had only begun to mechanize, and because of the Chinese preference for the durable, coarse cloth from the Southern mills, China presented to the South an immense market with insignificant competition from the higher-cost British exporters. In the decade ending in 1897, Southern textile exports to China more than doubled.[33] In the late

1800s, China purchased more than half of U.S. cloth exports, and more than half of U.S. exports to China were cotton textiles, with the great majority of this trade attributable to the Southern producers.[34] Many Southern mills sold virtually all of their output to China.[35] The Chinese market quite literally built the textile mills of the southern Piedmont region: A traveler in China reported back that in his wanderings through the country, "there was not a hole in the East where I did not find a Piedmont brand."[36]

The floods of cheap cotton clothing that flow today from China to the United States are almost a symmetric reversal of the trade flows of a century ago.

Once again, cotton textiles led the industrialization of a region. The cotton mills were the first factories in the American South, and the "mill villages" that soon turned into towns diversified the Southern economy away from agriculture and spurred the development of ancillary industries. Before long, the South had developed a capability in finer goods as well and had wrested the higher end of the domestic market from New England. For the 50 years ending in 1930, the New England mills gradually shuttered and reappeared in the South. By the mid-1930s, 75 percent of the yarn spindles in America were in the South.[37]

As had been the case in England and New England, most of the early Southern mill workers were drawn from ranks of the rural poor. Indeed, many of the Southern workers were former cotton sharecroppers, hard hit by low prices, the boll weevil, and the western movement of American cotton production to the factory farms of Texas. Melvin Copeland, a professor at Harvard in the early 1900s, described the Southern workers variously as "poor whites," "tackies," or "crackers" and appeared to hold his nose while describing the Southern mill workers who came from the surrounding farms and mountains. The mill workers

> eeked out a meager livelihood from their squalid patches of barren soil and the fruits of their rifles. Their food was simple and not abundant, their clothing scanty, and their home a small cabin with a dirt floor . . . they pay scant attention to literature and entertainment . . . and the vast majority are improvident.[38]

While Copeland goes on to criticize everything from their cooking to their clothing and cleanliness, he conceded that, for the low-skill demands of the cotton mills, they would do: "Although lacking ingenuity, foresight, and ambition, they were, however, adaptable to factory life."[39]

In the early part of the twentieth century, Southern girls entered the mills as young as age 7 and worked more than 60 hours per week. They had little to no education, poor nutrition, crowded living conditions, and a hostile and sometimes violent working environment.[40] Four generations of Piedmont women might have worked in the town's cotton mill.[41]

But just as the Southerners were declaring a decisive victory against the aging mills in the North, a new competitor loomed in the race to the bottom. By the mid-1930s, Japan would have approximately 40 percent of the world's exports of cotton goods.[42] While Japan's lead came a full century after Britain's, the role of cotton textiles in the development of Japanese industry was as great in Japan as it had been in Britain. In the late 1920s, more than half of Japan's industrial workers were employed in textiles, and textiles comprised two-thirds of the country's exports.[43] While Britain's economy had long since diversified, cotton textiles was the only developed global industry in Japan prior to World War II. And while over 90 percent of Japan's spinning capacity was destroyed in World War II, Japan had regained its preeminent position by the 1950s.[44]

Following the now-familiar historical pattern, Japanese leadership in the industry was based on low labor costs and poor working conditions, and especially the prevalence of "night work," which doubled the productivity of the textile machinery.[45] In the early 1900s, researchers sent by the U.S. government to examine the Japanese textile industries found that wages for cotton mill workers in Japan were 20 to 47 percent lower than wages in the United States and England, even when they accounted for productivity differences.[46]

The first cotton mill workers in Japan were young women escaping a life of subsistence agriculture in the countryside, driven into the mills by both rural poverty and natural disasters. Indeed, recruiting agents regularly scoured the affected regions following the floods, famines, and earthquakes that struck rural Japan with tragic regularity, because such events led to especially fruitful opportunities to recruit desperate young women.[47] The rural migrants were much preferred to suburbanites, whom the mills found to be frivolous and without endurance. According to the Japan

Cotton-Spinning Alliance, the ideal worker for a Japanese cotton mill was "unsophisticated, but honest, with great powers of endurance."[48] Or, as another manager put it, women from the rural areas were preferred because they were "naïve and diligent."[49] An American admirer observed the young women in the Japanese mills to be "docile, nimble, and deft."[50]

Female cotton workers in prewar Japan were referred to as "birds in a cage" given their grueling schedules—12-hour days and 2 days off per month—and captive lives in the company boardinghouses.[51] In most cases, the operatives were bound to the mills for a 3- to 5-year period, in a contractual arrangement not unlike indentured servitude. In the crowded boardinghouses the young women shared not only beds but even pajamas and they were confined to the premises by fences topped with bamboo spears and barbed wire. Food was scant, sanitation was poor, and disease was widespread.[52]

While textiles were in many respects a global industry as early as the 1800s, it was only in the 1950s that a similarly vigorous world trade began in clothing. Though Japan had leadership in both industries following World War II, by the 1960s Japan's share of world trade in textiles and clothing had begun to fall and new leaders in the race to the bottom began to offer yet lower labor costs and more docility (see Figure 5.2). By the 1970s, the Asian "NICS" (Hong Kong, Korea, and Taiwan) had passed Japan in the race to the bottom and had assumed leadership positions in the textile and apparel industries.[53]

By the mid-1970s, Hong Kong was the world's largest exporter of clothing, with a manufacturing base designed for the low end of the Western apparel markets. In 1976, textiles and apparel comprised approximately half of manufacturing employment in Hong Kong as well as half of exports.[54] In 1980, the industry's peak employment year, nearly 400,000 workers were employed in Hong Kong's textile and apparel industries.[55] Hong Kong's cheap and largely unskilled labor force—many refugees from famine in the Chinese countryside—fueled the development of other light industries as well. Similarly, in Taiwan and Korea, young women poured into the sweatshops from the rural areas and spun, wove, knit, and stitched the countries' way to the Asian economic miracle. In the mid-1970s, textiles and clothing comprised 35 percent of Korea's exports and

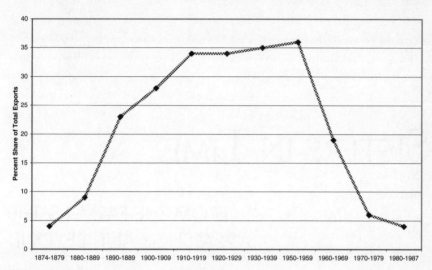

Source: Park and Anderson, 1991, p. 536.

FIGURE 5.2   *Japanese Textile and Apparel Exports as a Percent of Total Japanese Exports*

employed more than 20 percent of the workers in Taiwan's export zones.[56] Once again, the industry's destiny was driven largely by labor costs: Wages for textile workers in these countries were about 7 percent of the level in the United States and perhaps 15 percent of the level in Japan.[57] And once again, both admirers and detractors marveled at the docility and industriousness of the rural women with no alternatives.

But not far away Mao Zedong lay dying. China was waking and stretching from the nightmare of the Cultural Revolution, with wages perhaps 90 percent lower than those prevailing in Hong Kong. More important, China had millions and millions of young women—deft, nimble, desperate, and docile—who very much wanted off the farm.

SISTERS IN TIME

FROM THE FARM TO THE
SWEATSHOP AND BEYOND

Docility on a Leash

Jiang Lan works eight hours per day, six days per week in the Number 36 yarn factory in Shanghai. Her job is fixing broken yarn. She sits on a hard metal chair that is attached to tracks on the floor in front of a row of spindles. By depressing the pedal at her foot, Lan glides left and right along the tracks, stopping wherever she sees a flashing red light, the signal of broken yarn. With a deft and intricate move of her fingers, she repairs the yarn, then glides left or right to the next flashing light. Lan does this all day, wrapped in the steam and cotton flurries, blanketed by the metal noise. At the end of the day, Lan steps outside to the surprising quiet and walks across the gravel road to the company dormitory. And at the end of the month, she receives a paycheck of about $100. She saves pretty much all of it.

Yes, she says. She likes her job.

Jiang Lan, of course, is China's comparative advantage. Yet while the sheer number of Jiang Lans, as well as their low wages, are often put forth to explain China's dominance in light manufacturing, the truth is that these economic factors—the supply and price of labor—take us only part of the way toward understanding China's leadership position in this industry. The whole story requires that we understand not only supply and price, terms that have meaning everywhere, but also that we understand Lan's life in China, its limits and its possibilities. Since the rise of industry in eighteenth-century England, ideal workers for low-end textile and apparel work have been those that endure repetitive drudgery not just cheaply, but willingly and uncomplainingly.

Researchers from a wide variety of backgrounds and nationalities, examining disparate regions and different centuries, come again and again to the "D" word in describing the ideal textile and apparel worker. Docility, in turn, in Lancashire, Massachusetts, South Carolina, Japan, Taiwan, and Hong Kong has been the product of a lack of alternatives, lack of experience, and limited horizons. Ironically, while the founding principles of the modern Chinese state rest on the rights of the working class, the Chinese government has at the same time engineered a system of laws virtually assuring an almost unlimited supply of docility. The Chinese government controls Jiang Lan's life in ways that are bad for China's human rights record but very good for the production of T-shirts. Jiang Lan, in effect, is on a leash that restricts her choices, her experience, what she sees, and where she goes. It is not so much the labor market but the curse of anti-market forces in Chinese history that restricts her life and its possibilities.

Accidents of birth have always shaped destiny: race in America or class in England or caste in India. In China, the accident is *hukou*. To the worker, hukou is the leash, but to the textile industry, hukou is competitive strength, ensuring a stable and cheap labor force for the urban industry while at the same time ensuring that Jiang Lan and her colleagues bring their labor, but not themselves, to Shanghai. Roughly translated, hukou is a place of household registration. For a Chinese citizen today, the hukou specifies where you live, no matter where you actually are.[1]

The hukou system was devised in the 1950s to support the economic development plans of the new Communist China. The great majority of the country's citizens were assigned rural hukous: Those with rural hukous were required to remain in the countryside to produce quotas of food within their communes, and were normally barred even from traveling to the cities. Through the hukou system, China ensured a stable food supply for its cities while at the same time limiting the population of the urban areas. In reality, however, the masses in the countryside were "surplus labor," an academic term for people with nothing to do, people so "surplus" that their presence had no effect on the output of the commune. And while forcing the masses to remain idle in the countryside, China devoted its resources to the urban population, developing the cities' housing, education, healthcare, and infrastructure while leaving the rural population to fend for itself. As the cities developed, hundreds of millions of unskilled, barely educated people were held captive in their rural villages by their hukou.

In the late 1980s, however, China began to gradually liberalize the hukou system, lifting up the land away from the coast and pouring the rural masses to the coastal areas to produce T-shirts and sneakers and plastic toys. But even today, each rural citizen rolling toward the coast is on a leash. They can visit the city but they cannot easily stay; they can bring their labor but not themselves or their families. These workers are *liudong renkou*, which translates roughly to "floating people." As of the mid-1990s, 40 percent of the labor force in the Shanghai textile industry were "floating" girls and women from the rural areas.[2] Human Rights Watch in China estimates that the rural migrant population in China's cities is between 60 and 120 million.[3] In 2003, the AFL-CIO charged that China's exploitive hukou practices constituted an unfair trade advantage.[4]

The rural hukou defines and limits the worker's life in Shanghai. Floaters work 25 percent more hours per week but earn 40 percent less than those with urban hukous.[5] Because they are not residents of Shanghai, they do not have access to what is left of the urban residents' "iron rice bowl" services such as subsidized housing, childcare, healthcare, and pension benefits. Most of the Shanghai floating population lives at work, in dormitories, makeshift shelters, or in the workshop itself.[6] Some floaters are able to rent housing, but they pay six times as much as urban residents for half as much space. Toilets and kitchen facilities are the norm for the city dwellers and the exception for the migrants.[7] The workers come to the city alone; there is usually no living space, schooling, or healthcare for their spouses and children. The floaters are China's Bracero workers. In a more recent analogy, China labor specialist Anita Chan has likened the hukou system to South African apartheid.[8]

Sometimes China's floating workers show up in the city and hope for the best, but often the migrants have prearranged employment, especially in the textile and construction industries. Migrants risk not only economic failure but also detention and worse under China's regulations on "Custody and Repatriation." Under these regulations, a rural visitor with the "three not haves" (*sanwu renyuan*)—no papers, no job, no address—can be forcibly detained in a C&R center, or sent home. At best, detention is costly (citizens detained must pay to be released); at worst, it is tortuous.[9] And even those workers with employment live an uneasy life in the city, because the regulations governing migration to the cities are so byzantine that virtually every visitor is in violation of one rule or another. Depending on the city, a visitor might need an identity card, a temporary residence card, an employment registration card, a migrant identity card, a housing permit, and a family planning permit, each obtained from a different agency at significant cost.[10] In the cities studied by Knight et al., the permits necessary to avoid the C&R laws—if they can be obtained—cost more than half the monthly wage for the typical migrant worker.[11] Often, by the time the worker gets the final necessary document, the first has expired.[12]

Though China has recently increased migrant workers' protections under the C&R rules, many of these protections are only theoretical, because, as Anthony Kuhn found, the limitless supply of rural migrants means that only those who surrender their protections are likely to be hired.[13] Even government officials acknowledge that migrants are often not paid: In one survey the government found that 72.5 percent of migrants were owed back wages by their employers.[14] And though the law requires that the migrants have employment contracts, more than 90 percent of workers do not.[15]

The factories have an uneasy relationship with their floating workers. Managers report that the floating workers are critical to production, not only because they are cheaper than their urban counterparts, but, more important, because they "can bear more hardship" and are "more manageable."[16] Managers report that they hire floating workers for the simple reason that city workers will not take the dusty, steamy, noisy work of the construction and textile trades, and, even if they would, the city folk not only talk back, but are physically not up to the work.[17] Yet the factories' ability to hire migrants is restricted: Only some jobs are open to floating workers, and enterprises may have quota limits on the number of floating workers they may employ. The government uses the quota system as a labor market intervention: expanding the quotas during boom times and restricting the quotas during times of urban unemployment. The rural workers are the variable cost, ebbing and flowing with the American appetite for T-shirts.

Until today, each stop in the race to the bottom has been more fleeting than the last. Today, however, China's lead in the race to the bottom in textiles apparel is the same yet different from that of her predecessors. The characteristics of the ideal worker—particularly docility and desperation—have not changed, the repetitive drudgery of at least most of the work has not changed, the relentless cost pressure has not changed, and the role of the rural poor in powering the factories has not changed. Yet China's sheer size, and especially the remnants of the state-engineered hukou system, ensure that the supply of docile young women from the farm will be much greater than it was for China's industrial predecessors. China, for the foreseeable future, will likely lead in the race to the bottom.

As was the case for slaves, sharecroppers, and Bracero workers, it is not the perils of the labor market that block the path for Chinese textile and apparel workers. Instead, as was the case for these prior generations as well, it is a state-engineered system that limits the ability of these workers to participate in the market as full citizens.

Sure Beats the Farm

Like their sisters in time, textile and clothing workers in China today have low pay, long hours, and poor working conditions.[18] Living quarters are cramped and rights are limited, the work is boring, the air is dusty, and the noise is brain numbing. The food is bad, the fences are high, and the curfews inviolate. As generations of mill girls and seamstresses from Europe, America, and Asia are bound together by this common sweatshop experience—controlled, exploited, overworked, and underpaid—they are bound together too by one absolute certainty, shared across both oceans and centuries: *This beats the hell out of life on the farm.*

In mid-1800 Britain, a 9-year-old girl not engaged in textile work instead was busy:

> driving bullocks to field and fetching them in again; cleaning out their houses, and bedding them up; washing potatoes and boiling them for pigs; milking; in the field leading horses or bullocks to plough. . . . mixing lime to spread, digging potatoes, digging and pulling turnips . . . I loaded pack horses; went out with the horses for furze. I got up at five or six, except on market mornings twice a week, and then at three.[19]

Bertha Black was born in Trinity, North Carolina, in 1899, one of seven children of a rural family. Bertha's parents tried in vain to scratch a living from their 21 acres, and Bertha remembers well the family's exciting move up to the mill village, from picking cotton in the sun to spinning and weaving it in the shade:

> We all went to work in the Amazon Cotton Mill and we all worked there all our lives. We were all anxious to go to work because, I don't know, we didn't like the farming. It was so hot from sunup to sun down. No, that was not for me. Mill work was better. It had to be. Once we went to work in the mill after we moved here from the farm, we had more clothes and more kinds of food than we did when we was a-farmin'. And we had a better house. So yes, when we came to the mill life was easier.[20]

And today, literally millions of young Chinese women choose the factory over the farm, apparently preferring even the most grueling, worst sweatshop work to life in rural China. Liang Ying, a young woman interviewed by sociologist Ching Kwan Lee, remembered the day she escaped to the Shenzhen factory zone in southern China:

> That was the year when I turned sixteen. More than ten girls from my village planned the trip to Shenzhen. That day, we went to do the farm work in the fields as usual. We even went back for lunch with our parents. After our parents left for the field again, we took our luggage and left notes saying, "Dear parents, when you see this note in the evening, I will have already left for Shenzhen to find work. Please don't worry."[21]

For Liang Ying, almost anything was better than life on the family rubber farm and the choice between farm and factory was clear:

> It is really hard work. Every morning, from 4 am to 7 am you have to cut through the bark of 400 rubber trees in total darkness. It has to be done before daybreak, otherwise the sunshine will evaporate the rubber juice. If you were me, what would you prefer, the factory or the farm?[22]

He Yuan Zhi agrees with her sisters in time. Yuan Zhi has worked as a cutter at Shanghai Brightness for eight years. It was a good job for a girl from the farm, and it is an even better job now, she believes, as after several raises she earns nearly $150 per month. Yuan Zhi came to Shanghai from the mountainous area of Jiangxi province, because of the lack of opportunity at home in the village. She told me that she misses only two things about her home village: One is the spectacular scenery, and the other is her 12-year-old son, who is back in Jiangxi in the care of his grandparents. Everything else about life in Shanghai, she says, is better than that in the village. Jiang Lan of the Number 36 textile mill agrees. In the factory she gets to sit down, and is not outside in the sun all day. We can talk, she says, and the work is not so hard. What's more, Jiang adds, we each have our own bed.

The fact that low-skill factory work in textiles and apparel has represented a stepping stone from the drudgery of the farm is also illustrated by the manner in which many were denied the chance to step on the stone at all. In early New England, the Irish were denied any but the most menial work in the mills. In twentieth-century Shanghai, women from certain regions (in particular, Subei) who tried to make the move from night soil collector to cotton mill worker were openly discriminated against.[23] And in the American South, spinning and weaving jobs, albeit with separate toilets and water fountains, were opened to African Americans only in the 1960s. While in most cases the exclusion of blacks was simply inviolate custom, in South Carolina it was law. To assure plenty of agricultural production as well as domestic labor, and also to maintain workplace segregation, South Carolina law prohibited "anyone engaged in cotton textile manufacturing to allow . . . operatives . . . of different races to work together in the same room."[24] The law was on the books until 1960, but African Americans continued to be systematically excluded from the mills until the Civil Rights Act of 1965.[25]

The Subei natives, or the Irish, or the African Americans, could only walk by the cotton mills and think about what-ifs. At age 14, Billie Douglas started work, cooking and cleaning and looking after white mill workers' children. She would walk by the mill and think about what her life would be like on a mill worker's paycheck, where a day's work probably paid what she made in a week.[26] Johnny Mae Fields remembers a lifetime of obeying the white people, with her head down, in the postwar South. She used a simple philosophy of life handed down by her mother ("If the white woman want salt in her pie, put salt in her pie"). When the mills opened to black women, things were different.[27] Clest King remembered, too, "Before the mills opened up for black women, all they had was washing and ironing and cooking for white women."[28]

And in the late 1990s, Nicholas Kristof and Sheryl WuDunn, the Pulitzer Prize–winning *New York Times* correspondents, found that for many poverty-stricken Asians working as garbage pickers, prostitutes, or not working at all, a job in a sweatshop, if beyond their reach, was an aspiration they held for their children.[29]

For He Yuan Zhi and her sisters in time, factory work has provided not only a step up the economic ladder and an escape from the physical and mental drudgery of the farm, but also a first taste of autonomy and self-determination, and a set of choices made possible by a paycheck, however small. For some it was a choice to escape boredom, for others to escape a betrothal or a domineering father, for still others the chance to choose their own clothing. In the 1840s, a New England mill girl wrote home to a cousin to try to explain the variety of push and pull factors that had led her boardinghouse mates to the cotton mills. As the writer circles the dinner table in the boardinghouse, the new freedoms are almost palpable:

> I will speak to you of my acquaintances in the family here. One, who sits at my right side at table, is in the factory because she hates her mother-in-law. The one next to her has a wealthy father but like many of our country farmers, he is very penurious. . . . The next has a "well-off" mother, but she is a very pious woman, and will not buy her daughter as many pretty gowns and collars and ribbons . . . as she likes. . . . The next is here because her parents and family are wicked infidels, and she cannot be allowed to enjoy the privileges of religion at home. The next is here because she must labor somewhere, and she has been ill-treated in so many families that she has a horror of domestic service. The next has left home because her lover, who has gone on a whaling voyage, wishes to be married when he returns, and she would like more money than her father will give her. The next is here because her home is in a lonely country village and she cannot bear to remain where it is so dull. The next is here because her parents are poor, and she wishes to acquire the means to educate herself. The next is here because her "beau" came, and she did not trust him alone among so many pretty girls.[30]

In the early 1990s, sociologist Ching Kwan Lee went to live among migrant factory workers in southern China as part of her doctoral research.[31] For the young women from the rural villages, Lee found poor working conditions, limited freedoms, and a highly structured hierarchical labor system that limited the workers' conversations, their ability to use the toilet, and their diet. The conventional wisdom was that these women were an integral part of the family economy, sent to work in the city to send home money to keep the rural homestead afloat.

But as Lee gained the trust of the workers, much more complex motivations emerged. While the money sent home did indeed ease the burdens in the rural areas left behind, the women admitted, often embarrassed, that what had brought them to the factory towns was not so much money but autonomy of a kind that was impossible in the village where they were dominated by fathers and brothers. Many, Lee found, were attracted to factories not only to escape agricultural work but to write their own destiny and to escape their parents' plan for their lives.

Chi-Ying, a young single woman from Hubei, was interviewed by Lee.[32] Though Chi-Ying makes seven to eight times as much money at the factory as her father does at home, money is not at the top of her list of reasons for leaving the village for the factory. Chi-Ying has delayed marriage and ultimately decided against the husband her parents had chosen for her. With her wages, she repaid the young man for the gifts he had given her parents. In the city, she feels modern, free, and young. She likes buying a pair of cheap earrings with her own money, seeing a movie, or visiting the shopping mall. Chi-Ying compares herself to her mother and grandmother, and the striking differences seem to her to be not income but horizons. Mom and grandma never had their own jobs, or their own money. They never left the village, or saw a high-rise building. Actually, mom and grandma never saw a paved road.

The irony, of course, is that the suffocating labor practices in textile and apparel production, the curfews, and locked dormitories, the timed bathroom visits and the production quotas, the forced church attendance and the high fences—all of the factors throughout industrial history designed to control young women—were at the same time part of the women's economic liberation and autonomy.

One payday Lee went shopping with Hon-ling and Kwai-un, two migrant factory workers from the northern countryside. Walking into a boutique with money in their pockets, Hon-ling and Kwai-un were no longer peasants. Lee writes:

> A disposable cash income brought more than consumer items. It was a resource with which women workers from the north asserted their dignity in the face of society's imposition of an image of migrant peasant daughters as poverty-stricken and miserable.[33]

Lee found the young migrant workers eager to expand their professional horizons as well. Evenings were often taken up with night courses in business, typing, computers, and English, and many had entrepreneurial ambitions.[34]

More than 75 years ago, Ivy Pinchbeck closed her pathbreaking study of England's Industrial Revolution by concluding that its most significant legacy was the liberation of women. Similarly, researchers have found that the young rural women who powered South Korea's and Taiwan's economic miracle in the 1980s benefited from income but especially from increased autonomy and a chance at self-determination.[35] And 75 years ago, in Shanghai, young cotton mill workers banded together in groups called "pulochia." Roughly translated, these were independent women who had their own money and refused to get married, often, like Chi-Ying, repaying the bride price paid by her family. And 150 years ago, in Lowell, Massachusetts, the mill girls also gravitated to self-improvement opportunities: lectures, plays, and, most of all, to the lending libraries.[36]

In 1901, Sadie Frowne described her 12-hour days in a New York sweatshop. She made $7 per week, but at the price of frequent injuries, brutal bosses, and the exhausting pace of the piecework sewing system. At the end of each day, Sadie was so tired she wanted nothing more than to go to sleep. But she resisted the temptation:

> [O]ne feels so weak that there is a great temptation to lie right down and go to sleep. But you must go out and get some air, and have some pleasure. So instead of lying down I go out, generally with Henry.

Sadie enjoys a good time, and especially enjoys the independence that comes with her paycheck. Though she is clearly fond of Henry, Sadie also likes to dance and to shop:

I am very fond of dancing and, in fact, all sorts of pleasure. I go to the theatre quite often, and like those plays that make you cry a great deal. . . .

Some of the women blame me very much because I spend so much money on clothes. They say instead of $1 a week I ought not to spend more than 25 cents a week on clothes. . . . But a girl must have clothes if she is to go into high society at . . . Coney Island or the theatre. . . .

I have many friends and we often have jolly parties. Many of the young men talk to me, but I don't go out with any except Henry. Lately he has been urging me more and more to get married.

But the New York sweatshop, while brutal in some ways is liberating in others. Her paltry paycheck has given her a choice. She considers marrying Henry, but then decides:

I think I'll wait.[37]

Exactly 100 years later, author Peter Hessler followed the fortunes of Ma Li, a young girl from rural China who had been in his English class when he served in the Peace Corps. Ma Li had left home and gone to the southeastern factory town of Shenzhen where she worked in a jewelry factory with a lecherous boss and a night-time curfew. Hessler worried about how Ma Li was faring in the city and paid her a visit. He learned that:

Since coming to Shenzhen, she had found a job, left it, and found another job. She had fallen in love and broken curfew. She had sent a death threat to a factory owner, and she had stood up to her boss. She was twenty-four years old. She was doing fine.[38]

Factory women the world over arrived at the factory with docility bred by a lack of alternatives, and it was docility rather than intelligence or creativity that was and is the defining character trait of the ideal sweatshop worker. Yet the factory work itself proffered alternatives to the young women: They could choose a new hat or a new boyfriend or no boyfriend, and, as they became more skilled, even a new job. And just as their docility had been bred by a lack of alternatives, the choices presented by their new worlds gradually melted their passivity away. In country after country, and factory after factory, the women have stood up and stared down the bosses, expanded their horizons, made their own choices. In the process, they became less ideal workers for the textile trade, but better workers for the expanding industries requiring initiative, decision making, teamwork—industries that moved in as the race to the bottom progressed and the cotton mills closed.

Amazon.com and Dell Arrive at the Mill

In 1748, philosopher David Hume extolled the virtues of the race to the bottom:

> There seems to be a happy concurrence of causes in human affairs, which checks the growth of trade and riches, and hinders them from being confined entirely to one people. . . . When one nation has gotten the start of another in trade, it is very difficult for the latter to regain the ground it has lost because of the superior industry and skill of the former. . . . But these advantages are compensated in some measure, by the low price of labor in every nation which has not had an extensive commerce. . . . Manufacturers therefore gradually shift their places, leaving those countries and provinces which they have already enriched, and flying to others, whither they are allured by the cheapness of provisions and labor, till they have enriched those also, and are again banished by the same cause. . . . [39]

Manchester, England, the birthplace of the Industrial Revolution, today produces little cotton cloth. Manchester is today a brash and slightly seedy place, producing hard-core music, and angry dances with names like trip hop and acid jazz. The young and raging underclass shoots up and sniffs and smokes in the boarded-up cotton mills. But there is an ego, an edge, to Manchester today. The descendants of the cotton mill workers learn in grade school that it all began here: factories, corporations, global industries, modern industrial capitalism. So today:

> Despite a century of decline and eleven years of Margaret Thatcher, despite lousy weather and even lousier prospects, despite the grim housing estates, the boarded up buildings, the shallow obsessions of club culture, the drugs, the gangs, and garbage in the streets, Manchester still feels alive. That is an accomplishment, however long it lasts. The place survives through small acts of defiance. In and around the ruins of an empire, kids are dancing. [40]

Yet Manchester dominates a new industry today. It is the main home of the European "call center" business where touch-tone phones the world over will connect you to a young woman who cares about you, the customer. This industry now employs more than 400,000 Britons, mostly young women seeking flexible hours as well as job security. Some people liken the call center jobs to work in the early textile mills: relentless pace, unreasonable supervisors, too-short breaks. The comparison, thankfully, is nonsense.

Across the Atlantic in Manchester, New Hampshire, the economy is now dominated by technology, healthcare, and education. Manchester is the state's largest and most prosperous city, and frequently earns spots on national lists of "best places to live." But if the Internet now dominates Manchester's economy, the mammoth Amoskeag mills still dominate the skyline. In the mills are condos, offices, restaurants, and even a college campus. Today, what was the world's largest textile factory produces no cotton cloth at all. In fact, the largest textile complex in New England today is the American Textile History Museum, in Lowell, Massachusetts, the town named for the man who brought factories to America.

Charlotte, North Carolina, is also its home state's largest city. The former center of the Southern cotton mill kingdom today has one of the country's most robust growth records based on a diversified economy centered on the city's role as an international financial center. Bank of America and First Union Corporation, both headquartered in Charlotte, together employ more than 35,000 people, and IBM, BellSouth, and US Airways are also large employers. Charlotte has 23 colleges and universities in the surrounding area, and half a dozen advanced healthcare facilities. Just to the south, in Greer, South Carolina, is a new BMW manufacturing facility. The facility drew much of its labor force from the decaying cotton mills. Lane Jones, whose skin color would have kept her out of the cotton mills a generation ago, is an "associate" at BMW today, where she makes nearly $60,000 a year and drives a new BMW in the bargain.[41] Lane came to BMW from a denim mill: hot, dusty, boring, and work that never seemed to pay the bills. In Alabama, Honda, Toyota, and DaimlerChrysler have all built factories in former cotton mill country during the past decade, with Hyundai slated to join them in 2005. There is little doubt that the former mill workers prefer the jobs in the auto factories. In Campbellsville, Kentucky, an old Fruit of the Loom plant was reopened, refurbished, and expanded in 1999. The new tenant is Amazon.com.

In Japan, the cotton mills around Osaka have made way for some of the world's most successful companies. Twenty-nine firms in the Fortune

Global 500 are headquartered here, including Matsushita, Sanyo, Sharp, and Kyocera. Nearby is Toyota City, which began as a cotton spinning factory but by the 1980s had revolutionized the global automobile industry.

And while Hong Kong remains a prodigious clothing exporter, the city's apparel industry has moved from the sweatshop to the high tech. TAL Apparel, Hong Kong's leading firm in the industry, is led by Henry Lee, who has a doctorate from Brown University. TAL has solved the age-old apparel problem of the puckering seam—caused by the fact that thread shrinks more than fabric—and has patented and licensed its "puckerfree" technology in countries throughout the world. The firm has not only seamstresses, but researchers committed to improving mechanical and chemical engineering in garment production. And as the firm perfects mechanical processes, it is also setting standards in logistics and supply chain management. As shirts sell from the shelf of JCPenney in suburban America, inventory data are relayed to Hong Kong, allowing TAL to restock a hot-selling product in 27 to 29 days, down from 5 months only 3 years ago. And the next major innovation in garment production—size customization for each consumer—is now close to a reality in Hong Kong. The world's best-selling garment design computer program was developed in Hong Kong, and mass customization research is now under way at the Hong Kong University of Science and Technology. And Taiwan today dominates the computer industry, producing more than half of the world's laptop computers and more than one-quarter of its desktops. South Korea too has grown out of the sweatshop and into a world-class competitor in electronics, film, and automobiles.

The countries that have lost the race to the bottom are some of the most advanced economies in the world today, but they share a common heritage in the cotton mill and the sweatshop as the ignition switch for the urbanization, industrialization, and economic diversification that followed, as well as for the economic and social liberation of women from the farm. The now high-income workers have priced themselves out of work in the sweatshops, and these countries no longer have the desperate rural poverty that pushed and pulled women from the farms to textile and apparel factories. The workers are now neither cheap nor docile, and offer comparative advantages to other industries, in auto manufacturing, financial services, and information technology. While it was never a happy day when the mill closed, a padlocked cotton mill is also a sign that the economies, and the workers, by losing the race to the bottom, have emerged as victors.

Of course, all is not rosy in the countries that have lost the race to the bottom. While some textile workers laid off in South Carolina will get a job in the BMW plant, many will not, and life after the mill closes often gets worse before it gets better, especially for the thousands who quit high school because their future in the cotton mills seemed secure. For the workers who are not equipped to move up to BMW or IBM, or those who do not wish to leave the mill towns that still pepper the South, the loss in the race to the bottom is of course not a victory. In Chapter 7, we will see the rather unbelievable lengths to which many will go to keep T-shirt production from moving on to the next stop in the race.

But of all the rallying cries of the anti-globalization movement, the call to "stop the race to the bottom" is both the scariest and the most nonsensical, especially when it comes from rich country activists who owe their own prosperity to the very race they wish to halt for others. Who, we might ask, would these activists like to keep on the farm? Yet if some activists are misguided in their ideas about stopping the race to the bottom, others are a powerful force in changing the nature of the bottom itself.

Writing the Rules of the Race

Today's protestors are quick to point out that even if the conditions in the apparel factory are a step up from those on the farm, it does not follow that workers in developing countries should simply accept their fate, working day and night in poor conditions, for pitiful wages and with limited rights. While free trade advocates may wish to isolate the globalization activists as an uninformed fringe element, research shows that most Americans have reservations about the slippery slope in the race to the bottom and the working conditions in overseas apparel factories.[42] Both Bill Clinton and George W. Bush have nodded nervously toward the labor activists, "Global Labor Standards" has emerged as a topic on the agenda of the World Trade Organization, and the International Labor Organization (ILO) has endorsed a set of "Core Labor Standards" designed to serve as speed bumps in the race to the bottom. Many argue that the conditions of the working class in Asian apparel factories are comparable to, or worse than, those found centuries ago in Europe and America. The dark Satanic mills have moved but not shut down. How, the protestors charge, can the conditions so deplorable a hundred or more years ago in the West now be acceptable in the East?

The truth, however, is that this comparison too is nonsense, as even a cursory review of factory conditions across time and space shows. Today's protestors have sisters and brothers in time as well, generations of activists who gave their efforts and sometimes their lives to improve the condition of the working classes. Generations of activists—today's included—have changed the rules of the race and raised the bottom, making it a much better place than it used to be.

While the competitive market forces powering the race to the bottom are strong, there have, since the first factories emerged, been opposing forces at work. As production spiraled down to lower and lower cost locations, there have been generations of activists to throw sand in the gears and erect speed bumps in the race. These opposing forces, forces of conscience, religion, and politics, have continually rewritten the rules of the race and changed the nature of the bottom, making it not a good, but a better, place to be. The forces, then and now, have been governments and labor unions, religious leaders and international organizations, student activists, and most centrally the workers themselves. As the factory experience itself melted away their docility, the workers have stood up and stared down the bosses, raising the bottom for themselves and the workers who followed them.

These opposing forces, competitive markets on the one hand, political, religious, and labor leaders on the other, have long been identified as enemies of sorts, eyeing one another suspiciously and even venomously. Today's globalization activists identify the multinationals' pursuit of profit and free trade as the enemy of the poor and powerless, a greedy force to be stopped and never trusted. The business community, in turn, scornfully dismisses the activists as a lunatic fringe, a ragtag bunch of ill-informed obstructionists, blocking the only path available out of poverty. The battle has been put in these terms—greedy inhumanity versus naive and reckless troublemakers—since the first textile factories emerged.

In a larger sense, however, global capitalism and labor activisim are not enemies but are instead cooperators, however unwitting, in improving the human condition. As much as the CEOs would like to silence the activists and activists would like to silence the corporations, the fact is that the two sides need each other, and, most important, the workers at Shanghai Brightness Garment Factory and the Shanghai Number 36 textile mill need them both.

Dr. Thomas Percival, a physician and social reformer in the late 1700s, proposed a radical reform for the Manchester, England, cotton mills. Percival's proposal was radical first of all because it suggested that any sort of interference in the management of the cotton factories might be allowable, and second because it suggested that legislation might limit the hours (typically 14 at the time, including night work) that children were employed in the mills. Percival had in mind nothing so far-fetched as a ban on child labor, only a requirement that young children be given dinner breaks and be protected from working more than 12 hours per day.[43] Predictably, business interests charged that Percival and his allies were uninformed about the nature of their business, and thus began nearly a century of struggle in Britain, where successive waves of Factory Acts—in 1819, 1825, 1833, 1844, and 1878—gradually shortened children's working hours and raised minimum ages for work in the factories.

In the United States, Massachusetts, the birthplace of the American cotton textile industry, was the first state to limit the hours that children could work. Other states gradually introduced similar restrictions, and in 1916 President Woodrow Wilson signed the first Federal Labor Law restricting child labor. Yet representatives of Southern cotton mills battled the bill to the Supreme Court, where it was struck down by the now familiar arguments regarding the proper role of the government in the affairs of business. In 1941, however, the Supreme Court upheld the Fair Labor Standards Act, affirming the right of Congress to legislate to protect working children. In Japan, legal protections for child workers came a full century after similar developments in Britain, and in China, the Compulsory Education Act, passed in 1986, prohibits children under the age of 17 from working, and requires minimum schooling for children.

So just as the production of cheap cotton clothing ignited the Industrial

Revolution in countries around the world, it also sparked the forces of conscience for generations of activists determined to protect the most vulnerable from the unrestrained forces of capitalism. While the race to the bottom fueled demand for the cheapest and most docile labor of all, the opposing forces, at first lone, alleged lunatics, and then mainstream citizens, and finally lawmaking bodies, were gradually successful in implementing protections for children from factory work, and fostering the now nearly universal view that children belong in school.

Today, all of the world's significant textile and apparel producers have ratified the ILO's convention prohibiting child labor. Though child labor has by no means been eliminated from textile and apparel production, thanks to generations of noisy activists, the employment of children has moved from the ordinary and accepted course of business to the illegal and objectionable. Those who liken today's textile and apparel factories to those of a century or more ago in Britain and North America fail to note that however bad the current conditions, thanks to progressive activists around the world, the machinery is no longer powered by eight-year-olds.

And a job in textiles and apparel, however unpleasant, no longer presents appreciable risks of death or maiming. Thanks to textile machinery, missing fingers, hands, arms, and legs were so common a sight in Manchester, England, that Friedrich Engels likened Manchester to a place soldiers returned to after war.[44] In a two-month period in 1843, the *Manchester Guardian* reported that:

> 12 June, a boy died in Manchester of lockjaw, caused by his hand being crushed between wheels; 16 June, a youth in Saddleworth seized by a wheel and carried away with it; died utterly mangled. 29 June, a young man . . . at work in a machine shop, fell under the grindstone, which broke two of his ribs and lacerated him terribly. 24 July, a girl in Oldam died, carried around fifty times by a strap; no bone unbroken. 27 July, a girl in Manchester, seized by the blower (the first machine that receives the raw cotton), died of injuries received. August 3, a bobbin tuner died . . . caught in a strap, every rib broken.[45]

Even today, most older Southern mill workers recall machinery accidents as a common occurrence. Aliene Walser, who went to work in a North Carolina mill in the 1940s, remembers a coworker with long, beautiful blonde hair, scalped by textile machinery.[46] Machinery-related accidents that maimed or killed were also regular events in Japanese mills.[47] Thanks to activists from both the medical and labor communities, Britain began industrial safety inspections in the late 1800s.[48] In the United States, the Occupational Health and Safety Administration was formed in 1970 and today is advising an analogous body that is developing in China. Again, the point is not that industrial accidents no longer occur, but rather that, thanks to the efforts of generations of activists, workers in every country in the world have better legal health and safety protections than their predecessors.

Today, the most prominent health and safety issue in the apparel and textile industry is ergonomics. Repetitive motion injuries such as carpal tunnel syndrome affect millions of workers each year, according to Eric Frumin, health and safety director for the largest union of textile and apparel workers.[49] If history is a guide, Frumin and his colleagues will win, and textile and apparel workers will receive treatment, training, and compensation for ergonomics injuries in the near future. Business owners, of course, oppose the ergonomics regulations, echoing familiar objections voiced by their forebearers centuries ago. But thanks to his activist ancestors, Frumin can devote his energies to the ergonomics fight, as workers don't get eaten by textile machinery anymore.

Rose Rosenfeld died at the age of 107, a few months before September 11, 2001. Had she lived a few months longer, she would have no doubt felt a déjà vu horror. A lifetime ago, in 1911, only a short distance from where the World Trade Center would later be built, Rose had watched her friends' bodies fall flaming out of the sky. In a garment factory known as the Triangle Shirtwaist Company, 146 people were killed in one of America's worst industrial fires, in a building with no alarms, no sprinklers, and no escapes. Rose made it out in time to watch her coworkers hit the pavement. Though the factory reopened within days of the fire, Rose never returned to work there. She spent the rest of her life as an activist, speaking to college classes, reporters, and labor rallies. At the age of 106, she said of the fire, "I feel it still."[50] Thanks to Rose and her compatriots, fire safety at work, like child labor restrictions and safe machinery, is accepted as a right the world over.

Bysinosis, or brown lung, is a disease that has been largely eradicated. Caused by the inhalation of cotton dust, it slowly asphyxiated generations of textile and apparel workers. The disease is now virtually unheard of as OSHA-style cotton dust standards have been adopted in virtually all textile and apparel producing countries. And of course, early mill workers not felled by brown lung or maimed by machinery might still fall victim to the myriad of infectious diseases caused by poor sanitation, poor ventilation, and overcrowding. Life expectancy in Manchester, England, was under 30 in 1800 while 50 years later in Fall River, Massachusetts, it was 35. Today, life expectancy in Shanghai is 77, slightly ahead of that in New York City.

In the early 1900s, minimum wage legislation was virtually unheard of in the United States, though state-level legislation sometimes applied to women and children in certain industries. Only in 1938 did the U.S. Congress pass a national minimum wage law. Today, however, virtually all apparel-producing countries have legislated minimum wage levels, and have also placed limitations on hours of work and mandated overtime.[51]

And finally, a day's work in the cotton yarn factory is not at all what it used to be. Perhaps 100 years ago, children worked as "piecers," running from spindle to spindle watching for broken threads. Spotting a break, they would climb up, tie the piecer's knot, and resume their watching. Less than 100 years ago, women in Shanghai performed the same task, not climbing but tottering on bound feet. Today, however, the Shanghai Number 36 mill has many simple devices—the red blinking light, the chair on tracks, etc.—that make all the difference to the experience of a day's work. And at the cotton mills in the American South today, piecers are now industrial history: On a walk through an American spinning mill, one might see no people at all; the "piecers" are robotic devices who know where the broken threads are and how to fix them. Gradually, the worst jobs in the production of T-shirts are fading into old photographs.

In the mid-1990s, a variety of labor abuses came to light in factories that produced shoes and apparel for the Nike Corporation. Charges of underage workers, coerced or forced overtime, safety violations, and generally poor conditions began to surface, especially in factories in China and Indonesia. The factories, while supplying goods to Nike, were independently owned and operated. As a result, Nike argued, it bore no responsibility for conditions in its suppliers' facilities. Nike's general manager in Indonesia, while acknowledging that violations might exist, essentially argued that they were neither his nor Nike's affair: "I don't know that I need to know (about them)," he replied in response to questions.[52]

Thanks to activists from religious groups, NGOs, and college campuses, by the year 2000 Nike needed to know. In 1999, students from around the country staged protests at numerous universities, demanding that U.S. apparel companies disclose the names and locations of their supplier factories. In short order, the activists also demanded that the companies take responsibility for the conditions in these factories, that they allow independent monitors to audit the labor conditions, and that they enforce codes of conduct as a condition of continued business relationships. The companies at first protested, in echo of corporate response since the first factories: The new generation of Thomas Percivals did not understand the industry, the business, or the supply chain, and the activists' demands were both unworkable and unreasonable. Yet, unlike the activists of the 1800s or even the 1960s, the current generation is armed with technology. Through web sites, cell phones, and e-mail they joined forces, and within a few short years virtually all of their demands were met.[53] Corporate Codes of Conduct for suppliers to the footwear and apparel industry are nearly universal in the United States today, and factory disclosure and monitoring are accepted practices as well. The mainstream business press now routinely advises large companies on how to address labor conditions issues in Asia.[54] And like child labor, fire safety, minimum wages, and occupational health, the activists' fringe-like demands continue to go mainstream and work their way into law.

Of course, the effectiveness of the activists in raising the bottom is facilitated or limited by the extent to which civil liberties are present. It is not a coincidence that China—where neither workers nor activists enjoy effective political voice—has among the world's worst industrial safety records. And freedom of the press—also limited in China—was a prerequisite for the rapid success of sweatshop activists' very public "name and shame" campaign. Evolving political freedoms, then, as well as current trends toward democratization (which even in China are occurring on a small scale) will continue to facilitate improvement in working conditions.

The economic development led by the growth of the textile and apparel industries also plays a role in improving working conditions. As of the summer of 2004, growing demand for goods from Americans was fueling growing demand for workers in China, with the result that pay and benefits in China's Pearl River Delta were rising rapidly, and factories began to compete to keep workers happy with perks such as clinics, swimming pools, child care, and higher-end housing.[55] And researchers continue to confirm the commonsense proposition that better working conditions are a market-led result of higher-skill industrialization.[56] Yet markets alone do not generate child labor restrictions, worker safety protections, and other minimum labor standards. Instead, as Peter Dougherty argues, it is often the protections demanded by the activists that facilitate the development of the markets.[57]

Thanks to globalization, the sweatshop, and the race to the bottom, He Yuan Zhi of Shanghai Brightness doesn't worry about being stuck on the farm anymore. She married when and whom she chose, she makes her own living and her own choices. If current trends are an indication, her income will grow at more than double the rate of that of her Western sisters. And thanks to generations of backlashers—radical, unkempt, and uninformed—she works 50 hours per week and not 80, she can read and write, and her children can, too. She has never heard of bysinosis, and has never met anyone who has been hurt by machinery or burned in a factory fire. She will likely live to a ripe old age. The bottom is rising.

Yuan Zhi slices through fabric with her cutting machine and tosses T-shirt pieces into a piled-high basket. It is a practiced toss, a toss with an attitude. It is hard to know how long she will slice and toss, slice and toss. She is getting bored, and besides, the mills and garment shops are closing around Shanghai, moving away in search of lower labor costs and more docility. Patrick Xu told me that in the late 1990s alone, more than a third of the garment factories in Shanghai closed, and of the Shanghai cotton mills once numbered 1 through 40 only 6 remain. But General Motors is here now, and Cummins Engine, and Coca-Cola, Starbucks, Volkswagen, and even Amazon.com. Yuan Zhi is ready.

Representatives of the textile and apparel industries from the United States, Bangladesh, Turkey and Sri Lanka gather in Brussels in 2004 to discuss the looming China threat. From Left: Ghulam Faruq, Auggie Tantillo, Allen Gant, Cass Johnson, Fazful Hoque, Ziya Sukun, M. Cooray. (Photo courtesy of Ziya Sukun)

PART III

TROUBLE AT THE BORDER

MY T-SHIRT RETURNS TO AMERICA

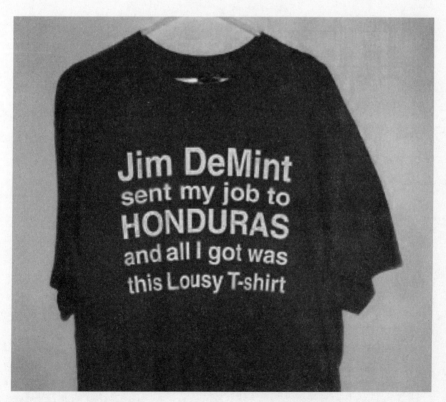

Textile trade issues assume prime importance in 2004 South Carolina Senate race. (Photo courtesy of Tanya Sisk, South Carolina Democratic Party)

DOGS SNARLING TOGETHER

HOW POLITICS CAME TO RULE THE GLOBAL APPAREL TRADE

Chinese T-Shirts versus American Jobs

The shipping container stacked with T-shirts boards the freighter in Shanghai and heads back across the Pacific.[1] The ship travels south along the western coast of Mexico and squeezes through the Panama Canal before heading north to the Miami port, and finally to the screen printing factory at Sherry Manufacturing. At this point, the T-shirts enter the most complex and challenging phase of their lives: trying to gain access to the U.S. market. Chinese T-shirts and Chinese immigrants have similar experiences in attempting to get to America. In both cases, the journey is expensive, risky, and often illegal. There is an army waiting on shore, ready to fight the invasion. The U.S. apparel industry has lost the race to the bottom, and while this may be the result of a "happy concurrence of causes" as David Hume suggested in 1748, not everybody is happy about it. Most of the American South has moved onward and upward from textile production, but there are pockets across the Carolinas and Georgia where the mills are still at the center of the economy and the community.

Losers in the U.S. textile and apparel industries are not going gracefully, especially not when losing to China. The textile and apparel trade is the most managed and protected manufacturing trade in U.S. history, or, as one writer noted, "the most spectacular and comprehensive protectionist regime in existence."[2] Whether the regime has at the same time been a spectacular success or failure depends upon one's point of view.

When Auggie Tantillo sees a T-shirt from China, he gets a bad feeling in his stomach, but his reflex is fight rather than flight. Auggie can go into Wal-Mart to buy soap or batteries, but he can't even walk by the clothing without the feeling coming back so he avoids that section of the store entirely. Auggie is executive director of the American Manufacturing Trade Action Coalition (AMTAC), an advocacy group dedicated to preserving manufacturing jobs in the American textile and apparel industries. Auggie represents not so much a "special interest" as a moral viewpoint. As the youngest of nine children in a traditional Sicilian family, Auggie is used to fighting for his fair share. He is soft-spoken, fiercely intelligent, and very sure that he is right. Auggie has spent his entire adult life on defense, trying to block or slow the waves of cheap clothing imports flowing into U.S. markets. For 25 years the waves have been growing bigger, but he keeps bouncing back, ready to block and punch.

But Auggie thinks the fight with China could be the last. Between 2000 and 2004, the U.S. textile and apparel industries lost more than one-third of their remaining jobs, and looming on Auggie's horizon—and on the horizon of manufacturers everywhere—is the China threat, as well as a new set of rules to govern global trade in T-shirts. U.S. producers of yarn, fabric, and apparel have no hope of competing with China, at least not under the radical new rules of the game scheduled to take effect in 2005. Unless somebody stops China, it will be all over, Auggie believes. Waves of T-shirts, socks, underwear, caps, sweaters, pants, and ties will come flooding in, and will drown the American textile industry within the decade, along with the industries in dozens of other countries. Unless somebody stops China, there won't be another war to fight because there won't be an industry left to save.

Auggie used to have a bigger army in the war against apparel imports, but one by one his fellow soldiers have dropped out, or worse yet, defected to the dark side. The AKA (American Knitwear Association), AAMA (American Apparel Manufacturers Association), ASA (American Sweater Association) are all gone now, the industry associations having no raison d'etre without an industry. In 2003, I met with executives of the American Textile Manufacturers Institute (ATMI), which for half a century had been the booming voice of the industry in Washington, where hundreds of Congressmen would answer their calls on the first ring, and even U.S. presidents made sure to stay friendly. When I went back a year later the ATMI was gone, having shrunk and consolidated with other gasping textile associations into a shadow of itself, a shadow that often did not get its calls returned from Capitol Hill. Worse than the soldiers who have faded away, however, are the defectors. A Rolodex full of former government officials and even members of Congress are now across enemy lines, arguing not just for free trade in general but for free trade in T-shirts in particular.

Auggie understands the pull to the dark side. Increasingly that is where the paymasters are, the rich retailers, the powerful China lobby, and all of the American apparel firms that are now just importing machines. Auggie understands that there are more realists than idealists in Washington, though he himself isn't one of them. For most of his life, the manufacturing job news released every month has been bad news, and Auggie seems to take each layoff personally. But he also knows that without his relentless scuffles, there would be fewer jobs still, so he keeps going. Auggie also knows that, in the long run, he will lose. But on the way to losing there are victories, and these keep him energized. When Auggie can keep a factory open for a few more years, then a community will stay intact a while longer, a few more children will grow up with working parents, and a few more of them will be able to go to college. Every day an American textile mill stays open is a win for Auggie Tantillo, and every day somebody keeps a job is a good day.

Though Auggie's army is smaller than it once was, the troops are rallying in the fight against China. After 10 years of squabbling and splintering, there is a renewed unity and purpose in the face of a common enemy. In

July 2003, the leaders of the ATMI, AMTAC, NTA, AYSA, AFMA, NCC, ASIA, ATMA, CRI, GTMA, THA, AFAI, NCMA, and TDA joined forces in a powerful alphabet army to demand that the Bush administration take action against China.[3] They demanded that the U.S. government institute "safeguard" quotas restricting Chinese textile and apparel imports, and also demanded that apparel from other countries be restricted in its use of Chinese fabrics. Weeks later they fired off more specific requests, demanding immediate limits on Chinese knit fabrics, brassieres, dressing gowns, and gloves. In the meantime, a delegation from China flew to Washington to stop the madness, and the Bush administration had to decide whether to anger the Chinese—just when it needed China's cooperation on dozens of other issues, ranging from North Korea to semiconductors to intellectual property—or anger Auggie, just when it needed his help in the upcoming election. The Bush administration sided with Auggie and restricted the imports from China.

Several months later, the alphabet armies lined up 117 Congresspeople behind a request for a meeting of the WTO to consider responses to the looming China threat.[4] John Kerry was on board, but Bush was on the spot, torn between his commitments to China and the wrath of the voters in the textile mills. During the summer of 2004, the administration was trying to leave itself some wiggle room: room to side with Auggie, room to side with China, or more likely, room to split the differences somehow in a web of Washington deal making. But as the 2004 election heated up in the fall, Auggie played his best card: In mid-October, AMTAC filed about a dozen safeguard petitions to restrict Chinese imports of goods such as T-shirts, cotton pants, and underwear.[5] As George W. Bush rushed around the swing states in the days leading up to the election, the administration had to decide whether to reject or accept the petitions for consideration. The deadline for the administration to respond? November 1. Few were surprised when the administration sided with Auggie.

Julia Hughes, Washington representative for the U.S. Association of Importers of Textiles and Apparel, is a leader in the opposing army, and has sat across the table from Auggie many times over the years. While Julia respects Auggie's integrity and commitment, she just thinks that Auggie is wrong, and that he and his troops should stop whining and join the twenty-first century. And besides, from Julia's perspective, almost every-thing has gone Auggie's way. As Julia sees it, Auggie's army has had unfair advantages for nearly 50 years. Where Auggie sees a flood of T-shirts from China washing American jobs away, Julia sees the Chinese T-shirts as underdogs with both hands tied behind their backs, hopelessly handi-capped against the political power of Auggie's troops.

Most economists, of course, are on Julia's side. Under the widely accepted doctrine of free trade, the best course of action for both the United States and China is for everyone to clear the ring and let the best T-shirts win. This is the best course for the United States, where access to the best T-shirts at the best prices will boost incomes; it is the best course for Charlotte, North Carolina, which is now a regional hub in the global economy; and it is the best course for developing countries, where, as we have seen, exports of textiles and apparel provide a route from rural poverty and a first step onto the development ladder.

But free trade may not be the best course—at least in the short run—for Kannapolis, North Carolina, where nearly 5,000 textile workers lost their jobs on a single day in 2003. My T-shirt's perilous journey home shows that the best economic policy from the perspective of the United States or even North Carolina does not make for the best politics, and that trade in T-shirts is not (yet) a contest of faster better cheaper on the part of competing businesses, but is instead a contest played out in the realm of politics. While the market forces powering the race to the bottom are strong, the political forces pushing back against the markets are strong as well, particularly in the United States. Trade flows in T-shirts are the result of economic forces but also the result of thousands of deals cut in Wash-ington, Geneva, and Beijing, and politics are at least as important as mar-kets in understanding the T-shirt's journey. Many of the firms still standing in the U.S. industry do not believe that they should have to compete with sweatshops that pay their workers 50 cents an hour, and especially not with China where cheating of almost every type is rampant. Better to build a fence to keep out the lions than to run an unfair race that can't be won. The fence hasn't worked as well as many U.S. producers would have liked, but it has slowed the competition down, and most of all it has confused them.

The effects of political barriers to Chinese apparel into the United States are readily apparent. While Chinese apparel has captured approximately 80 percent of apparel imports in several other industrialized countries, as of 2003, China's share of the U.S. apparel imports was approximately 14 percent.[6] China's victory in the race to the bottom is obvious when we examine its overall exports, but is far less striking when we examine its performance in the U.S. market (see Figure 7.1). My Chinese T-shirt, in particular, was one of the lucky ones. As Figure 7.2 shows, U.S. imports of cotton knit shirts from other regions have grown far more

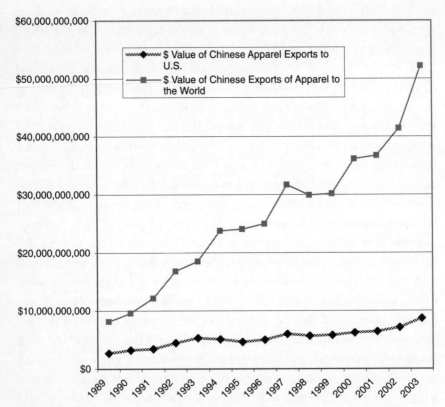

Sources: United Nations COMTRADE database; OTEXA, U.S. Department of Commerce.

FIGURE 7.1   *Chinese Apparel Exports to the United States vs. Total Chinese Apparel Exports*

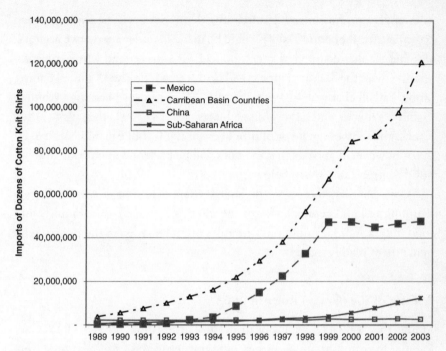

Source: OTEXA, U.S. Department of Commerce (apparel categories 338 and 339).

FIGURE 7.2   *Cotton Knit Shirts Imported into the United States, by Region*

rapidly than have imports from China. As we will see, it is trade policy, not comparative advantage, that explains these patterns.

Auggie Tantillo and Julia Hughes spend their days in a Washington dance, following each other around the Commerce Department, the Congress, Customs, and the office of the U.S. Trade Representative, with Auggie trying to plug holes in the import dike and Julia trying to punch them open. Because Auggie and Julia are in constant motion, the trade policies governing apparel are in constant motion as well. Textiles and apparel are subject to not only a higher level of trade protection but also a higher level of trade protection complexity than any imports into the United States outside of agricultural goods.

During the time that I was writing this book the rules governing apparel imports into the United States often seemed to change almost daily. The rules governing how many T-shirts of which types could be sold by which countries; the fabric the T-shirts could be made of under alternative regimes; whether a collar counted as a "component" or a "trim" (and whether it mattered); where the T-shirt's fabric could be dyed and "finished"; and, of course, tariffs, had all changed. In 1999, the rules did not look so bad for a Chinese T-shirt trying to enter the United States, but by 2003, the rules shifted against the Chinese in favor of producers in the Caribbean and Mexico. By 2005, however, it appears that the rules will be back on China's side, though not if Auggie Tantillo can help it.

Gary Sandler, the owner of Sherry Manufacturing in Miami, faces a daunting task in keeping apace of the rules governing T-shirt imports into the United States. Simply put, the rules are nuts, as even the people who made them readily agree.

A Taste of the (Crazy) Rules in 2003

Under the 2002 U.S.–Caribbean Trade Partnership Act (CBTPA), Gary Sandler may import apparel from 24 countries in the Caribbean free from tariff and duties.[7] However, free access applies only to clothing that meets the American "yarn forward" requirement, which requires that both the fabric and yarn from which the clothing is constructed be made in the United States. Both dyeing and finishing of the fabric must also occur in the United States, and the fabric must be cut into pieces in the United States, as well. However, apparel pieces may be cut in the Caribbean countries if U.S.-made thread is then used to stitch the components together.

Apparel that is "knit to shape"—rather than made from fabric that is knit and then cut into pieces—may be made from fabric formed in the Caribbean country, as long as the fabric is made from U.S.-made yarns and the imports are below a certain limit. However, there are more restrictive provisions for socks and T-shirts. Brassieres have their own astonishingly complicated rule book, which allows them free access only if the firm producing the brassieres has used components in which at least 75 percent of the value of the fabric has been sourced in the United States for certain *prior years'* exports of brassieres to the United States. A debate over which parts of the brassiere "count" toward the 75 percent went on for some time, and was finally negotiated to include cups, sides, wings, and backs but to exclude straps, bows, and labels.

T-shirts are also privileged with their own special rules. T-shirts made from Caribbean-made fabric using U.S.-made yarn may enter the United States freely, but only to a limit of 5,651,520 dozen in 2003. The special T-shirt cap was negotiated at the insistence of Fruit of the Loom, which tried to match the quantitative limit to its own productive capacity. This maneuver gave free access for the firm's T-shirt products into the United States while at the same time dissuading competitors from setting up rival T-shirt manufacturing plants in the Caribbean.

Julia, Auggie, and the alphabet armies negotiated for years over the CBTPA provisions, in a telling example of the dominance of politics over markets in T-shirt trade flows. U.S. retailers wanted to simply lift the gates and allow free access to whatever apparel the Caribbean countries produced. Roger Milliken, a billionaire South Carolina textile magnate and self-proclaimed "economic nationalist" joined forces in an unlikely alliance with the textile and apparel workers trade union (UNITE). Together, along with Senator Fritz Hollings and other like-minded Congresspeople, they opposed any free access at all for Caribbean-made apparel, believing, both procedurally and substantively, that "giving away" access to the U.S. market was bad policy. The ATMI, as well as a number of U.S. producers, lobbied for the U.S. fabric requirement, while other producers—such as Fruit of the Loom and Russell Mills, along with the Caribbean countries— fought to gain benefits for apparel produced with Caribbean-made fabrics.

The complexity of the rules is perhaps inevitable, given the nature of these multiple opposing forces. In the end, the rules were hammered out in the only way possible given the disparate interests involved: sock by sock, bra strap by bra strap. It may be hammered out all over again in a few years, as the CBTPA is set to expire in 2008.

A similar set of rules—though different enough to keep importers like Sandler confused—govern T-shirt imports from Sub-Saharan Africa under the African Growth and Opportunity Act (AGOA) and from Bolivia, Columbia, Ecuador, and Peru under the Andean Trade Preference Act (ADTPA).[8] Under the North American Free Trade Agreement (NAFTA), still other rules apply to T-shirt imports from Canada and Mexico.

To Julia Hughes, the only thing more outrageous than these rules is to hear them referred to as "free trade" agreements. According to Julia, a free trade agreement should make it easier, not harder, to trade. The poorest countries of the world, especially those in Africa, already handicapped on almost any dimension, cannot possibly succeed in such a byzantine tangle of rules, Julia believes, and many U.S. importers take one look at the rules and walk away. Trade from these areas is not free at all. It is easier and cheaper (at least once the time is factored in) just to pay the tariff and source from preference-free countries. Julia Hughes once tried to make sense out of the various free trade area provisions for her retail clients. She found, however, that she could not put them on a grid; they were all just too different. Auggie, for his part, believes that the retailers are responsible for the complexities: The complications, as Auggie sees it, are simply the result of all the exceptions that were made for Julia.

In 2003, cotton T-shirts that did not meet the requirements for "preferential treatment," either because they came from countries outside the membership of AGOA, the CBTPA, ADTPA, or NAFTA, or because they did not meet the requirements regarding the origin of the fabric or yarn, were charged an import tariff of 17.4 percent, except if they were from Jordan, in which case the tariff rate was 10.9 percent, or Israel, in which case the tariff rate was 0.[9]

Complexities are apparent in the tariff schedule as well. For some apparel, the power of particular companies is evident. Tariffs are nearly 30 percent on some categories of clothing, including, for example, Harmonized Tariff Schedule category 6102.30.20, which are:

> womens' or girls' overcoats, car coats, capes, cloaks, anoraks (including ski jackets), windbreakers, and similar articles, knitted or crocheted, of man-made fiber, containing less than 25% leather by weight and containing 23% or less wool or fine animal hair.

It might be hard to imagine such a garment, but it is clear from the tariff rate—nearly the highest of any on apparel—that someone in the United States manufactures them.

As of 2003, U.S. apparel imports for an additional 40 WTO member countries were limited under the umbrella of the Agreement on Textiles and Clothing (ATC).[10] The ATC, in turn, is the phase-out mechanism for

U.S. Import Limits for Cotton Knit Shirts, 2003

Country	Quota Limit (in dozens)
China	2,525,562
Vietnam	10,463,635
Turkey	17,777,705
Pakistan	12,407,951
India	5,777,025
Egypt	4,717,195
Poland	3,533,491
Cambodia	4,187,637
Philippines	3,633,517
Sri Lanka	2,635,755
Romania	1,270,216
Oman	922,140

Source: U. S. Customs.

FIGURE 7.3   U.S. Import Quota Limits for Cotton Knit Shirt Quotas, 2003

the Multifiber Agreement (MFA), which had set quantitative limits, or quotas, on clothing and textile imports from dozens of countries since 1974. In 2003, the United States had quota limits on cotton knit shirts from 27 countries; some of these are shown in Figure 7.3. Though the ATC is scheduled for expiration at the beginning of 2005, a number of quota regimes will remain in place for U.S. apparel. First, the China safeguard allows importing countries to impose quotas on Chinese apparel imports through 2008. Second, quotas will remain in effect for a number of countries that are not WTO members.

All in all, the restrictions and regulations governing apparel imports are written, administered, and enforced by hundreds of lobbyists and lawyers, as well as bureaucrats from the Department of the Treasury, the Department of Commerce, the Congressional Textile Caucus, the U.S. Trade Representative, and the interdepartmental Committee for the Implementation of Textile Agreements. In fact, a leading textbook illustrates the interlocking webs of government involvement in textile and apparel trade policy with a full-page map containing 11 boxes linked together by a dozen arrows.[11] While the United States is the largest offender, it is not alone. As Richard Friman has shown, other rich countries also employ complex "patchwork" approaches to protecting their domestic textile industries.[12]

Beginning in 2002, the web site of the United States Association of Importers of Textiles and Apparel showed a clock with days, minutes, hours, and seconds ticking by. With the MFA scheduled to expire on January 1, 2005, apparel importers could go to the web site for an exact calculation of the length of time they had to contend with perhaps the most tortuously complex set of trade protections in U.S. history. The regime, as we will see, had many effects: good, bad, and mostly unintended. When the clock strikes zero, there will be more surprises still.

According to many, it will be the last nail for the U.S. industry in the sad story of plant closings and job losses that has lasted nearly 50 years. It will also mean the last nail for Auggie Tantillo and the alphabet armies who have fought to save the U.S. industry from the waves of cheap imports. "It's about time," many people told me. More than a few Washington insiders muttered "dinosaurs" when I asked them about Auggie Tantillo's troops. The Southern textile interests are living in the past, clinging to something that makes no sense in today's global economy, people told me over and over again.

The dinosaur label doesn't bother Auggie. "We're not extinct," he told me, "not yet."

Snarling Together

How did the United States—as the self-anointed free trade champion of the universe—end up with such a dauntingly complex and downright silly mass of barriers to the import of T-shirts? Why, in an era of progressive trade liberalization and increasing deference to the market mechanism, has the role of politics remained so pervasive in this industry?

The first factor to explain the dominance of politics in the trade is the size of the textile and apparel manufacturing base, even today. While textile and apparel employment in the United States peaked shortly after World

War II at approximately 2.5 million workers, the industries in 2004 employed about 700,000 people, which accounts for about 5 percent of manufacturing employment.[13] Given the size of the employment base, the unrelenting job losses related to the global race to the bottom have strengthened the political voice of the industry, as the "groans of the weavers" have become both louder and more sophisticated. Winning industries do not groan, and losing industries' groans become louder with the extent of their misfortune. The U.S. textile industry felt the first serious threat from imports immediately after World War II, and foreign competition since that time has been growing steadily and sometimes exponentially, which has led to compensating cries for help in Washington.

Yet the withering of America's competitive position in these industries is not sufficient to explain their political power, as industries from toys to bicycles to televisions have faded away with few rescue missions from Washington. Political response to industrial demise is the result of not only the demise itself, or even the size of the industry, but the strength of industry alliances and the access the alliances have to policymakers.[14] Or, as Jock Nash, perhaps the American textile industry's most colorful voice in Washington, reportedly advises, when a pack of dogs snarl together, people have to listen. The extent to which the industry can speak with one voice—or snarl together—goes a long way toward explaining its political influence.

Erik Autor, the chief lobbyist on trade matters for the National Retail Federation, is continually frustrated by the "snarl together" phenomenon. Though retailers ranging from a beachfront tourist shop to Saks Fifth Avenue to Wal-Mart all benefit from access to cheaper T-shirts from abroad, such diverse groups of businesses find it difficult to speak with a single voice. Southern textile leaders, however, share a cultural and historical bond that allows them to speak together. (They all know each other, Erik told me. Their daddies all knew each other. Their granddaddies all built the mills, and they all knew each other, too.) Related to the historical and cultural bond that strengthens their collective voice is the geographic concentration of the U.S. textile industry. More than 60 percent of apparel and textile manufacturing is located in Georgia, South Carolina, and North Carolina, and there remain many Congressional districts where the textile industry—or even a single firm—is the major employer. A geographic swath of Congresspeople remains beholden to the industry, even as its fortunes wane. The U.S. retail industry, in contrast, while employing significantly more people than the textile and apparel industries, is not only unable to snarl in unison, it is spread across the country in a manner that leaves it nobody's Congressional priority.[15]

A third factor that lends support to the regime is that the American public is nervous about trade, especially trade with China, and especially when the trade is believed to have severe effects on small American communities. The "It coulda been me" syndrome leaves many American voters far more tolerant of complex trade protections than we might expect them to be. While North Carolina now has a diversified economy that has "moved up" from textiles, many towns, along with many less-skilled workers, have not moved up alongside Charlotte.

I was not able to find anyone in Washington and certainly no one in China who was happy with the rules governing imports of T-shirts into the United States, or indeed anyone who tried to defend these rules. Participants from across the spectrum agreed that the deal-making process often showed Washington politics at its worst. But observers on all sides also agree that access to the American apparel consumer is currency in Washington, and this currency, like any good money, can and has been traded for almost anything. Often, the currency has been traded for votes, which has left generations of Congresspeople and even a few presidents indebted to the textile industry. Access to the American apparel consumer has also frequently been traded for foreign policy favors, from crushing Communism in Central America to crippling terrorists in Pakistan. Ironically, however, perhaps the most common use of the currency has been to pay Auggie Tantillo and his troops to move out of the way of broader trade-liberalizing initiatives. Beginning with Dwight Eisenhower and ending with George W. Bush, every U.S. president has paid the U.S. textile industry to be quiet so that America could get on with the business of free trade.

Auggie Goes to Washington

Auggie had thought little about politics and even less about trade policy as he neared his college graduation from Clemson University in 1980. He didn't know what his next step would be, and it was a fluke and a stroke of luck that led to a job as an assistant in Senator Strom Thurmond's office. Auggie left for the big city, having no idea what to expect. If he had opinions about politics, he doesn't remember them. Whatever illusions he might have had, however, were shattered at the ripe old age of 21, when he saw how Washington really worked. Auggie likens his Washington awakening to the day he discovered that Santa Claus was a fake. Santa Claus was President Ronald Reagan.

Strom Thurmond had figured critically in Reagan's 1980 election. Though the U.S. textile industry had a variety of trade protections in place at the time, Asian imports were gushing through new holes in the dike by the day. Between 1976 and 1979, textile and apparel imports into the United States had increased by nearly 50 percent.[16] In exchange for Thurmond's support, Reagan promised, if elected, to put a stop to it. In a letter to Strom Thurmond several months before the election, Reagan promised to limit the growth in textile and apparel imports to the growth in the domestic market.[17]

Thurmond kept his end of the deal and delivered a large Southern vote to Ronald Reagan. Reagan, however, shuffled his feet as Asian imports continued to soar. Auggie was just a note-taker and a gopher, but he remembers Thurmond's outrage as he raced around Washington meeting with Edwin Meese, George Schultz, and James Baker. He pounded the table, shoved the letter under their noses, as mill after mill closed and imports surged. "You've got to do something about this. *You promised.*"

Several people who had been involved with the negotiations in Washington told me that the infamous Reagan textile promise would have been impossible to keep, even with the best of intentions. It would have been a foreign policy disaster to renege on the deals already in place, which allowed imports under quota to grow at a rate of 6 percent, rather than the approximately 1 percent growth in the domestic market. It also would have required the United States to bring under quota many countries that had never been under export restraints, as well as to limit many categories of textiles and apparel that had also been without quota.

But to Auggie, Strom Thurmond, and the still millions of textile and apparel workers, a deal had been a deal. So Auggie Tantillo's introduction to Washington was the broken Reagan textile promise. It was Auggie's first experience in the value of textile promises as currency, but it was not the last. Strom Thurmond, who died in 2003 at the age of 100, had played this game before and he would play it again. In fact, every post–World War II president has made his own version of the campaign textile promise to Strom Thurmond, and, beginning in the 1960s, to Fritz Hollings and Jesse Helms as well. Some of the promises have been kept, and some have not.

But since the end of World War II, every U.S. president has also publicly supported the doctrine of free trade. Indeed, scholars of presidential rhetoric cite free trade doctrine as a "remarkably consistent rhetoric" across both time and party lines.[18] For some presidents, free trade was a foreign policy choice, designed to keep Communists or war at bay. For others, it was a clear case of the best economic policy. For yet others, a free trade posture was a matter of moral consistency. The United States had been the architect of the postwar General Agreement on Tariffs and Trade (GATT), a set of rules with free trade principles at its very core. For more than half a century, the United States has been the world's self-appointed champion of free trade, in word if not in deed.

Regardless of what has motivated the free trade rhetoric of U.S. presidents, all have found it impossible to implement the rhetoric without paying the textile and apparel industries to get out of the way. While a long list of trade liberalizing initiatives—from tariff reductions to NAFTA to China's WTO accession—has been championed by the United States, these initiatives have only been politically possible by making exceptions for Southern textile interests. In television appearances and public speeches, each postwar president has eloquently advanced the case for free trade on the grounds of freedom, prosperity, and morality.[19] But away from the cameras, in private phone calls, furtive telegrams, and secret meetings, each of them has assured the domestic textile industry that he had not really been talking to them. For 50 years, U.S. policymakers have played a balancing act with Auggie and his troops, trying to toss (or promise) them enough crumbs to get their votes and cooperation, but not so many as to make an obvious mockery of the free trade rhetoric. Almost every postwar president has needed help from the senators and governors in the Carolinas, who in turn needed help for their textile towns. Each special deal for the industry was labeled a temporary measure, but many of them, in one form or another, are still in place.

Making Deals and Making Exceptions

The first groans of the weavers came shortly after World War II as cheap Japanese cotton goods took the lead in the race to the bottom. Though official U.S. policy was to open trade with Japan to encourage prosperity and thus stave off the Communist threat in Asia, the mill owners in both New England and the South felt a much more immediate threat from the growing imports from Japan than they did from the Communists. The American Cotton Manufacturers Institute (ACMI) announced that a crisis was at hand:

> We are face to face with a life or death question of whether our own govern-ment will stand idly by and permit low-wage competition from Japan to seri-ously cripple our industry. Must there be closed mills and breadlines before the administration in Washington concedes the possibility of irreparable damage to our industry?[20]

In order to quiet the groans and especially to advance its broader trade-liberalizing agenda, the Eisenhower administration persuaded Japan to "voluntarily" limit their exports of cotton textiles to the United States to allow temporary breathing room for the U.S. industry. Like much else from the 1950s, from today's perspective the Voluntary Export Restraint (VER) agreement with Japan looks charmingly simple and innocent. The agreement was only temporary, and it dealt with only one country, Japan. Only one alphabet troop, the ACMI, had been involved, and the agree-ment covered only a narrow range of goods. Though Eisenhower saw no choice but to toss the crumbs, he was clearly not happy about it. In his diary he later wrote of the "short-sightedness bordering on tragic stupid-ity" of the protectionists, and worried that unless the United States opened its markets, Japan would "fall prey to the Communists."[21]

In what would become a long epic of unintended consequences, the politics served to accelerate rather than slow the race to the bottom. The VERS, which limited imports from Japan, supplied not so much protection for the U.S. textile industry as an opening for Japan's competitors in the race—especially Hong Kong and Taiwan—to supply the U.S. market. In a pattern that continues to this day, the effect of plugging one hole in the dike was to increase the force of imports gushing through others. Between 1956 and 1961, imports of cotton goods from Hong Kong rose by nearly 700 percent.[22]

The soaring imports led to predictable cries lamenting the imminent collapse of the U.S. industry.[23] In the 1960 presidential campaign, John F. Kennedy promised Governor Ernest Hollings of South Carolina that he would help. Kennedy fulfilled his promise by instituting the Short Term Arrangement on Cotton Textiles (STA) as temporary assistance to the industry. The arrangement allowed the United States to negotiate import limits from other countries—not just Japan—in cotton textiles. The effect was a bigger program, covering both more countries and more goods than the original Japanese VER.

Of course a reprieve of one year was not enough to save the U.S. industry. In response to the continuing groans, on the expiration of the STA the Kennedy administration created the Long Term Arrangement for Cotton Textiles (LTA), effective from 1962 to 1967. Just as the STA was a bigger VER, the LTA was a bigger STA, covering more countries, more products, and more years. In effect, the LTA imposed quotas to limit import growth from the major producers—particularly in Asia—to annual growth of 5 percent per year.

In exchange for protecting its own industry against imports, the ACMI dropped its fight against Kennedy's Trade Expansion Act and allowed the Kennedy Round trade liberalization to continue. The Kennedy Round resulted in tariff cuts on U.S. imports of 30 percent, but textile and apparel tariffs were off limits in the negotiation. They maintained their already high levels and were, in the case of apparel, even increased.[24] Representative Carl Vinson of Georgia proudly wrote the ACMI that, "Thanks to their good friends in Congress, the industry had been singled out for special treatment by President Kennedy and his Cabinet."[25]

The "temporary" LTA was renewed in 1967 and again in 1970, each time as a bribe to allow Lyndon Johnson and then Richard Nixon to seek trade liberalization in other ways. By 1973, the LTA was restricting hundreds of categories of cotton textile imports from dozens of countries.

With the passage of the LTA and its extensions, U.S. trade policy for textiles and apparel took the seemingly irreversible step to a complexity that
left it unintelligible to all but a few.

However, just as blocking the flow of clothing from Japan had resulted
in an even more forceful flow of imports from Hong Kong, blocking
imports of cotton textiles and apparel also served to accelerate rather than
slow the race to the bottom.

By limiting imports of cotton textiles and apparel, U.S. policy unwit-
tingly encouraged its trading partners to upgrade their production and
sales efforts to wool and to the increasingly popular man-made fibers such
as nylon and polyester. Predictably, imports of man-made fiber apparel
from Asia soon soared, with U.S. imports of these fibers from developing
countries increasing 2,500 percent between 1964 and 1970.[26] Just as predictably, U.S. textile interests extended their groans to these other sectors.
The ACMI morphed into the ATMI (American Textile Manufacturers
Institute), and U.S. textile interests began an intensive campaign to extend
the LTA to other fibers, calling for the implementation of a Multifiber
Agreement (MFA).

In his 1968 presidential campaign, Richard Nixon promised Senator
Strom Thurmond that he would seek to broaden the LTA into an MFA and
would extend quotas from cotton to wool, man-made fibers, and blends.[27]
Once elected, Nixon faced the familiar challenge of reconciling his free
trade rhetoric with his campaign promise. On the one hand, Nixon had a
vision of trade as a path not just to economic growth but to political freedom.
On the other hand, there was the MFA promise telegram to Thurmond that
had been printed in newspapers all over the South. Nixon's rhetoric showed
the balancing act, and was typical of rhetoric from Dwight Eisenhower to
George W. Bush: Free trade was good, but textiles were a special case:

> By expanding world markets, our trade policies have speeded the pace of our
> own economic progress and aided the development of others. . . . We must
> seek a continued expansion of world trade, even as we also seek the disman-
> tling of those other barriers—political, social, and ideological—that have
> stood in the way of a freer exchange of people and ideas, as well as of goods
> and technology. . . .
>   [H]owever, the textile import problem, of course, is a special circum-
> stance that requires special measures.[28]

In the end, MFA I, in effect from 1974 to 1977, was signed by 50 countries and covered approximately 75 percent of U.S. textile and apparel imports.[29] In painstaking bilateral negotiations, country after country hammered out with U.S. negotiators how much of which categories of textiles and clothing could enter the U.S. market. Though largely successful in satisfying the domestic textile interests, the MFA was, as William Cline wrote, "an embarrassing breach of the GATT principles," principles that the United States had authored and continued to espouse.[30]

In the 1976 campaign Jimmy Carter promised to extend the "temporary" MFA. MFA II, which extended the arrangement through 1981, was more restrictive still in allowing access to U.S. and European markets. In the meantime, Carter and then Reagan also wished to maintain the free trade momentum on a new round of trade liberalization talks—the so-called Tokyo Round. Once again the textile and apparel industries were largely exempt: The United States cut its import tariffs on manufactured goods to an average of 6.5 percent, but apparel tariffs, while reduced from their postwar highs, remained at an average of 22.5 percent.[31]

Though Ronald Reagan had not kept his election-year textile promise to Strom Thurmond, Reagan had little choice but to toss some crumbs in the direction of the textile industry. Reagan would have to show his face in South Carolina in the 1984 campaign, as Thurmond kept reminding him. With MFA III, the temporary regime of textile and apparel quotas was extended yet again. In effect for the 1981 to 1986 period, MFA III was the most restrictive yet.

Jobs for Bureaucrats

With the implementation of the MFA and its extensions, the administration of the quota regime became—and remained in 2004—a small industry both in Washington and in the exporting countries, as the mind-numbing complexity of the regime increased over time in response to the groans from certain companies, industries, or Congressional districts. In the simplest case, the United States negotiated a bilateral agreement with each country, which allowed the country to export to the United States certain quantities of various categories of textiles and apparel, such as men's woolen sweaters or women's cotton knit shirts.[32] In some cases, the country is allowed to use the quota for any garment in the category, but in other cases there are limits on subcategories. For example, while the Chinese quota for all cotton knit shirts was 2,373,699 dozen in 2002, T-shirts and tank tops were limited to 1,801,137 dozen of this amount.

Even where quota allocations appear to be identical, market access to the United States can differ. Throughout the year countries might apply "swing" (borrowing T-shirt quota from another category of textiles and apparel quota from the same country), "special shift" (borrowing T-shirt quota from a prespecified list of other categories of quota), "carryover" (shifting last year's unused T-shirt quota to the current year), or "carryforward" (borrowing against next year's T-shirt quota).

In order for quota to be traded across time and categories, each category is assigned a square meter equivalent (SME) of cloth.[33] A dozen cotton knit shirts (category 338 or 339) is convertible to 6 SMEs of cloth while a dozen handkerchiefs of man-made fiber (category 630) are convertible into 1.4 SMEs. As a result, a country that applied swing from cotton knit shirts to polyester handkerchiefs could trade the right to sell 1 T-shirt for the right to sell 4.29 handkerchiefs. Some apparel is measured by weight rather than quantity—a kilogram of silk ties is convertible to 6.6 square meters of cloth, making a kilogram of ties "worth" slightly more than a dozen T-shirts for the purpose of quota swing.

Another whole mini-industry must deal with MFA "origination" requirements. If a T-shirt is sewn in China from fabric pieces that were cut in Hong Kong but knit in Malaysia from yarn that was spun in the United States, where *is* the T-shirt from, and whose quotas should it count against? While the general rule for most of the MFA's history was that fabric cutting conferred origin, the rules have been fluid, and since the mid-1990s have specified that it is generally the stitching, rather than the knitting, spinning, or cutting, that determines where the T-shirt is from for MFA purposes.

The MFA, then, while designed to save the U.S. textile and apparel industries, actually at the same time created its own industry, with hundreds of bureaucrats around the world to negotiate, implement, and enforce the innumerable bilateral deals that collectively have comprised the MFA. Each minute provision of each bilateral agreement is the result of a push-pull negotiation among multiple parties, and each provision also by necessity creates its own supporting bureaucratic structures. To see the SME equivalents, the swings or shifts, and of course the product and country lists themselves in action is to appreciate the MFA not so much as a protectionist regime but instead as a marvel of bureaucratic engineering.

Unity 1985 to 1990

In what had become a predictable pattern, even with the stricter quotas under MFA III, the crisis continued in the U.S. industry and the groans of the weavers were unabated. Though the speakers had changed, the speeches had not. In 1985 Representative Ed Jenkins of Georgia told his House colleagues that the industry was experiencing its "last gasp," while a textile association president threatened that "in five years, the industry will cease to exist."[34]

The renewal of the MFA also did little to lessen the sense of betrayal that still stung from Reagan's unfulfilled promise to Strom Thurmond, and once Reagan had won a second term, the industry's hopes for justice were further dashed. Strom Thurmond's leverage over Reagan was gone, and White House aides had stopped picking up the phone. Ronald Reagan would not have to go back to South Carolina. Yet there was a silver lining in the betrayal: The injustice united the industry in a manner seen neither before nor since. Snarling together, they almost achieved the impossible.

If the White House would not listen, the Congress would have to. The mid-1980s were a golden era of sorts for the domestic textile and apparel industries. Though their fortunes were shrinking and their plants were closing, there was an energy and unity of purpose that propelled them forward. It was a pinnacle, according to Auggie Tantillo and many others with whom I spoke, where standing upon each other's shoulders they had made their greatest reach, coming within only inches of achieving justice. All of the alphabet armies in the U.S. textile and apparel complex, from yarn spinners to fabric producers to apparel manufacturers—the ATMI, AFMI, AYSA, and AAMA—along with the unions representing the workers—began to snarl together. Auggie Tantillo, still young but by now an expert in the areas of both textile trade policy and the ways of Washington, accepted a position to open the Washington office for Russell Mills, one of America's largest T-shirt producers. United, the troops formed an industry coalition, the Fiber, Fabric, and Apparel Coalition for Trade (FFACT) to battle the imports.

Auggie and his troops sought legislation that would keep the Reagan promise. The Jenkins Global Quota bill would limit the growth of imports not from particular countries, but instead place a global cap on U.S. textile and apparel imports, and also give the United States unilateral power to restrict imports, rather than requiring negotiations with each trading partner. The bill would roll back quotas for the largest Asian suppliers, as well as negate more than 30 existing bilateral textile and apparel trade agreements.[35] Ronald Reagan and his administration were nervous. Once Auggie and his troops got into the U.S. Capitol, there was no telling what would happen.

Though the framers of the U.S. Constitution placed responsibility for formulating trade policy on the shoulders of the Congress, during the past 50 years it has become increasingly clear—perhaps especially to Congress itself—that they are not up to the task of formulating rational trade policy. A Congressperson seeking election or reelection is often forced into a protectionist posture, but can only obtain protection for his interests by offering the same to his colleagues. "The political logic of protection leads to protection all around" wrote an observer in 1935, because Congress's natural tendency is a spiraling protectionism extending trade barriers into the districts of each Congressperson.[36] A vote for free trade, according to another early observer, is an "unnatural act" for a Congressperson.[37] Only a very few die-hard constitutional literalists believe that the U.S. Congress should be in charge of trade policy.

Julia Hughes understands this all too well. While she has some free trade allies in Congress, nobody wins elections by promising free trade or help for the apparel consumer. Auggie, however, has comrades in Congress who will fall on their sword, or at least pretend to, to help the U.S. textile industry. From North Carolina through Georgia and Alabama, in town after town the voters will choose the candidate who promises to keep the mill open. What members of Congress most want, however, is to make protectionist speeches without having to take protectionist actions.

Indeed, as Destler notes, by surrendering power to make trade policy decisions, Congresspeople are more freely able to spout protectionist rhetoric, secure in the knowledge that they will be unable to take action:

> A Congressman, no matter how keen his desire to help the toy marble makers, does not want to be given the right of voting them an increase in tariff rates. He prefers to be in the position of being allowed merely to place a speech in their favor in the Congressional Record . . . free to indulge the responsibility afforded those who do not participate in the final decision.[38]

But FFACT, having been spurned by the Reagan administration, began knocking on the doors of members of Congress. The Jenkins Bill passed easily in both the Senate and the House, where it had 230 cosponsors. But this victory was only the first step, as Reagan swiftly vetoed the bill. Some of those involved in the negotiations told me that at least some Congresspeople were able to vote for the bill because they felt assured that Reagan *would* veto it. Dan Rostenkowski, chair of the House Ways and Means Committee, though sympathetic to the plight of the mill workers saw the bill as being fraught with unworkable elements. "This bill is garbage," he allegedly remarked to Tip O'Neill. O'Neill, surveying the political landscape, replied, "Yeah, but move it along, Dan. Move the garbage."

The override received 276 votes, just 8 votes short of the two-thirds needed to undo Reagan's veto.[39] Yet it was a win of sorts. As Auggie Tantillo remembers, "We scared them good."

To many observers, the close vote was a terrifying brush with insanity, an example of the madness that can result if trade policy is left in the hands of elected representatives. Economist William Cline estimated that the bill would have cut back imports of textiles from Hong Kong, Korea, and Taiwan by nearly 60 percent, and would have cost U.S. consumers approximately $43,945 per U.S. textile job saved.[40] In addition, by the sheer force of its hypocrisy when placed against American free trade rhetoric, it would also have likely tied U.S. hands in pursuing other trade negotiations. And finally, swift and disabling retaliation against U.S. exports was virtually assured.

But, like Auggie said, they had been scared. They had seen the whites of Auggie's eyes, and were willing to talk. The USTR was willing to talk, Hong Kong was willing to talk, and even Reagan was willing to talk. The

MFA IV, signed for a five-year period ending in 1991, was the most restrictive yet. For the first time, quotas were placed on fabrics not even produced in the United States, such as silk, ramie, and linen. The only fibers now exempt from U.S. quotas were jute and abaca, though U.S. negotiators warned that these too would be dealt with if imports surged.

In the meantime, Auggie Tantillo had moved up yet again. After serving a stint as Strom Thurmond's Chief of Staff, Auggie was appointed by President George H.W. Bush as Undersecretary of Commerce for Textiles and Apparel. The job was the top textile post in Washington, and carried with it the chairmanship of the Committee for the Implementation of Textile Agreements (CITA), an interdepartmental policy committee with representatives from the Departments of State, Labor, Treasury, and the USTR.

Snarling Back

From the pinnacle of political power they held in the late 1980s, the U.S. textile and apparel industries' influence declined rapidly in the 1990s. While their power remained the envy of virtually any other industry, compared to their influence in the heady days of the Jenkins Bill the troops were tattered and weakened. First, FFACT itself began to splinter, with infighting that weakened its collective voice. More important, however, other political voices began to rise in volume, not drowning out but at least softening the snarls from the U.S. industry.

The apparel industry was the first to splinter off from the cause. Under the industry's new business models, Auggie was starting to sound like a bit of a dinosaur. For the firms who continued to produce apparel in the United States, access to cheaper and more fashionable foreign fabric was a necessity. By limiting their access to foreign fabrics, trade restrictions were making it more, not less, difficult to keep their production in America. For other apparel firms, such as Warnaco and Liz Claiborne, it was becoming more attractive to source their clothing from abroad, partly because of the restrictions associated with gaining access to their fabrics of choice, and partly because of the increasing quality and price competitiveness of the Asian producers. The American Apparel Manufacturers Association made a clean break with Auggie in 1990, when they refused to sign on to support the 1990 version of the global quota bill. They did not cross the line to the dark side at first, but instead made clear that they were not going to help. By the mid-1990s, however, the AAMA was the enemy, fighting in direct opposition to Auggie's efforts to contain textile and apparel imports, and a short time later, the AAMA was gone.

The textile workers' union (UNITE), as well as the yarn and fabric sectors, also began to splinter into different directions. While the fabric producers wanted a freer rein to use imported yarn in production, the yarn spinners predictably preferred to limit the use of foreign yarn in U.S.-made fabrics. As trade agreements started to be negotiated, further splits appeared. The yarn and fabric guys squabbled over the provisions in the agreements, and the union workers generally opposed any agreements at all. Unable to snarl in unison, the industry became an annoyance rather than a threat on Capitol Hill.

As FFACT's united political front crumbed, other alphabet armies began to snarl in unison. For the first time, the U.S. retail industry formed a collective voice on the subject of trade in general, and apparel imports in particular. The Retail Industry Trade Action Coalition (RITAC) led by Sears, JCPenney, and Dayton Hudson, had first been formed to counter FFACT on the Jenkins Bill, but soon took on the larger goal of doing away with all quotas.[41]

Gone On Long Enough

RITAC was soon bolstered by another collective force as the developing countries that had been constrained by quotas also began to speak with one voice. The International Textiles and Clothing Bureau (ITCB), a coalition of developing country textile and clothing exporters, began to echo RITAC's call for the end of quotas. In a foreshadowing of the collective clout they would display in 2004, poor countries banded together to shape the global trade agenda.

Many of the family businesses in Asia had first come under quota under John F. Kennedy's administration, and some business owners remembered when their grandfathers had been assured that the quotas would be temporary. ITCB members were running out of patience in the globalized economy, where the MFA appeared increasingly anomalous and hypocritical, and was viewed as a rich country plot that stood in the way of poor country fortunes. In a twist on the well-worn historical pattern, America would now have to pay the developing countries to move out of the way of broader trade liberalization.

George H.W. Bush and then Bill Clinton were eager to see a successful conclusion of the Uruguay Round, the third major round of postwar trade liberalization talks. While both the Kennedy and Tokyo Rounds had focused on and achieved tariff reductions (though not for U.S. textile and apparel imports), U.S. aims for the Uruguay Round were more complex. In particular, U.S. negotiators wanted developing countries to liberalize rules for trade in financial and other services, and for foreign investment, and they also sought new agreements in areas such as intellectual property. The United States had little left to offer in return besides the MFA. Thanks to the successive rounds of liberalization, the United States maintained few trade barriers of any kind, save for those in place for agriculture and textiles, as tariffs for imports into the United States were close to zero for most goods outside of these industries. The ITCB made clear that they were willing to negotiate only if the MFA was on the table.

As Uruguay Round negotiations progressed, the MFA was extended twice more as the final agreement was hammered out. In the end, the negotiation took seven years and produced 22,000 pages of agreements.[42] With Auggie's troops in splinters, the new voice of the retail industry rising in the background, and, most important, the developing countries united for the first time in history, the rich countries agreed to abandon the MFA.

The Slow Unraveling

If there were doubts about the political staying power of the U.S. industry, they were dashed as it became clear that an agreement to end the MFA was not the same thing as the end of the MFA. While retailers and developing countries wanted to yank the thread to unravel the regime in a few pulls, the textile interests pushed the other way, and ultimately made sure that the unraveling would proceed at a snail's pace. Negotiations over *whether* to end the MFA were simple compared to the negotiations over *how* to end the MFA.

Should the MFA be phased out over 5, 10, 15, or perhaps even 25 years? Should the poorest countries be freed from quotas first, or should the bigger exporters be allowed to go first? Or perhaps each category of clothing should be freed from constraint at the same time for all countries? The tortuous complexity that had characterized the administration of the MFA for decades was in the end trumped by the even more daunting complexity of the regime's undoing. Finally, the countries agreed to a 10-year phase-out, beginning in 1995. The countries also agreed to lift the quotas in stages by product. In 1995, goods comprising 16 percent of SME imports were freed from quotas; the subsequent 2 tranches, in 1998 and 2002, freed 17 percent and 18 percent, respectively, of SME imports from quota.[43] The final tranche, set for liberalization in 2005, liberalizes the remaining 49 percent of imports.

However, the term "phase-out" is quite a misnomer, because the agreement does not phase out quotas steadily but instead leaves most in place until the "cliff" in 2005. The agreement specifies that certain percentages of *imports* be freed from quota, but it does not require that the goods freed be those that were under quota to begin with. As a result, during the first two tranches, very few quotas were removed, because most of the goods specified in the tranches had not been under quota. Approximately 85 percent of quotas were scheduled to still be in effect until December 31, 2004.[44] Indeed, in the first tranche, the United States lifted only one quota: that for work gloves from Canada.[45]

Julia Hughes and Erik Autor could only shake their heads at the beginning of the "phase-out" as nonexistent quotas were rescinded on parachutes, kelims, silk sport bags, and laparoscopy sponges. Thanks to the weakened but still snarling domestic industry, they would have to wait another 10 years to see the quotas vanish (maybe) on things that people actually buy, such as cotton T-shirts, underwear, or pants.

PERVERSE EFFECTS AND UNINTENDED CONSEQUENCES OF T-SHIRT TRADE POLICY

No More Doffers

What have been the effects of the dominance of politics over markets in world trade in apparel? The stated purpose of the protectionist regime was and remains to protect manufacturing jobs in the Western textile and apparel industries, and judged against this benchmark the regime's success has been quite limited. But the influence of politics in redirecting trade has had a number of other consequences—mostly perverse and unintended—but both positive and negative, for rich and poor countries alike. In addition, despite the limited success of the regime in protecting employment, the American public remains much more sympathetic to trade protection than we might expect.

John Edwards, the 2004 Democratic vice-presidential nominee, is the son of a textile mill worker and is one of the latest generation of politicians to sign on to the cause of saving textile jobs in the American South. The mill in which Edwards' father worked closed years ago, and Edwards can speak firsthand about the effects of low-wage competition on Southern textile towns. Edwards has argued for a reconsideration of the MFA phase-out, and throughout the 2004 campaign stumped passionately on the cause of job losses. Though his story was compelling in a sound bite, the truth is that while the trade regime has indeed saved thousands of jobs, the employment effect has largely been in Washington among the armies of lobbyists and bureaucrats who hold the regime together, as well as their counterparts in developing countries. Textile and apparel jobs in the United States have been vanishing, and will continue to vanish, with or without protection from imports.

Over the past 50 years, an entire vocabulary has become extinct in American textile mills as capital and technology have replaced labor in textile and apparel production. The "piece up" (thread tying), "doffing" (removing full bobbins), and "draw in" (starting the warp threads) jobs are

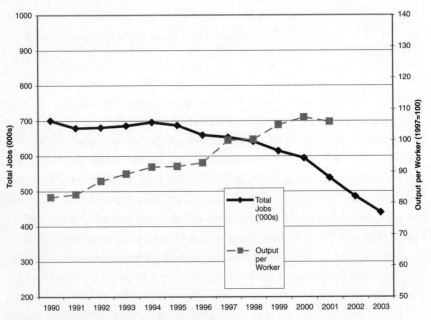

Source: BLS (NAICS 313, 314 combined).

FIGURE 8.1   *Employment and Productivity in the U.S. Textile Industry, 1990 to 2003*

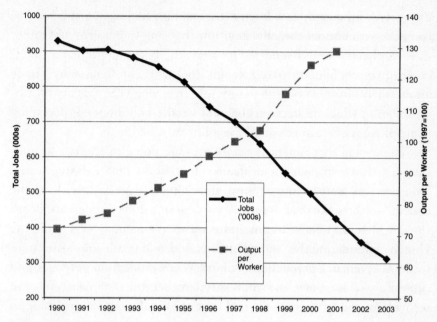

Source: BLS (NAICS 315).

FIGURE 8.2   *Employment and Productivity in the U.S. Apparel Industry, 1990 to 2003*

all gone now, the victims not of competition from China but of technological progress and mechanization. While employment in the U.S. textile and apparel complex fell by approximately 60 percent from 1990 to 2004, production output in this sector has been relatively steady.[1] In 2001, U.S. textile and apparel workers produced between 40 and 125 percent more goods per hour of work than they had in 1990 (see Figures 8.1 and 8.2).

This pattern mirrors that of many other manufacturing industries in the United States: While employment is falling, production is steady or even rising. Indeed, for the period 1970 to 2002 manufacturing employment in the rich countries fell by approximately 25 percent, but manufacturing output has more than doubled.[2] While the textile trade regime has had some effect in keeping *production* in the United States by increasing the price of imports, the stated goal of the regime—to save manufacturing jobs—has been undermined much more by mechanization and technological progress than by foreign competition.[3] Even if U.S. textile firms were completely protected from foreign competition they would still have to compete with one another, and any firm choosing to preserve jobs rather than mechanize would soon wither from the better performance of its competitors. While the rationale for the series of "temporary" trade arrangements has always been to save jobs by giving U.S. industry breathing room in which to become competitive, the only hope for becoming competitive is often to get rid of the jobs.

The charge that America's textile jobs are going to China also must square with a remarkable and inconvenient fact: China is losing textile jobs, too, and losing more of them more rapidly than has ever been the case in North or South Carolina. According to a 2004 Conference Board study, China lost almost 10 times as many textile industry jobs as did the United States during the 1995 to 2002 period, and textile jobs losses were the most severe of any industry in China. While production, revenues, and exports are soaring, employment is shrinking because of rapid advances in technology and labor productivity.[4] In short, textile jobs are not going to China; textile jobs are just going, period.

Own Worst Enemy

Not only has the regime failed to deliver its intended consequence—employment—it has also had the unintended consequence of reducing competitiveness across the U.S. textile and apparel complex, as members of the alphabet armies create higher costs for one another at each stage of a T-shirt's production. Or, as Erik Autor told me, the armies are often their own worst enemies. Cotton agricultural interests such as the National Cotton Council (NCC) have succeeded in erecting import barriers for raw cotton, which has increased the raw material costs for AYSA (American Yarn Spinners). The AYSA, in turn, lobbied for the tariffs and quotas on yarn imports, which have limited the ability of American fabric producers—represented by ATMI—to obtain the best yarn at the best prices. And finally, the quotas and tariffs applied to fabrics not only increase costs for U.S. apparel producers, they also limit the ability of apparel producers to respond to the rapidly changing fashion whims of the American consumer. The narrow successes of each step in the value chain in keeping foreign competition at bay has, collectively, imperiled rather than enhanced America's chances at remaining competitive across the production complex.

As we have seen, trade agreements such as AGOA, CBTPA, and NAFTA contain innumerable side deals designed to protect American producers. But these provisions often undermine rather than help the competitive position of U.S. firms. For example, free access under the CBTPA requires that apparel fabric be produced in the United States from U.S.-made yarn in order for the clothing to gain free access to the U.S. market. This "yarn forward" requirement actually often handicaps American yarn spinners, who are discouraged from both exporting their yarn to the Caribbean and from shifting production to more cost-efficient locations. The rules also handicap American cotton producers because, by limiting Caribbean yarn spinning capabilities, cotton exports are limited as well.

The regime has also introduced a regulatory risk into the already significant challenges of staying alive in this industry. Because T-shirt and apparel producers are never quite sure which types of textile trade policy currency will be traded away and for what, the risks inherent in forecasting policies are added to the already high normal business risks in the industry. For example, as a fabric "dyeing and finishing" provision was recently debated in Congress, firms had to consider for the better part of a year where and how to invest assets in printing technology in order to evade—or take advantage of—the new provisions. Trade Agreements such as CBTPA may be extended (or not) at the whim of the Congress, and if extended, the fabric provisions may (or may not) be modified. In attempting to carve out and preserve a piece of the pie for U.S. firms, the "preferential" agreements challenge an already debilitated industry to forecast not just markets but politics.

The economic costs of protecting the U.S. textile and apparel industries from imports have been estimated by many researchers. Though the results vary widely, most researchers conclude that the costs fall under the general category of Very Big Numbers. Surveying this literature in 1999, the U.S. International Trade Commission estimated the annual cost of textile and apparel import quotas to be between $7 and $11 billion.[5] The USITC estimated that the removal of all textile and apparel quotas and tariffs would have resulted in an economy-wide gain of $10.4 billion in 1996, but at a cost of 117,150 American jobs. Using these estimates, textile and apparel protection in the United States cost approximately $88,000 per year in the mid-1990s for each job preserved. Hufbauer and Elliott estimated the consumer cost of protecting an apparel job in 1990 to be $138,666, while a later USITC study estimates the cost of textile and apparel quota at between $7 and $12 billion.[6] Using the USITC's most conservative estimates, 2002 textile and apparel quotas cost $174,825 per job saved.[7] Finally, Schott and Buurman concluded that the combined tariffs and quotas in effect in the early 1990s represented an effective tax on clothing of 48 percent.[8] The costs of protection are not only high in dollar terms, they represent a regressive tax, which falls disproportionately on the lower-income workers that the regime is designed to protect.

Other self-defeating consequences result from apparel import quotas. As of 2004 the United States still had quotas on T-shirt imports from approximately 30 countries, and some of these will likely remain even after the expiration of the Agreement on Textiles and Clothing in 2005. The most predictable and obvious effect of the quantitative limits on apparel imports has been "upgrading" by the exporting countries. When China, for example, is allocated a quota of 2,523,532 dozen cotton knit shirts or 211,076 dozen cotton dresses, producers in China have an incentive to use the quota for high-end rather than low-end products. Chinese producers are loath to "waste" cotton knit shirt quota by using it to sell a cheap T-shirt when the quota could instead be used to sell a high-end, combed cotton polo shirt to L.L. Bean. The quotas have therefore encouraged China and other potential low-end producers to become high-end producers, and have in effect encouraged more high-margin, expensive clothing production to be shifted abroad. Again, my lowly $5.99 T-shirt was lucky to have made it in at all.

Race to the Quotas

The quotas have also driven much of the investment in apparel production worldwide, with firms locating production in countries with quotas rather than in countries that make sense for other business reasons. By plugging the apparel import dikes from dozens of countries over the past generation, the United States encouraged a myriad of detours and otherwise irrational moves by firms who were—and are—forced to engage in what Andrew Tanzer has called "The Great Quota Hustle." Indeed, the astoundingly creative entrepreneurial maneuvers that have been undertaken to deal with the quota regime are as strong evidence as anything of the business acumen among Chinese managers. Managers who grew up learning to deal with the irrational regime of Mao Zedong have an advantage, it appears, in dealing with U.S. trade policy.

The Esquel Corporation, today the world's largest producer of cotton shirts, started in Hong Kong in the late 1970s, but, unable to obtain quota to sell to the United States, shifted production to mainland China.[9] When the United States tightened Chinese shirt quotas in the early 1980s, Esquel moved production to Malaysia. When Malaysian quota also became difficult to obtain, Esquel moved yet again, this time to Sri Lanka. The globe hopping continued, with the Chinese shirt producer setting up operations in Mauritius and Maldives. Other Chinese firms played the game as well, shipping Mongolian goat hair to tiny islands that had extra cashmere sweater quota. A difficulty with the system is that the countries with quota often had no expertise and few workers, so the firms were forced to ship Chinese workers to Mauritius and Chinese managers to Cambodia. The Chinese were still producing the clothing, though travel time and complexity had of course increased markedly.

The image of globe-trotting corporations often presented by antiglobalization activists as well as by textile interests in Washington demonizes corporations for their lack of loyalty, and especially for their fleeting moves to cheaper and cheaper production locations. While this "race to the bottom" story is indeed descriptive, it is important to note that the globe hopping we observe in the textile and apparel industries is also the result of the very policies that have been erected by the textile interests. Indeed, it has been politics as much as markets that has fueled the race to the bottom, even as politics alters the course of the race. As the *Financial Times* reports, the apparel industry has globalized in response to trade barriers rather than in response to open markets.[10]

Under the quota system, cheating, by all accounts, is rampant. Though the United States employs hundreds of customs inspectors and regularly raids Chinese factories, billions of dollars in clothing made in China is labeled as if it were from other countries. This "transshipment" game is complex, as Chinese producers first find out which countries have quota available for which goods, and then find a way for the clothing to be shipped to the country with quota and then onto the United States while confounding U.S. Customs. One apparel importer told me that he had visited a factory of his Chinese supplier and seen "made in" labels for numerous countries on the sewing tables, and that his Chinese supplier had offered him goods "made in" Cambodia, Kenya, or Lesotho. Though U.S. penalties for transshipment are severe, they make only a small dent in the illegal trade.[11]

Perhaps the most perverse consequence of all from the U.S. system of apparel quotas is the extent to which it has made the wrong people wealthy. Quotas are in effect options, and, as any investor knows, options have value. By allocating quotas to dozens of countries around the globe, the U.S. government has parceled out valuable options—that is, the right to sell to American consumers—as gifts from the U.S. government.

Many exporting countries auction or allocate through under-the-table payments the apparel import quota granted to them by the U.S. government, and the cost of the quota adds directly to the price of the clothing. There is an active secondary market in apparel quota that functions much like a stock exchange, with quota buyers seeking to acquire quota at low prices and resell it at higher prices. A number of industry participants in China told me that the quota market was rife with speculation and manipulation, where, for example, a trader with "inside information" about a large shirt order from a U.S. retailer would buy up the necessary quota in advance and resell it at a profit. According to Roy Delbyck, an American trade lawyer, quota profits are found in Hong Kong's stunning skyline, where the riches from the quota trade have been invested in the property market.[12] While they may not have helped South Carolina's textile workers, the quotas have quite clearly helped Hong Kong's storied real estate investors.

As of 2004, quotas were in place on dozens of categories of clothing from China, including several categories that had been decontrolled for all other countries. Most observers expected that many quotas would stay in place at least through 2008. Because of the tight constraints, Chinese apparel quota is actively traded and very valuable. Figure 8.3 shows examples of the prices at which Chinese apparel quota was trading in mid-2004. As the table shows, T-shirt quota (category 338/339) was selling for approximately 67 cents per shirt, though the quota prices for cotton knit shirts with collars (e.g., polo shirts) were close to $2.50. Quota costs added a little over 70 cents to the cost of each pair of underwear from China, and nearly $54 to the cost of a woman's wool coat. Based on the market prices prevailing in the summer of 2004, the apparel quotas granted to China during that year represented a gift of approximately $905 million to the Chinese government.[13]

Category	Description	Quota Price per Dozen
333	Men's and Boys' cotton blazers	$21.00
644	Women's and girls' suits, MMF*	$67.00
338/9	Cotton knit shirts (T-shirts)	$8.00
338/9-S	Cotton knit shirts with collar	$30.00
435	Women's and girls wool coats	$650.00
342	Cotton skirts	$46.00
445/446	Wool sweaters	$170.00
636	Dresses, MMF	$70.00
352	Cotton underwear	$8.80
651	Pyjamas, MMF	$13.00
448	Women's wool trousers	$170.00

*Man-made fiber
Source: Hong Kong Trade and Development Council
http://tdc-link.tdc.org.hk/quota/China/chinaquota.asp
accessed August 18, 2004.

FIGURE 8.3   Market Prices for U.S. Import Quota for Apparel from China, August 2004

It is hard to know where to start in discussing what is wrong with this picture. First, perhaps the chief complaint against China made by the U.S. textile industry is that the Chinese government subsidizes its industry, through subsidized inputs, easy bank loans, and tax credits. But if the Chinese government is subsidizing its industry, then the United States is subsidizing the Chinese government with, as we have seen, a gift of close to a billion dollars. In exchange for this gift, however, few jobs have been saved in South Carolina, though they have clearly been saved for the hundreds of bureaucrats around the world who administer the regime, and they have also been saved for workers in countries such as Bangladesh and Sri Lanka who supply the goods that China cannot when it runs out of quota. While the quota regime was allegedly put in place to protect the American worker, it is difficult to construct a story that concludes that the Chinese quota saves American textile jobs. And if the $905 million in Chinese quota could be allocated instead to the 98,000 U.S. textile and apparel workers who lost their jobs in 2003, each worker could be paid more than $9,000 in job retraining or other benefits.

Even if the nonsensical maze of U.S. textile trade policy did protect American textile and apparel workers—which it doesn't—the question remains: Why do the 99.99 percent of Americans who are *not* textile and apparel workers put up with it?

Auggie and Aristotle versus Wal-Mart

Needless to say, when free traders get going on textile and apparel trade policy, it is hard to get them to stop: The whole system is a blight on world trading, an island of reactionary irrationality in a forward-moving universe, and it is ineffective to boot. Today, the doctrine of free trade has virtually unanimous support among professional economists, a group almost without exception who scorn protectionism in general and the MFA in particular.[14] Indeed, Douglas Irwin, the noted economic historian, suggests that the doctrine of free trade is not only a good idea but is even the best useful idea ever generated by economists:

> The case for free trade has endured because the fundamental proposition that substantial benefits arise from the free exchange of goods between countries

has not been overshadowed by the limited scope of various qualifications and exceptions. Free trade thus remains as sound as any proposition in economic theory which purports to have implications from economic policy is ever likely to be.[15]

Nearly a century earlier, Frank Taussig noted that even the strongest political pressure cannot change the quality of an idea:

[T]he doctrine of free trade, however widely rejected in the world of politics, holds its own in the sphere of the intellect.[16]

There is perhaps no other issue, however, in which the professional opinion of economists differs so markedly from the opinion of the American public. While economists are near unanimous on the superiority of free trade as policy, the American public has grave reservations.[17] Though the public is not necessarily supportive of U.S. textile interests, it is also not supportive of unrestrained gushes of cheap goods from China. What accounts for this gaping divide between professional and public opinion?

In general, economists judge policies by their effects on national wealth and income, or "global welfare," and it is inarguably true that this metric supports free trade over most, if not all, forms of trade protection. The American public, however, has other metrics in mind: metrics that are less well defined, and certainly more difficult to measure. Whether the spigot pouring T-shirts into the United States from China should be closed, open, or left to dribble through an administrative maze is therefore a debate not about the best *economic* policy but instead about economic policy versus all of the other factors that weigh on policymakers' decisions. It is easy to be outraged over the dominance of special interest politics over sound economic policy, but we must also recognize that it is not only special interests, but also the American public, that remains uneasy about free trade.

Trade has always made people nervous. Douglas Irwin writes that the ancient Greeks, in particular Aristotle, were highly suspicious of international trade, even as they acknowledged its economic benefits.[18] While conceding that trade brought more goods more cheaply, they were concerned about a number of negative influences on civil society. This same tension today is crystallized in the many and varied debates surrounding Wal-Mart, which supplies about 25 percent of the U.S. apparel market with goods that are virtually all imported from abroad. While Wal-Mart's provision of cheaper and cheaper imports is unquestionably a boon to the apparel consumer and to the economy at large, virtually every aspect of the firm's behavior has drawn protests, and the very behavior that gives consumers a windfall is at the same time the target of critics.[19] Protestors want Wal-Mart to stop their union-bashing, and to improve its pay and benefits for employees. The company is also criticized for its merciless squeeze on supplier pricing, and for its failure to effectively monitor the working conditions in the overseas factories that produce the apparel for its stores. The cheap apparel itself is blamed for the demise of South Carolina textile mills, and the laid-off textile workers complain that the only jobs left when the mills closed were as checkout clerks behind the enemy lines, because Wal-Mart had also squeezed out the smaller stores on Main Street. Auggie Tantillo describes the Wal-Mart squeeze cycle, in which Wal-Mart's squeeze on its American suppliers has bankrupted them, and led the firm to China where it squeezes Chinese suppliers, who in turn squeeze their own suppliers as well as their sweatshop workers. At the end of the squeeze cycle, we can buy our T-shirts for 25 cents less, so on average we are richer, but at what cost?

Auggie Tantillo has a moral view on the Wal-Mart squeeze, and he shares this view with a storied line of ancestors, beginning at least with Aristotle, as well as with an uneasy American public. A bit more stability, a bit more community, a bit more of a dike against the bashing waves from China are worth more than small savings for each of us on the cost of a T-shirt.

Another divide between professional and public opinion relates to differing perspectives: While economists view matters nationally or even globally, many Americans take a local perspective. While free trade increases global welfare, some local workers, companies, and communities are the losers; the economic benefits of free trade are diffuse, while the costs are typically concentrated. When the benefits of cheaper T-shirts for millions across the country are placed alongside the costs of job loss for a few thousand in a North Carolina mill town, the public's internal calculator often works much differently than does an economist's. Judging from the political rhetoric in the 2004 election, it is worth something, perhaps a lot, to keep the manufacturing jobs—or to try to keep the jobs—in a community that is on the edge. Even when it looks futile, Americans seem to want to try.

Economists do not deny that free trade may bring concentrated losses to certain industries and workers, but the solution, most economists argue, is "the compensation principle." The best economic policy is not to erect trade barriers but instead to compensate the losers. The rationale behind a variety of Trade Adjustment Assistance (TAA) programs that have been undertaken in the United States is that by taxing the millions who have benefited from cheaper T-shirts and funneling the compensation to the thousands who have lost their jobs, we can both gain the economy-wide benefits of free trade and at the same time mitigate the negative local effects.

It works better in economic theory than it does in practice. While some towns in the textile South have moved beyond this industry and never looked back, others that used to produce textiles and T-shirts it seems now produce only news stories or documentaries on life after the mill closed. These stories have a common thread: It is not just that the jobs are gone, but that the communities are gone, too, and the future is uncertain and scary. The paycheck can be replaced by the compensation principle, but everything else, as the ad says, is priceless. Especially in low-tech industries such as apparel manufacture, the losers stay losers once their jobs are gone.[20]

(Unintended) Winners

If the 45-year regime has not served its intended purpose of saving jobs in the United States, have there been any positive effects at all? It is certainly true that the regime has softened and delayed the landing for many textile firms and their communities. With hindsight, however, it is clear that the primary beneficiaries of the textile and apparel trade regime have been not U.S. workers but the dozens of small developing countries whose textile and apparel industries were effectively created by the MFA. By restraining textile and apparel exports from the large and competitive producers such as Japan in the 1950s, Hong Kong in the 1970s, or China in the 1990s, while at the same time allocating quota to Bangladesh and Mauritius, the

MFA provided an incubator for the industrial development of dozens of these small developing countries. However unsuccessful the quota regime has been in protecting U.S. jobs, it has been successful indeed as foreign aid, or economic development assistance, to dozens of poor countries.

While it is no doubt true that broader economic development in these countries would have been a preferable outcome, it is not at all clear that this would have occurred without the MFA. The developing countries that have never been allocated textile and apparel quotas—primarily in Africa—are not only not broadly industrialized but are barely industrialized at all. The quotas given to Mauritius and Bangladesh not only opened sewing factories but indirectly built roads, ports, and communications systems, and at the same time fostered the development of a wide variety of trade-related services. This is not to argue that this positive "industrializing" influence outweighs the variety of costs associated with the MFA, but is instead simply to point out that there are at least some (unintended) benefits to outweigh these costs.

More broadly, trade barriers in business can serve the same purpose as any other type of barrier. While the conventional wisdom associates free markets with forward progress and prosperity, barriers, too, can lead to progress. Sometimes a wall limits our fortunes; other times a wall can incite much more creativity than an open door. It was a barrier that led Eli Whitney to invent the cotton gin, and a different sort of bottleneck that led James Hargreaves to invent the spinning jenny. While the world in aggregate would have been richer without the trade barriers, the world also would have been a different place. Trade barriers, like other barriers, can blow the future apart. Consider this parable from long ago, when Auggie Tantillo's protectionist ancestors first tried to block the cheap cotton clothing flowing in from Asia.

Let the Dead Be Forced to Wear It

In the early seventeenth century, the English woolen industry had no rivals. The industry was highly successful both domestically and internationally, and it formed the backbone of entire communities in much the same way cotton mills dominated early twentieth-century North Carolina. Employment was also great in ancillary industries such as weaving and embroidery. Writers on the topic of English wool often became mired in what Thomas called "poetic ecstasy": The more restrained lauded English wool as the "foundation of English riches," while the less restrained compared English wool to Samson's locks.[21]

Poetic ecstasy notwithstanding, the term "English woolens" does not compel one to jump out of bed each morning to dress. Though the fabric was indeed central to the economy, the woolens were also expensive to the average consumer, so the English middle class had very little variety of dress. And then, as now, woolens were itchy, they were hard to clean and dry, and they were hot and clammy in the damp English summers. It is hard to imagine how even the most passionate patriot would, if given a choice, prefer woolen underwear to cotton.

The handmade Indian cotton calicoes and muslins that began to pour into British ports in the mid-1600s were a consumer boon not unlike today's cotton T-shirts from China. For socks, children's clothing, and frocks, there was a marvelous new alternative: It was cheap, it was light, and it was washable. It came in a variety of bright colors and prints, and it was soft instead of itchy. The directors of the East India Company wrote India in 1691 that any quantity, and any type, of Indian cotton cloth should be sent: "You can send us nothing amiss at this time when everything of India is so much wanted."[22] Defoe worried that the cheap cottons from India had:

> crept into our houses, our closets, our bedchambers; curtains, cushions, chairs, and at last beds themselves were nothing but Callicoes. . . . everything that used to be made of wool, or silk, relating to either the dress of women or the furniture of our houses, was supplied by the Indian trade.[23]

Readers can no doubt predict the response of the British woolen industry to the torrents of cheap cotton clothing flowing in from Asia. As consumers clamored for the soft and cheap clothing, the "groans of the weavers" quickly reached the British Parliament.[24] The mill owners told of crises and even starvation in the shadow of the shuttered woolen workshops, and of the unemployed fleeing to Holland and Ireland. Even the mills that stayed open had cut their employment drastically, and the related industries, as well as woolen district shopkeepers, also suffered and added their voices to the cacophony of groans. In many districts unemployment was above 50 percent, leaving half the men, and most of the women and children, dependent upon the parishes for support. And the cheap cotton imports cost not only jobs but lives. The 1700 *England's Almanac* reported that:

> Lord Godophins's and Duke of Queensbury's sisters were burnt to death by muslin head-dresses and night-rails; the Lady Frederick's child burnt to death by a calico frock; a house belonging to St. Paul's School burnt by a Calico bed and curtains, a playhouse at Copenhagen with 3 or 400 people burnt occasion'd by calico hangings.[25]

The new underwear was dangerous.

The war against cotton imports that raged through the English Parliament in the late 1600s pitted the woolen interests against the reasoned voices of those who argued that cotton was a superior fabric in some settings, especially in summer. Like snarling dogs today, the woolen interests tried to reserve some piece of the pie for the domestic industry. This act, introduced in Parliament in 1689, for example, reserved cottons for use in the summer only:

> All persons whatsoever to wear no garment . . . but what is made of sheep's wool . . . from the feast of All Saints to the feast of Annunciation.[26]

Other attempts to shore up the market for woolens involved legislating the dress of particular groups in order to support the domestic industry. If the groups could be made big enough, perhaps wool could be saved. An act introduced in 1699 stipulated that:

> all magistrates, judges, students of the Universities, and all professors of the common and civil law . . . [must] wear gowns made of the woolen manufacture [at all times of year].[27]

When this attempt to dictate dress failed, the woolen interests turned their attention to less powerful groups. It was argued quite shamelessly that even the poorest could afford a bit of wool in their wardrobe: An act at the same time introduced to the Parliament required all female English servants earning 5 pounds or less to wear only woolen hats. As in today's trade agreements, there was an attempt to keep some piece of the pie for the domestic industry. If the woolens could have some part of the calendar, or some part of the population, then their well-publicized misery would be eased.

But in the end, by 1700, Parliament had granted woolen's wishes for only one group of consumers, a group that didn't get itchy in wool, the one group that was less powerful than female servants. An act, passed easily, stipulated that:

> No corpse of any person . . . shall be buried in any shirt, shift, sheet or shroud . . . other than what is made of sheep's wool only.[28]

For this event, like many others, there was a little poem:

> *Since the living would not bear it*
> *They should when dead be forced to wear it.*[29]

Of course, each British citizen only died once, and once dead did not change clothes, so this limited market was not enough to restore the fortunes of the English woolen industry. With the landowners and the churches on their side, the woolen workers could not be easily dismissed. In 1701, the Parliament responded with an astonishing rule for the living: Beginning on September 29, 1701, people simply could not wear this slight and tawdry cloth anymore. For all people, and at all times of year:

> all calicos painted, dyed, printed, or stained (in Persia, China, or the East Indies) which are or shall be imported into this kingdom, shall not be worn or otherwise used within this kingdom of England.[30]

Notably, the act did not exclude simple utilitarian muslins that had not been dyed or printed.[31] Presumably, anyone with a legitimate "need" for cotton fabric could have it met with the plain muslins. The "calicoe madams," however, who had embraced the new fashionable prints, had best dust off their woolens. Yet while the Calicoe Laws of 1701 appeared at first to be a victory for the woolen interests, it became clear almost immediately that Parliament could not legislate the woolen industry's salvation.

Predictably, the barriers ignited entrepreneurial instincts. With consumer demand still rampant, and the plain, undyed muslins still flowing in at very low prices, entrepreneurs in England figured out quite quickly how to print and dye cotton cloth, and had soon mechanized the process.

A new industry was born in England, and it was successful almost immediately. In 1702, barely a year after the act had gone into effect, the Commissioners of Trade and Plantations bemoaned the unintended consequences of the trade barriers:

> Though it was hoped that this prohibition would discourage the consumption of these goods, we found that allowing calicos unstained to be brought in has occasioned such an increase of the printing and staining calicoes here that it is more prejudicial to us than it was before passing the Act.[32]

In putting up a wall to keep out Indian printed cottons and save the domestic woolen industry, the protectionists had instead constructed a warm and profitable incubator for the cotton printing and dyeing industry in Britain. The woolen workers were behind where they had started. By 1719, they had taken their battle to the streets. Woolen weavers declared war, quite literally, against the calicoes that had stolen their livelihood. The woolen weavers—all men—began not only to "plunder" and protest in the streets of London, they began to attack the women. The news reports of the day are replete with references to "disorders" and "outrages and abuses" on bodies of persons wearing calicoes.[33]

The woolen weavers won the war, clearly and decisively. On December 25, 1722, it became illegal to wear—or to use in home furnishings— almost all types of cotton cloth.[34] And the law was not a brief insanity: The ban on cottons would not be lifted for decades, forcing a generation of Britons into hot, itchy, and expensive clothing, all in the name of saving the domestic textile industry.

Being forced into woolens in the damp English summers got people thinking, and before long the British gushed forth with a stunning string of ideas about how to manufacture cotton cloth in England: power looms, spinning jennies, factories, the Industrial Revolution itself. By blocking access to cheap cotton clothing from Asia, protectionist dinosaurs had launched the modern world.

40 YEARS OF "TEMPORARY" PROTECTIONISM ENDS IN 2005— AND CHINA TAKES ALL

The More Things Change

Though the most complex protectionist regime for textiles and apparel is unraveling, the broad historical pattern that created the trade policies governing T-shirt imports continues today. Waves of trade liberalization are ongoing, but the liberalization is facilitated by continuing exceptions for this still-powerful industry.

Bill Clinton, arguably the most free-trade–friendly president in U.S. history, undertook a wide-ranging set of trade-liberalizing initiatives during his two terms as president. In trade agreements such as NAFTA, CBTPA, and AGOA, broader trade liberalization progressed only at the expense of protections for U.S. textile interests. Perhaps Clinton's most noteworthy initiative in the trade arena was his fight—ultimately successful—to gain admission for China into the WTO. Once again, however, it was a victory made possible by making exceptions. China's WTO accession agreement does not grant the country the full benefits of the MFA phase-out agreement, but instead makes provisions that allow quotas to be imposed on Chinese goods through 2008.

As we have seen, divergent interests by necessity create numbingly complex trade policy outcomes. For every broad proclamation on the blessings of free trade, complex side payments in response to the groans of the weavers continue. In 2002, George W. Bush received the one-vote majority (215 to 214) he needed to obtain fast-track authority to negotiate trade agreements by promising Rep. Jim DeMint (R-SC) that fabric used to make apparel in the Caribbean countries would only receive preferential market access if it was dyed and finished—as well as manufactured—in America. In just a quick whirl of the sausage machine, printing presses closed down in Honduras and powered up in South Carolina. While the dyeing and finishing deal was being worked out, the "sock dispute" stalled another trade measure as textile interests held up a tariff reduction bill in exchange for a requirement that toes be sewed shut in the United States in order for Caribbean-knit socks to gain preferential market access.

The brain-numbing minutiae of the bribes to the textile industry appeared especially surreal in the days following September 11, 2001.

Wal-Mart Backs Musharraf

In the days following the terrorist attacks on the World Trade Center and the Pentagon, world leaders arguably had more vital matters to discuss, but T-shirt imports into the United States were the subject of discussions at the highest level, including President George W. Bush, Secretary of State Colin Powell, Secretary of Commerce Don Evans, and U.S. Trade Representative Robert Zoellick.[1] Pakistani President Pervez Musharraf had aligned himself solidly behind the United States and was rewarded with an aid package worth billions, including grants, the removal of myriad economic sanctions, and debt relief. But Musharraf, as well as his commerce minister, Abdul Dawood, quickly made it clear in conversations with President Bush and Secretary Powell that perhaps the most important reward for Pakistan's solidarity with the United States would be a loosening of the restrictions limiting textile and apparel imports into the United States. Textile and apparel represented more than 60 percent of Pakistan's industrial employment and its exports, and the United States was by far the country's biggest customer. But even so, Pakistan's apparel and textile sales to the United States were restricted by tariffs as high as 29 percent and by tight quota restraints limiting imports of dozens of categories of textiles and of apparel. Even by September, many of the annual quotas were nearly full.[2] Musharraf argued that the war against terrorism would be best served if Pakistan's textile and apparel factories stayed open and the workers kept their jobs. This, in turn, would happen only if Wal-Mart, Target, and other U.S. retailers could more freely import cheap cotton clothing from Pakistan. Both George W. Bush and Colin Powell assured Musharraf that they would do what they could.

So as the ruins of the World Trade Center still burned and America's military was mobilized for the war in Afghanistan, the alphabet armies mobilized for another type of war. The American Textile Manufacturers Institute (ATMI), the American Yarn Spinners Association (AYSA), the National Retail Federation (NRF), the American Apparel and Footwear Association (AAFA), the United States American Associations of Importers of Textiles and Apparel (USA-ITA), and the Union of Needletrades, Industrial, and Textile Employees (UNITE) readied for a fight, bolstered on both sides by members of the U.S. Congress.

Ron Sorini, the chief textile negotiator under George H. W. Bush, represented Pakistan. Alongside him were Erik Autor of the National Retail Federation and other kindred spirits representing American importers. They argued that U.S. firms such as Wal-Mart would only continue to purchase clothing from Pakistan if the quotas were lifted and the tariffs rescinded. Wal-Mart did not have to stay in Pakistan, Autor argued. There were a dozen other poor countries willing to meet the T-shirt orders at the click of a mouse. If the factories were to stay open in Pakistan, then the United States had to loosen the noose on Pakistani apparel imports.

Not so fast, said the other letters of the alphabet. Why should the U.S. textile and apparel industry be made to pay the cost of U.S. foreign policy? The ATMI pointed to its obituaries, showing the recent demise of more than 100 U.S. textile mills and 60,000 jobs across the American South. Members of Congress weighed in with letters detailing the dire straits of the U.S. textile and apparel industries, and urged the administration not to grant Pakistan's request. The textile industry's argument was that while assistance to Pakistan was a fine and noble goal, taking the assistance out of the industry's hide was not.

The two sides opened with extreme bargaining positions and began to wheel and deal. Pakistan requested the suspension of tariffs on all textiles and apparel through 2004, and a 50 percent quota increase for most categories of textile and apparel, as well as more flexibility in shifting unused textile and apparel quota to other categories. The U.S. textile industry opened with an offer to suspend tariffs on handmade carpets (then approximately 2 percent), period. The administration countered with a proposal to allow Pakistan to borrow from the following year's quota for T-shirts, pillowcases, underwear, pajamas, and mops. Not a chance, responded the textile interests. The wrangling started before the first U.S. bombs dropped on Afghanistan and was still going on as the new government took charge and the U.S. military tanks retreated. By mid-February, however, the alphabet armies had hammered out a compromise, though both sides agreed that the final deal was much more responsive to the U.S. textile industry than it was to Pakistan.

Pakistan's request for tariff relief was rejected completely. Tariff rate changes would have required Congressional approval, and Bush knew as well as anyone the perils of taking trade matters to Congress. For a two-year period, quotas were expanded by 15 percent for seven categories of apparel, though quotas were not loosened on the largest volume items such as T-shirts. The deal included a special two-year "swing" provision, allowing Pakistan more flexibility to shift quota from one category to another. The amount of special swing that Pakistan could use varied by product category, and ranged from zero for some goods to 25 percent for others. No swing was allowed for sheets and towels, for example, for which there were several vocal producers in North Carolina. By April 2002, Pakistan had used up its entire year's T-shirt quota.

A year and a half later, the Bush administration unveiled another ambitious aid program for Pakistan. It contained no provisions at all on textile trade. "They knew better than to ask us for anything," an official at ATMI told me.

In the end, the concessions to Pakistan had amounted to little, and, in any case, the military phase of the "real" war in Afghanistan had concluded as the negotiations dragged on, so the original motivation—to help an ally in the war—was no longer so pressing. The political opposition to Pakistan's requests had been organized, swift, and powerful. At the end of the day, George W. Bush swallowed his rhetoric about the glories of free trade as well as his black and white moral rhetoric to do "everything possible" to help his key ally in the war against terrorism. At the end of the day, he followed in the noble tradition of every U.S. president since Dwight Eisenhower: In staring down the U.S. textile industry, he blinked.

Whither the Dinosaurs?

It won't be long now, political insiders told me over and over again, as if we were all standing over a comatose patient. The days of rampant textile and apparel protectionism and unintelligible trade barriers will be over soon. The companies are dying, the venerable ATMI is dead, and the most legendary fighters are either dead or over 80. Strom Thurmond, the industry's most infamous soldier on Capitol Hill, died in 2003 at the age of 100. He had been a steadfast ally since he entered the Senate in 1954, and had elicited textile promises in virtually every presidential election since then. Thurmond had not been much of a player while in his 90s, Auggie Tantillo told me, but at least they could always count on him for a vote. Jesse Helms retired from the Senate about the time of Thurmond's death, and Fritz Hollings—perhaps the only senator to proudly still call himself a protectionist in 2004—announced his retirement a short time later. Together, Thurmond, Helms, and Hollings had served as a triumvirate textile power bloc for 30 years. Some of the young guys have their hearts in the right place, but it is just not the same. According to Auggie Tantillo, U.S. textile interests today have about half as many die-hard supporters in the Congress as they did in the late 1980s.

Though the industry's political and financial fortunes are waning, Roger Milliken, by all accounts, is still going strong. Milliken is the reclusive chairman of Milliken Industries and, according to Forbes, one of America's richest men. Milliken, like Auggie, believes in manufacturing in America, and believes that to surrender manufacturing to low-wage countries is to surrender our communities and our future. Milliken destroys his old textile machinery rather than see it shipped used to China, and supports organizations that see things his way on the subject of textile trade. Milliken is also the founding member and chairman of AMTAC, which Auggie directs. Auggie Tantillo and Julia Hughes—who agree on so little—agree on this: When Roger Milliken goes, things will be different. Milliken, while a force in the 2004 elections, turned 88 that year.

As the textile industry fades, the political power and influence of apparel retailers are growing rapidly. Wal-Mart's PAC donated $1.5 million in the 2004 elections, making the retailer the second largest corporate donor to federal candidates. As recently as 1998 Wal-Mart's Washington presence was negligible, but by 2003 the firm was spending $1.7 million a year to maintain three resident lobbyists in Washington.[3] Lowering trade barriers remains a crucial political objective for Wal-Mart, and they are joined in their efforts by Sears, JCPenney, Target, and others.[4]

There is a moral to the story of the 2004 Senate election to replace retiring Fritz Hollings, surely the Senate's ranking protectionist. South Carolina had had the worst job record in the country during the several years leading up to the election, as mill after mill closed and manufacturing jobs evaporated. The remaining textile organizations—AMTAC, NCTO, and the NTA—wanted to force the candidates to commit on the issue of trade, to make public their positions on textile job loss, on China, and on the burgeoning trade agreements. The alliance composed a survey of five point-blank questions to force the candidates' views on trade out into the open, and, more important, force their hands once they entered office. The questions allowed no wiggle room; the tone and the wording were obviously designed to force the candidates to stake their space on the right side of the line in the sand. In each case, the right answer was "yes." The questions, along with the candidates' answers, were posted on AMTAC's web site:

1. Do you commit to the continuation of quota restraints on Chinese imports of textiles and apparel beyond December 31, 2004?

2. Will you oppose any free trade agreement that would grant duty-free access to the U.S. market for goods that fail to use U.S. or signatory country fiber, yarn, thread, fabric, and fabric dyeing, finishing, and printing?

3. Will you vote against the proposed Central American Free Trade Agreement that was negotiated in 2003 but has not yet been submitted to Congress?

4. Will you oppose any reduction of U.S. textile and apparel tariffs through the World Trade Organization?

5. Do you support preserving and expanding the Berry amendment and other federal Buy American purchase requirements to ensure the survival of a viable textile and apparel component to America's military industrial base?

Virtually all of the dozen or so declared candidates answered yes to every question. After the minor candidates were flushed out, the contest for the Republican nomination to the Senate was between Jim DeMint, a member of the House, and David Beasley, the former governor, while Inez Tenenbaum, the former superintendent of education, emerged as the leading Democratic candidate. Beasley and Tenenbaum had answered yes to each of Auggie's questions, in the tried-and-true tradition of potential senators from a textile state. Jim DeMint, remarkably, answered yes to none of them. DeMint broke rank with every senator from the Carolinas in the past 50 years, and not only failed to support the protectionist position, but went to the other extreme and campaigned openly as a free trader, making a break even with his own past in which he had shamelessly extracted the dyeing and finishing bribe from George W. Bush. Trade was the only issue on which Beasley and DeMint differed. As Beasley promised to build trade walls, AMTAC went to work to support his campaign. AMTAC plastered billboards in the small textile towns ("Have You Lost Your Job . . . Yet?") and undertook a drive to register textile and apparel workers to vote. As Beasley promised to build trade walls, DeMint promised to tear them down. Free trade was the hope for South Carolina's future, said DeMint, in a message not heard in South Carolina in more than half a century. DeMint pointed not to the sputtering mills but to the other factories that had come to roost in South Carolina in recent years: BMW from Germany, Michelin from France, Pirelli from Italy, Fuji from Japan, and even Haier from China. He urged South Carolinians to look forward to the role that they could play in the global economy, not backwards to the wheezing textile mills.

DeMint beat Beasley in the primary, in a 60 to 40 trouncing that surprised virtually everyone, and then went on to handily defeat Inez Tenenbaum. On inauguration day in January of 2005, Ernest Hollings, the Senate's most ardent and unapologetic protectionist, was replaced by an almost rabid free trader.

It won't be long now, retailers and government officials told me over and over again in the summer and fall of 2003. A year later, though, as I finished this book, the patient was perking up, and the last of the perverse consequences was emerging. Another whole army—or many armies actually—had come to shore up Auggie and his troops from the Carolinas. They came from Bangladesh and Mauritius, Turkey and the Philippines. The developing country clothing exporters who had sided with Julia in her efforts to get the quotas lifted were having second thoughts. In dozens of different languages, they began to snarl together with Auggie.

The Last Fight

The master narrative, largely unquestioned since the early 1960s or earlier, was that rich country protectionism for textiles and apparel was yet another example in the long history of rich countries tilting the playing field against poor countries through hypocritical policies. While pressing developing countries to liberalize trade and open markets, the United States kept in place a suffocating quota system and high tariffs that prevented the developing countries from sewing and weaving their way to prosperity. But like all master narratives, this rich versus poor divide story is only partly true.

U.S. tariff policies conform to the master narrative. Textile and apparel tariffs have been largely immune from the broad cuts that have characterized trade negotiations for the past 40 years. As a result, trade between rich countries is now close to tariff-free—but imports to rich countries from poor countries face disproportionate tariff barriers because of the heavy reliance of poor countries on textiles and clothing exports. Edward

Gresser estimates that U.S. tariff "peaks" (i.e., tariffs exceeding 15 percent) are virtually never applied to U.S. imports from Germany, Norway, and Japan, but are applied to almost half of the primary imports from Bangladesh, Mongolia, and Cambodia. Indeed, the United States collects more tariff revenue from Cambodian underwear than it does from Australian wine or Japanese steel.[5]

Whether the MFA and its antecedents, as well as the quotas that will remain after 2005, are also consistent with the master narrative is a more complicated question. While the intent was to protect rich country industries by limiting imports from poor countries, the effect of these import restraints has been neither uniform nor uniformly bad for poor countries. While the major cost-competitive exporters—Japan in the 1950s or China in the 1990s—have undoubtedly been constrained by the quota system, and while the global welfare losses for poor countries in aggregate have been great, the argument that the MFA has stood in the way of all developing countries' fortunes is less compelling.

With the introduction of textile and apparel quotas, and especially with their growing reach and complexity, the effect was to constrain the large competitive exporters, but also to "divvy up" the lucrative U.S. market and grant pieces to dozens of developing countries that might have never sold to the United States at all. It was quota allocations, not market forces, that granted U.S. market access to baby clothes from the Philippines, underwear from Sri Lanka, and men's shirts from Mauritius. And along with access to the U.S. market, the MFA also facilitated other forms of economic development. But the prediction that the end of the quota system will allow these countries to increase their fortunes is a shaky one: The end of the quota system will not so much allow the Philippines to sell more baby clothes as it will allow other countries to capture the baby clothes market that had once been reserved for the Philippines. Observers on all sides of the debate now agree that however unsuccessful the MFA had been in protecting the U.S. industry, it was successful indeed as foreign aid for dozens of small countries. Most large retailers plan to source their clothing from only five or six countries in the post–MFA world, whereas they had been forced to find suppliers in more than 50 countries under the quota regime.[6]

As of mid-2004, the very countries who had argued—demanded, even—the MFA phase-out had taken a step back to look at the future. Maybe not, they decided. Maybe this was a bad idea after all. One by one, they called and e-mailed Auggie Tantillo.

When the third tranche of products was lifted from quota in 2002, some of the poorest countries in the world got a frightening glimpse of the future. China had been admitted to the WTO in 2001 and for the first time would be eligible to have its apparel exports removed from quota. Not only did it appear that the Philippines or Sri Lanka or Mauritius would not get a bigger piece of the pie when the quotas were lifted, it appeared instead that China would get everybody's pie. Throughout the regime's history, observers had become used to the gushes that followed when holes had been poked in the dike, but no one had been prepared for the gushes from China.

In most of the categories that were released from quota in 2002, China's exports to the United States surged by more than 100 percent, with commensurate declines in the exports of the countries that had held the quota. For a number of textile and apparel categories, the gushes from China were more forceful than anything that had been observed in the postwar era. Chinese exports of baby clothes (category 239) surged by more than 2,000 percent, robes (category 350/650) by more than 1,500 percent, and knit fabrics (category 222) by an astonishing 21,000 percent.[7] Overall, China increased its U.S. import market share of the apparel released from quota from 24 to 86 percent.[8] At the same time, Chinese suppliers were slashing their prices, with wholesales prices often falling by more than half. Of course, the price declines were partly the result of the quota regime itself, as exporters no longer needed to purchase quota in order to sell to the United States. As Figure 9.1 shows, the gains for China meant losses for virtually everybody else.

Retailers were giddy at the prospect of unrestrained sourcing from China. China was the gazelle of the global apparel industry: the fastest, the cheapest, the best. Firms ranging from JCPenney to Liz Claiborne announced plans to shift most of their sourcing to China.[9] Estimates vary on the degree to which China will dominate the global trade in the post–MFA world, but there is unanimity on the fact that China will dominate. More conservative estimates suggest that China will triple its market share of U.S.

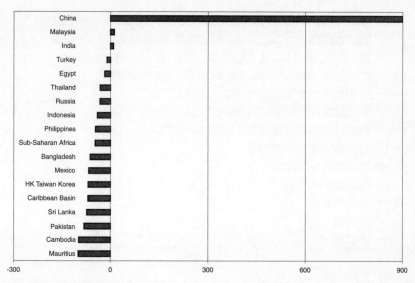

Source: OTEXA. Author's calculations for the 16 categories of apparel fully released from quota on January 1, 2002.

FIGURE 9.1   *Percentage Increase or Decrease in U.S. Imports of Quota-Free Apparel (2001 compared to 2004, year ending in August, in square meters)*

clothing imports, from 16 to 50 percent, while some industry experts predict that China could eventually supply 85 percent of U.S. apparel.[10] In mid-2004, the Esquel Corporation, which had been forced by the quota system to build factories in Mauritius, announced that they were closing up shop on the island and moving back to China.[11]

If the surges from China will hurt South Carolina, the effects will be far worse in a number of developing countries. Textile and apparel exports comprised more than half of manufacturing exports for a dozen countries, including Bangladesh, Mauritius, Honduras, and Sri Lanka, where the industries also provide the largest number of manufacturing jobs (see Figure 9.2). In many of these countries, the majority of the clothing exports were to rich countries that had quota constraints on Chinese apparel.[12] While the U.S. textile and apparel industries have lost approximately 300,000 jobs since 2000, the most dire predictions suggest that the end of the MFA could mean the loss of up to 30 million jobs in the developing

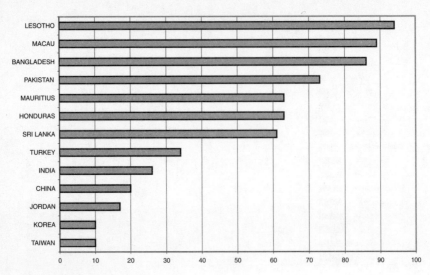

Source: USITC, 2004, Table 1.1.

FIGURE 9.2   *Textiles and Apparel Exports as a Percent of Manufactured Exports, 2001*

world.[13] In addition, each job in textiles and apparel may generate two jobs in ancillary services such as transportation or insurance, and these jobs are also at risk.[14]

In North Carolina, the lucky laid-off workers will get jobs at IBM and the less lucky will get jobs at Wal-Mart. The least lucky get unemployment benefits and trade adjustment assistance, and, if worse comes to worst, food stamps. In Bangladesh, however, there is little other industry and no safety net of any kind. Indeed, the closest thing to a safety net that Bangladesh has ever known was the secure market share provided by the MFA. It is hard to imagine the ultimate outcome of the trend shown in Figure 9.3, which shows drastic relocation to China at Bangladesh's expense. Bangladesh's market share in the goods released from quota fell by nearly 90 percent, while China's share more than tripled. While the global welfare benefits of the removal quotas are likely to be sizeable, these benefits are even more abstract in Dhaka than they are in Kannapolis, North Carolina.

A few countries believe that they can take on China. India and Pakistan are likely to be price and quality competitive with China, and will also serve

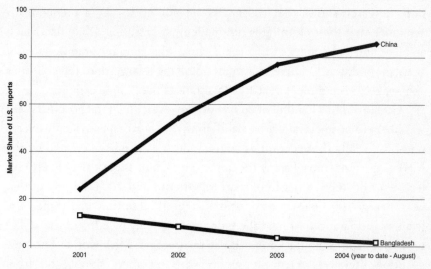

Source: OTEXA.

FIGURE 9.3   *Market Share of U.S. Imports of Apparel Released from Quota in 2002, China vs. Bangladesh*

as suppliers of choice for the retailers who do not wish to put all of their eggs in the China basket. A few Central American countries, especially Honduras, believe that their proximity to the U.S. market—and resulting delivery speeds—may give them a chance against China, especially under the tariff breaks offered by the CBTPA.[15] These tariff breaks, of course, require that the Central American countries use U.S. fabric, which handicaps them back in the other direction, but that is a fight for another day.

Interestingly, thanks largely to anti-globalization activists, tiny Cambodia also believes that it stands a chance. Rather than compete in a spiraling race to the bottom, Cambodia believes that there is a way to win on the high road. When the United States first granted apparel market access to Cambodia in 1999, it required in return a wide-ranging commitment on "anti-sweatshop" labor protections, and, in fact, offered Cambodia quota bonuses for meeting targets in improving labor standards.[16] As a result, for companies wishing to avoid the laundry list of sweatshop abuses so commonly heard regarding Chinese factories, Cambodia offers a "socially responsible" choice by which businesses and consumers have the assurance of rigorous monitoring sponsored by the International Labor Organization. Research shows that consumers are willing to pay a premium for assurance that their clothing is not made in sweatshops, while firms such as Nike and GAP are loath to see T-shirt sales hurt by graphic tales of sweatshop abuses.[17] There is a niche, perhaps a large one, for countries able make the credible "sweat-free" assurances that China cannot.

Outside of this handful of countries, however, life in the post–MFA era was likely to be uncertain at best and disastrous at worst as virtually everyone—especially those countries whose industries had been created by the MFA—loses to China. Facing the impending China threat, an unlikely collection of bedfellows began to snarl together in mid-2004. By July of that year, nearly 100 industry associations from 47 countries had signed the Istanbul Declaration, which called for an emergency meeting of the WTO to address the looming China threat in the post–MFA world. The new coalition literally circled the globe, with members signing on from Argentina to Zambia.[18]

Adding to the multilingual groans from across the world were the escalating cries of crisis from the U.S. industry. The National Council of Textile Organizations (NCTO), which had resulted from the merger of the ATMI and the AYSA, remained the master of the groans, as the industry continued to define itself in terms of its miseries. While many industry associations boast of their products, their customers, or their business models, textile groups continue to be most well known for their injuries. On the NCTO's web site in mid-2004, the web surfer could click on not products but problems:

- 💼 textile crisis
- 💼 plant closings
- 💼 job losses

As had been the case for half a century, the U.S. textile and apparel industries were still closing plants, laying off workers, and going bankrupt. AMTAC, NCTO, as well as textile CEOs from across the South were calling and writing Washington in what some said was the most unified show of political force seen since the late 1980s.

Auggie Tantillo had help from other quarters as well, as a wide assortment of groups from across America began to descend on Washington to charge that China was cheating. The groups ranged from the National Association of Manufacturers, backed by a substantial number of congresspeople, who charged that China was rigging its currency at artificially low levels in order to subsidize exports, to representatives from a range of industries who charged China with intellectual property violations and rampant piracy. The AFL-CIO charged that China's repressive labor policies—in particular the hukou system—constituted unfair trade practices, and manufacturers both outside and inside China complained that state-owned sectors continued to attract both unfair favors and subsidies from the Chinese government. An anti-China swell rose up in Washington, making its way even into the 2004 Democratic Party platform, which contained strikingly harsh "get tough with China" language.

And finally, at Georgetown University, where this book was born at a student protest, college students began to snarl, too. In a few short years the students had won codes of conduct for factories producing university-licensed apparel, and had shamed Nike, Reebok, and hosts of other companies into better behavior in apparel factories all over the world. Now, activists from NGOs and universities across the country took on the MFA cause, and demanded that U.S. companies stay loyal to their factories in the poorest countries rather than "cut and run" to China.[19]

In 2004, then, a new generation prepared to sit down at the table. The U.S. textile industry was newly energized by its mounting crises. Some developing countries were lined up to preserve the status quo, while others were lined up to make sure the MFA would be history once and for all. A number of countries were treading carefully on both sides, afraid for their future but also afraid to anger China. Some members of the U.S. Congress were railing against abuses by China, secure in the assurance that they wouldn't have to do anything. Other members, continuing in the long tradition of textiles as foreign policy currency, were pushing special tariff breaks for Muslim countries. George W. Bush was trying to tread lightly, wanting to keep the goodwill of voters in the Carolinas while not stepping too egregiously on China's toes, and also supporting his "War on Terror" allies. Julia Hughes and Erik Autor were shaking their heads: *They have had 10 years*, both of them kept saying. The U.S. apparel companies were trying to quiet the activists. Most of the Central American countries were on the sidelines, not sure whether to throw their negotiating weight behind Auggie or behind a push for more liberal fabric provisions. New alphabet armies were at the table, too, according to several people with whom I spoke. The CIA and NSA (National Security Administration) had developed an interest in the MFA as they began to ponder the security threat posed by perhaps 10 million unemployed textile and apparel workers across the Islamic world. As the disparate interests converged upon Washington in late 2004, it was clear that a political deal would be cut. Something would be worked out across the table, and the deal would likely have something for Auggie, something for Julia, something for Mauritius, and something for China.[20]

The old system, of course, was untenable. But the looming alternative, real free trade, seemed impossible, too. Since the British had been forced into woolens in the early 1700s, rich Western countries have been protecting their apparel industries from cheap goods from Asia, and the politics seemed unlikely to vanish on New Year's Eve of 2004. As of 2004, things were still being worked out in the realm of politics rather than markets, and it wasn't yet clear whether the best negotiators, or the best T-shirts, would win.

"See," Auggie Tantillo told me, pointing out his new allies from around the world who were suddenly huddling under his umbrella of politics, seeking protection from the markets and especially from China. "We're not just a bunch of guys from South Carolina howling at the moon."

PART IV

MY T-SHIRT FINALLY ENCOUNTERS A FREE MARKET

THE GLOBAL TRADE IN CAST-OFF T-SHIRTS

A Just-Opened Bale of American Used Clothing Near the Manzese Market. (Author's photo)

Geofrey Milonge at His T-Shirt Stall at the Manzese Market in Dar Es Salaam. (Author's photo)

WHERE T-SHIRTS GO AFTER THE SALVATION ARMY BIN

JAPAN, TANZANIA, AND THE RAG FACTORY

Meet Me in the Parking Lot

In the wealthy and normally well-mannered Washington suburb of Bethesda, Maryland, the competition is heating up.[1] It is Saturday morning, and soccer moms are in a race to throw things away. First in line is a Lexus SUV, followed by a Town and Country minivan, and then a Lincoln Navigator. The first three vehicles alone cost well over $100,000, which would buy about one-tenth of a house in much of the surrounding neighborhood. The Salvation Army truck sits outside the Sumner Place Shopping Center, but the truck has only so much room, so it pays to be early and to be tough. The wait to dispose of last year's stuff is longer than the wait to buy more stuff inside the shopping center, and often, by 10:00 A.M., the van is full and the weaker competitors are turned away until the next week. Mostly, the moms are giving away clothing—large Hefty bags stuffed to bursting with perfectly fine clothing that someone is tired of. Some of the moms admit that later in the afternoon they were headed to

175

the mall to buy more stuff, and that next year they would likely be unloading that as well. A few of the moms express an altruistic motive for lining up behind the van, and all say that they will use the tax deduction. More than anything, though, the moms are here because they need to clean out their closets to make room for new stuff.

T-shirts? Yes, they agree, lots of T-shirts. They shake their heads, not sure how they ended up with so many T-shirts. It is easy to see the simple market dynamic of secondhand T-shirts in a wealthy U.S. suburb: all supply and no demand.

The high wages that have caused the demise of U.S. textile and apparel manufacturing have a flip side. The very wages that have stripped America's manufacturing might have at the same time led to a new comparative advantage: Rich Americans—or even middle-class Americans—excel at throwing things away, and the richer we become, the bigger the mounds of cast-off clothing swell. The Salvation Army at one time tried to sell all of the clothing in its stores or to give it away, but the supply now so far outstrips domestic demand that only a fraction of the clothing collected by the Salvation Army stays in the United States. There are nowhere near enough poor people in America to absorb the mountains of castoffs, even if they were given away.

America's castoffs, however, have customers the world over, and clothing thrown away by Americans forms the backbone of a highly successful global industry. While the United States has experienced an unbroken string of merchandise trade deficits for more than a quarter century, recycled clothing has been a consistently successful export industry. Between 1990 and 2003, the United States exported nearly 7 billion pounds of used clothing and other worn textile products to the rest of the world (see Figure 10.1), and the industry now has customers in more than 100 countries.[2] The United States also has close to a 40 percent market share of the world's used clothing exports.[3]

Observers have sharply conflicting views about the global trade in cast-off T-shirts. Is the recycled clothing business a villainous industry—a shadowy network that exploits the goodwill of charities and their donors, and suffocates the apparel industries in developing countries under mountains of castoffs? Or is it a great industry, a model of nimble, free market dynamism

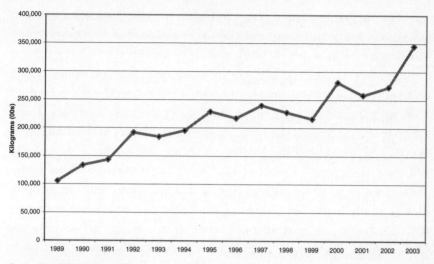

Source: USITC Dataweb.

FIGURE 10.1   *American Exports of Used Clothing, by Weight*

that channels charitable impulses into clothing for the poor? People who hold opinions about this business hold them strongly, but most people, of course, do not think about the industry at all, and while tossing T-shirts into the collection bins have only the vaguest and usually wrong idea of where the T-shirts might be headed and what will happen to them next.

The industry is all but invisible except to insiders: It has no household names and no big global players. Firms go in and out of the business almost daily, and though there are some factories, there are mostly networks of small family businesses scattered around the globe. The networks are often linked by ethnicity or family ties, and most of the businesses have only fleeting advantages in demand or supply. It may look easy, a simple matter of funneling the mountains of clothing that rich people no longer want to the poor who never have enough. But there are multiple complications and many challenges with an industry that links the moms in the Bethesda parking lot with the moms in African villages. Each leg of the journey has another set of competitors, and it is impossible to know ahead of time what will get thrown away in Bethesda and who in Africa might want it. Both suppliers and customers are fickle, and increasing competition has sent selling prices on a downward trend for more than 30 years.

For now, I've decided to keep my T-shirt. But one day I will toss it into a Salvation Army bin, and it will encounter a myriad of new experiences. Most important, it is only in this final stage of life that the T-shirt will meet a real market. Unlike the U.S. cotton producers, North Carolina textile mills, or the Chinese sewing factories, the clothing recyclers are on their own, without help, or even notice, from governments or lobbyists. There are no walls to keep out the lions, so successful players in the used clothing trade have no choice but to compete by punching rather than ducking, and each survives only by excelling in an exhausting race of faster better cheaper with hundreds of competitors, a race that leaves little time for politics. It is only in this last chapter of the T-shirt's life that world trade patterns are fashioned by economics rather than politics. While subsidies likely explain much world trade in cotton, and tariffs, quotas, and trade agreements explain much world trade in finished T-shirts, once the T-shirt is tossed into the bin its remaining life story is a story about markets and little else.

The global used clothing industry is also a fascinating study in the market for "snowflakes," as almost every item of clothing that enters the trade is unique. At the raw cotton stage, any bale of similarly graded cotton is interchangeable for any other, and once certain characteristics are specified, plain white T-shirts, too, are interchangeable. But if the moms lined up in Bethesda toss away 100 T-shirts, each will be different, and this snowflake factor has important implications for how the industry is structured and what it takes to win. In brief, the snowflake factor means that the most successful firms in the industry are those with highly developed expertise in picking out special snowflakes, and with worldwide but personal relationships that allow them to match snowflakes with customers. It is hard to see how a big multinational could pull it off. Here, finally, is a global industry for the little guy.

Panning for Gold on the East River

The Stubin family of Brooklyn, New York, has been a player in the industry for more than 50 years. Trans-Americas Trading Company, the family firm, occupies a five-story warehouse and factory on the Brooklyn side of the East River. Ships used to dock here, factories used to produce here, and people used to live here, but the neighborhood went downhill in the 1960s and 1970s, and today not much is left but the Stubins. New York City planners are talking about developing the waterfront, musing about river walks and condos, but for now there is little activity and even less traffic. It is not so much a bad neighborhood as a non-neighborhood. Though the factory is a mere 10 minutes from Manhattan, the lone traffic seems to be the trucks pulling in and out of Trans-Americas' loading dock. Even though it now appears to be a wasteland, the Greenpoint section of Brooklyn was of course a first stop for generations of immigrants, especially from Europe. Morton Stubin, who arrived from Poland in 1939, was one of them. Family lore is a bit hazy on how Morton started in the used clothing business, but somehow he found buyers and sellers of used clothing and built a business bringing them together.

Ed Stubin, Morton's son, hadn't planned to join the business. His plan was to become an academic, and he went so far as to obtain his Ph.D. in psychology. But Ed found himself facing a weak academic job market and the demands of a growing family, so he joined his father in the business in the 1970s. Today, though Ed is completely committed to the business, and is considered by many to be the industry's leader and voice, he doesn't really believe he is a natural businessman, and he still thinks about what he might be able to do with his psychology training once he retires. Eric Stubin, Ed's son, also did not plan to join the business, but after college and a few years climbing the corporate ladder, he came back to Brooklyn and joined his father. Sunny Stubin, Ed's wife, also works at Trans-Americas.

The U.S. textile recycling industry consists of thousands of small family businesses, many now in their third or fourth generation of family ownership, and Trans-Americas is both the rule and exception in the industry. Like its nearly 3,000 competitors, Trans-Americas is a family-run firm involving multiple generations in the day-to-day operations of the business.[4] Every year the Stubins watch many of their competitors go belly-up, and every year the failures are quickly replaced by new and nimble players. In this fluid network of start-ups and failures, however, the Stubins stand out for their longevity. Ed Stubin repeats this often, usually with a tone of amazement: "We're still here," he keeps telling me, as if he can't quite believe it. The Stubins also stand out for their size: Trans-Americas has about 80 full-time employees, whereas 30 to 50 is more typical.

The Stubins buy clothing from charities within a 1,000 mile radius of New York, and on an average day will receive about 70,000 pounds of clothing onto the loading dock. The charities charge what the market will bear, which in recent years has ranged between 5 and 7 cents per pound. Prices tend toward the higher end of the range when the castoffs come from wealthier neighborhoods, and toward the lower end in seasons that generate less desirable castoffs. In general, winter clothing has a more limited market than summer clothing, so prices trend down during periods when suburbanites are disposing of cold-weather clothing, and per pound prices are higher in warmer climates.

Used clothing buyers can't be choosy or averse to risk. They have no choice but to buy what has been thrown away and deemed worthless by somebody, and they never know exactly what will be buried in the truckloads from the charities. The most successful buyers are like successful stock traders, buying at low points, seizing timing opportunities, and hoping competitors are looking the other way.

Unfortunately, the best stuff has been picked off by the time the clothing reaches Trans-Americas. The larger charities—Goodwill and the Salvation Army—sort through donations for the goods that are saleable in their stores, so by the time the donations reach the Stubins, they have already been cast off twice, by the original owner and by the charity. But astute buyers not only know what types of goods get tossed to which charities and when, they also know which charities tend to skim off what.

Ed Stubin has seen a shift in the very nature of the business during the past 30 years. For many years, the business was essentially a sorting business. The tons of clothing pouring through the loading dock were sorted into three basic categories: for sale as clothing, wiping rags, and fiber. Each category had ready buyers, and, more important, each category was profitable. Whether the clothing coming into the warehouse was to be shredded into fiber, cut into rags, or worn as clothing, most of the prices paid for the raw material were sufficiently below the selling prices that the Stubins could make a profit. The business was simpler and easier then, and it was this appearance of easy profits that began to attract competitors.

Increasing competition in the 1970s led to a downward trend in selling prices that continues to this day. With selling prices falling and buying prices rising, it was no longer enough to sort and sell in the three categories, as most of the selling prices were below the Stubins' cost. The business changed from a sorting operation to a mining operation. Mining usually requires more skill than sorting, and also entails significantly more risk. While some firms in the industry simply "sort and sell," others, like Trans-Americas, have developed significant expertise in mining.

The clothing enters the Trans-Americas warehouse on a conveyor belt that moves quickly past the workers who stand on either side of the belt. Like an *I Love Lucy* rerun, the workers grab the clothing whizzing by and toss it into or onto one of a number of bins, chutes, or belts. At this stage, little skill is required; the "rough sort" simply entails identifying the product and tossing to the appropriate place. The choices include, for example, skirts, men's pants, household materials, and jeans. T-shirt material has its own category, but includes not just T-shirts but also other articles made of cotton, T-shirt-like fabric.

Clothing in the T-shirt category drops through a hole to the floor below, where it lands on a belt surrounded by another team of workers. The workers quickly examine each snowflake and decide its fate. The shift is subtle but distinct: The workers are now miners and graders, rather than sorters, and the job requires more skill and more attention, and is rewarded with more money. The workers also categorize the clothing by amount of wear, ranging from like new to slightly worn, to unsaleable as clothing. As the workers grade and categorize, they are also panning for gold, because certain types of clothing, even that in poor condition, have an upscale and eager market. So-called "vintage" clothing has the highest value of all, though it is not easy to explain what exactly "vintage" is. If a worker identifies an article of clothing as "vintage," the clothing is singled out for special treatment on the top floor of the factory, where Sunny Stubin matches special clothing with special customers. While it may not be clear what "vintage" means, what is clear is that the business depends on the workers' ability to spot it, because to let it whiz by with the flotsam is like flushing gold down the river along with the firm's profits. Spotting the snowflakes that have special value is a skill that management experts call "tacit knowledge." In other words, it's hard to explain.

Some aspects of the panning business are easier than others. Everyone knows to watch for Levis and Nikes, because hip young Japanese have a penchant for these brands, and just the right pair of used jeans or sneakers can sell for thousands of dollars in Tokyo.[5] The Japanese also love Disney, and a perfect-condition Mickey Mouse T-shirt can easily be sold for 10 times the price of a less well adorned T-shirt. Because of its insatiable demand for Americana, Japan is the largest customer for American used clothing.[6] However, Japan's demand is limited to both high-end and quirky items; so while Japan is the largest dollar volume customer, the country absorbs only a tiny volume of America's castoffs. Most of the truckloads that are dumped into the Stubin factory have little of interest to the Japanese.

Once the likes of Mickey Mouse have been picked off, panning for gold in the T-shirt river becomes more inexplicable. The value equation might be flipped upside down, with worn items sometimes having greater value than new, and sometimes not. Old tie-dye, for example, is gold, new tie-dye is not, but the equation is reversed for sports team shirts. Somehow, Sunny Stubin just knows when she sees a T-shirt, whether it will appeal to one of her upscale customers, and somehow, the higher-paid workers are expected to know, too. How to explain to a worker from another culture that a ratty Led Zeppelin T-shirt (what is Led Zeppelin anyway?) should be skimmed off while a newish JCPenney T-shirt should be sent down the chute? How to explain why some "event" T-shirts (David Faulkner Memorial 2001 Motorcycle Ride) have high value and others (Kidz in the Zoo Fun Day 2002) do not? Sunny Stubin shrugs repeatedly: You just have to know your customers, she says over and over again.

Certain T-shirts are hot right now, especially in Europe, New York, and Los Angeles. Sunny has customers willing to pay top dollar for 1970s rock bands, for example, so the viability of the business depends on the workers' ability to spot such gold and send it onto the "vintage" belt for special handling. Sending an old Rolling Stones T-shirt to Africa is a lose-lose, as African consumers could care less about the Rolling Stones and also do not like visible wear and tear. Just the right Rolling Stones T-shirt—from the band's 1972 tour, for example—can fetch about $300 at a hip vintage store.[7] If such a shirt ends up in an Africa-bound bale, then the Stubins have not only a foregone profit from their vintage customers, but they have created an unhappy customer in Africa.

The T-shirts singled out for special treatment as vintage are matched with certain customers and are often sold by the piece, though sometimes by the pound. A nice Mickey Mouse can go for $3.00, and a rare rock band can bring much more. The vast majority of the T-shirts flowing onto the conveyor belts are not gold, however, and not bound for London, Los Angeles, or Tokyo. Like the leftovers from Nelson Reinsch's cotton production, old American T-shirts end up in surprising places.

T-Shirts in the Afterlife

Approximately half of the clothing arriving at Trans-Americas has another life to live as clothing. Where rich Americans see garbage, much of the rest of the world sees perfectly fine clothing that can be worn to work or even to weddings, and can clothe another child or two. Since the fall of Communism, American used clothing has found an eager market in the so-called "second world," and American processors now ship large volumes of used clothing to the former Soviet bloc. According to the Department of Commerce, America ships used clothing to Poland, the Ukraine, and Russia, and used clothing Internet message boards often contain expressions of interest from the poorer side of Europe. An advantage of the Eastern European market is its climatic similarity to the United States, as well as its similar fashion sensibilities. Other common destinations for American used clothing include the Philippines, Chile, and Guatemala. Virtually all of the clothing shipped to these markets is in fine condition; the only thing wrong with most of it is that an American got tired of it.

But most of the clothing whizzing by on Trans-Americas' conveyor belts is headed to Africa, on a journey from the richest to the poorest place on earth. For more than a dozen countries in Sub-Saharan Africa, used clothing represents one of America's leading exports (see Figure 10.2), and for several, it is often America's largest export.

The countries appear to have come from a list of World Bank basket cases, places where women still carry water and babies are born in mud houses. The basket case imagery is often used by critics of the used cloth-

Country	Rank of Used Clothing as Import from United States, 2003
Tanzania	1
Benin	3
Togo	3
Republic of Congo	4
Dem. Republic of Congo	5
Liberia	5
Niger	5
Uganda	6
Burundi	7
Ghana	7
Guinea	7
Senegal	7
Sierra Leone	8
Somalia	8
Burkina Faso	9
Kenya	9
Equatorial Guinea	10
Guinea-Bissau	10

Source: USITC Dataweb.
FIGURE 10.2 *Countries for Which Used Clothing Is Among the Top 10 Imports from the United States*

ing trade, where observers like to describe how insult is added to injury when the poorest countries of the world serve as a dumping ground for America's rags.

Ed Stubin has traveled to many of these countries, traipsing through Niger, Mozambique, Angola, and Benin to meet with customers and drum up business. He is still haunted by images of swollen bellies and especially of land-mine amputees. But to Ed Stubin, Africa is not a dumping ground or a basket case but a customer, or rather hundreds of different customers, each with exacting demands for quality, service, and price. Stubin is mildly offended but mostly amused by the notion that he dumps castoffs into Africa. Such a business model would never allow him to survive, not when his competitors are eagerly trying to meet the demands of the African consumers. As Americans continuously clean out our bigger and bigger but still too small closets so that we can head back to the mall to buy more, we create an exploding supply of used clothing that shifts the balance of market power to the African customer. Whether the African customer is seeking khakis, baby clothing, or T-shirts, he has hundreds of potential suppliers from the networks of exporters in the West, and Stubin survives only by figuring out what his customers want and delivering it in good time at a competitive price. The underlying principle is not original, but it is critical: The customer is king, and Stubin is in a faster better cheaper race to make the customers happy. Dumping ground, indeed.

Like clothing customers anywhere, Trans-Americas' customers in Africa want their clothing free of stains and tears. In addition, the hot climate means a preference for light cottons. But modesty is an important value in most of Africa, and so shorts have little appeal except for children. Miniskirts, too, are out, as is anything sexually suggestive. Most of Ed's African customers prefer darker colors, because they do not show dirt so easily. The Africans are every bit as fashion-conscious as the Americans, and know whether lapels are wide or pants have cuffs this year, and make their demands accordingly. T-shirts are perfect for the African weather, though the market is particular about the pictures or script on the shirt.

Most of Trans-Americas' clothing is baled according to customer specification and sold by the pound. Typically, the bale size is 500 pounds, though it can be smaller or up to 1,000 pounds. The bale's size and contents, as Stubin keeps stressing, are whatever the customer wants. Stacked in the warehouse ready to leave the loading dock are literally hundreds of bales marked "women's cotton blouses," "baby clothing," "men's khaki pants," "cotton polo shirts," or just "socks." In their incessant quest to meet the exacting customer specifications, Trans-Americas today sorts clothing into more than 400 different categories.

T-shirts are their own mini-industry. In all, the Stubins sort T-shirts into approximately 30 different categories, for example, pocket tees, ringer collar tees, four-color pictures, script, two-color pictures, and sports teams. While some customers will order bales of mixed styles of T-shirts, others will specify in detail their T-shirt style preference. Today, the market price of used T-shirts in good condition is between 60 and 80 cents per pound. Because T-shirts average three to a pound, this means that the Stubins sell T-shirts to their African customers for 20 to 25 cents apiece. Ed Stubin likes to stress that he can send a nice T-shirt to Africa for less than the cost of mailing a letter. The cost is also approximately half of the value of the raw cotton in the shirt.

My T-shirt from the Florida beachfront shop is well suited to the African market. African customers do not like "in your face" logos (e.g., "Ya got a problem with that?") or suggestive messages (e.g., "Hot Chick"). But my T-shirt's colorful picture of the parrot and palm tree is cheerful and inoffensive, and the shirt could be worn by a man or a woman. The T-shirt is still in good shape, with no holes or stains. It has been washed a few times, but the print is still bright.

My T-shirt is among the lucky ones, however, because about half of the shirts that enter the Trans-Americas factory do not have another life as clothing, as there is virtually no demand from the world market for clothing that is torn, excessively worn, or stained. Of the clothing that is no longer wearable, T-shirts are among the most valuable: Most of them will end up as wiping rags in the world's factories. There are few better wiping rags than an old T-shirt, according to Ed Stubin. Suppose, he asks, you have a pile of old clothing at home and you spill your coffee: What would you wipe it up with—the jeans, the sweater, or the T-shirt?

Approximately 30 percent of the clothing entering the Trans-Americas factory is destined to become a wiping rag. Trans-Americas provides bales of worn T-shirts for sale to rag cutters, who pay the firm about 5 cents per pound. Many industrial processes require white rags, so white T-shirts are baled separately and sold for a higher price. At this stage, the value proposition reverses again, as a T-shirt with an elaborate four-color picture will sell for a lower price than a plain white T-shirt, because the material used to make the print impairs the cloth's absorbency. Very dark T-shirts (whose dyes can react with some chemicals) and those containing some polyester (which impairs absorbency) can also sell for lower prices.

In order for an old cotton T-shirt to be saleable to a rag cutter, there must be enough left of the T-shirt so that the cutter can cut a rag of about 15 square inches. Some T-shirts are too ratty, or too covered with paint or prints, to be sold to the wiping rag manufacturers. There is a gasp of breath left in such a T-shirt, however, as it enters yet another market to become "shoddy."

A T-shirt becomes shoddy once it is shredded into bits by a machine called (aptly) a mutilator, in a process that is a bit like turning tree trunks into mulch. Shoddy has a market value of 1 to 2 cents per pound, and it also has customers across the industrial landscape. Bernie Brill, executive director of the Secondary Materials and Recycling Textiles (SMART) Association, told me that used T-shirts are contained in, for example, automobile doors and roofs, carpet pads, mattresses, cushions, insulation, and caskets. And finally, in a fascinating full-circle story, high-quality cotton shoddy can be spun back into low-grade yarn and turned into cheap clothing again.[8]

Ed Stubin finds a use and a market for almost all of the textile articles thrown away by Americans. The high-end items with quirky appeal will be sold to vintage shops all over Europe and North America, and the Japanese will get most of the Levi's. Winter coats will go to Eastern Europe, and old cotton sweaters will go to Pakistan to be turned into new sweaters. Shoddy will go to factories everywhere and also to India, where it is transformed into cheap blankets that are passed out to refugees. Italy is a customer for old wool, where an industry is built on recycling fine cashmere.

The heart of the business, though, is the trade with Africa, where the exploding supply of castoffs from the rich meets the incessant demand for clothing from the poor.

How Small Entrepreneurs Clothe East Africa with Old American T-Shirts

Mitumba Nation

Poverty in Dar Es Salaam is a languid and sultry state that has settled on the city like a heavy wash of paint. Though Tanzania is one of the poorest countries in the world, the poverty is not one of frenetic wretchedness as one finds in Calcutta or even Nairobi, but is instead a peaceful way of being, a slow-moving and purposeful means of navigating life's rhythms: sleep, eat, shop, laugh, smile, sing, be poor. Poverty is the weather in Tanzania. It is just there—there when the Africans go to sleep, and there when they wake up, there every day of their very short lives. Like the weather, poverty doesn't change enough to be a topic of conversation. Poor just is.[1]

Tanzania's socialist dream is in shambles, crumbling like the colonial buildings left by the British. Julius Nyerere, the country's post-independence leader, had a dream for Tanzania of self-reliance: After generations of bowing to slave traders and colonial masters, Tanzanians would produce their own goods, grow their own food, write their own destiny.

Nyerere's vision of "Socialism with Self-Reliance" was a road map to escape the past.

Under Nyerere's leadership, Tanzania in the late 1960s was the most committed of the socialist countries of Africa, and Nyerere was a spokesperson not only for socialism but for the poorest of the poor around the world. But like many of her African neighbors, Tanzania found that the socialist road led to dead end after dead end with factories that didn't produce, workers who didn't work, and farmers who didn't farm. Throughout the 1970s, incomes were falling, investment was contracting, and the majority of Tanzanians lived below the poverty line.[2] By 1980, Tanzania had the second lowest per capita income in the world. The Tanzanians who had for so long been exploited by the British were now exploited by an ideal—an ideal that could deliver pride, and perhaps a theoretical self-reliance, but could not deliver goods, food, jobs, or medicine.[3]

Today, free market economics is supposed to be the way forward for Tanzania, but this seems like an almost surreal prescription for this dusty, peaceful place of brilliant smiles. Babies in Tanzania die at 100 times the rate of babies in the United States, often from diseases that vanished from the West generations ago. AIDS has eviscerated villages and families, and has brought the average life expectancy in Tanzania down to 43, lower than it was a generation ago. The majority of the country's population survives by subsistence agriculture and still lives below the poverty line. How to define and measure poverty and well-being has been a challenge for development experts for generations, but it is not a challenge at all to see that by virtually any measure—income, calories, wealth, life expectancy, access to water, or brick housing—Tanzania holds down the bottom of the graph—a graph that in many cases is moving in the wrong direction.[4] During the past generation, as China's per capita income has quintupled, Tanzania's has barely budged. In 2001, Danielson and Skoog estimated that at then-current minuscule growth rates, Tanzania would reach a per capita income of one dollar per day in 2045.[5]

The most stunning scenery in Tanzania is not the savannah landscape but the African women. They stand taller and prouder than women anywhere, perhaps from years of carrying bananas and flour on the tops of their heads, perhaps from years of holding the country together. The white women—European backpackers, lunching diplomatic wives, missionary aid workers—fade away in comparison, graceless and silly in the shadow of the African queens. Many of the African women in Dar Es Salaam are draped in the brilliantly colored native cloth, graceful folds wrapping their strong bodies and stronger spirits. They are brilliantly colored splashes across the poverty and grief of Tanzania.

The men are a muted background to this scenery. They work, or they sit under shade trees, not as proud, not as strong, not as busy. There are some men in Muslim skullcaps and a few in Indian dhotis, but none at all in traditional African dress. Almost all of the men and boys in Dar Es Salaam wear *mitumba*—clothing thrown away by Americans and Europeans, and many are in T-shirts. Julius Nyerere would turn over in his grave at the sight of it: Used clothing from the West was among the first imports banned under his prideful policy of Socialism with Self-Reliance. What could be less self-reliant or more symbolically dependent than a nation clothed in the white-world's castoffs? Yet, it is difficult to see exploitation or dependence in the human landscape clothed in mitumba. I found that most of the men on the streets of Dar Es Salaam looked natty and impeccable.

In 2003, used clothing was by far America's largest export to Tanzania, and Tanzania ranked fourth worldwide as a customer for America's castoffs, with competition from countries such as Benin, Togo, and the Republic of the Congo.[6] Though it would take an average Tanzanian about 170 years to earn enough to buy the Lexus SUV in the Bethesda parking lot, thanks to a nimble network of global entrepreneurs Tanzanians can dress well for very little money. In this small piece of the Tanzanian experience, the markets work just fine.

Two for a Penny

The Manzese market in northern Dar Es Salaam is the largest mitumba market in Tanzania. The market runs along busy Moragora Road for more than a mile and contains hundreds of tiny stalls. Like a suburban shopping mall, different stalls gear their products to different customers. Stalls specialize in baby clothing or blue jeans, athletic wear or Dockers, or even curtains. The higher-end stalls boast this year's fashions, tastefully displayed, but the perfect Dockers are priced at $5.00, far out of reach for the poor and accessible only to Tanzania's upper classes. Blue jeans, too, are high-end items, and the shoppers poring over the blue jeans are discerning consumers, often with a better sense of what is in (how many pockets? how much flare?) than the original purchaser. The young people in Dar Es Salaam are as fashion savvy as young Americans, with a flawless sense of the hip and unhip.

The market mechanism is considerably more flexible than in an American department store. The Dockers with waist sizes in the low 30s sell for more than those with sizes in the 40s, as Tanzanians in general lack Americans' paunches. Otherwise identical polo shirts can vary in price as well, with more popular colors and sizes commanding a premium. Prices trend up at the end of the month when many workers get paid, but drift lower during periods between paychecks.

Perhaps the most interesting pricing behavior is evident in the divide between men's and women's clothing, as both supply and demand influences lead to significant price discrimination against the men. First, because Western women buy many more new clothes than men, they throw away many more clothes as well. Ed Stubin estimates that the bales arriving from the Salvation Army contain between two and three times as much women's clothing as men's. Women are also more particular about the condition of their clothing, so about 90 percent of what is cast aside by women is still in good condition. Men, however, not only buy less clothing but wear it longer, so only half of the clothing received by the used clothing exporters is in good condition. On the supply side, the bottom line is that world supply contains perhaps seven times as much women's clothing in good condition than it does men's. African demand exacerbates this imbalance, as African women's clothing preferences exclude much of Western fashion while men clamor for the limited supply of T-shirts, khakis, and suits that are in good condition. The end result of this supply and demand dynamic is that in the Manzese market, similar clothing in good condition may cost four to five times as much for men as it does for women.

Geofrey Milonge runs a T-shirt stall near the center of the Manzese market. Geofrey stands tall and shiny-black, with the languid pride and gentle manner that seem to be the national traits of the Tanzanians. Geofrey arrived from the countryside more than 10 years ago, hoping to escape the rural poverty of his village in the interior. Today, he is a mitumba trade success story, having started out on the sidewalk with just a single 50-kilo bale of clothing, which he had purchased on credit. Geofrey buys and sells about 100 bales of clothing per month, and runs three mitumba stalls in the Manzese market, each catering to different types of consumers. His T-shirt stall is neatly laid out, with hundreds of T-shirts lining the walls on hangers. Geofrey sells between 10 and 50 T-shirts per day, usually for between 50 cents and $1.50. Almost all of Geofrey's T-shirts are from America.

The labels show that most of the T-shirts were originally born in Mexico, China, or Central America, and most of the T-shirts also reveal something about their life in America. The college and professional sports team shirts (Florida Gators, Chicago Bulls) are ubiquitous, and winning teams' shirts fetch higher prices. Washington Redskins shirts move slowly, but Geofrey had earlier in the morning received $2.00 for the Pittsburgh Steelers. U.S. sportswear logos are popular, too—Nike, Reebok, Adidas—but Geofrey's customers can easily tell the fakes (cheaper, coarser cotton) from the genuine. Middle-American suburbia hangs neatly pressed as a backdrop to the more valuable sports logos. Across the back of the stall is a Beaver Cleaver caricature of America: Weekend activities (Woods Lake Fun Run 1999), family vacations (Yellowstone National Park—Don't Feed the Bears), social conscience (Race for the Cure), and neighborhood teams (Glen Valley Youth Soccer) are some of the customers' choices.

Geofrey buys his T-shirts in 50-kilo bales, and, because of the snowflake challenge, he is very careful about where he buys from. The sellers can hide all kinds of garbage in the middle of a bale, so it pays to know your suppliers and to make sure that they know that if they give you garbage you won't be back. Geofrey prefers to buy bales that have been sorted in the United States, rather than in Africa. The U.S.-sorted bales cost a bit more, but the jewels are less likely to have been skimmed off and you get a lot less junk. In the world of mitumba, an unbroken U.S.-sorted bale is a high-end luxury good.

In her study of the secondhand clothing trade in Zambia, anthropologist Karen Hansen found the perverse manifestations of the preference for castoffs fresh from American bales.[7] In the world of mitumba, Hansen found, consumers seek out "new" clothing that is wrinkled and musty-smelling. A fresh-pressed or clean-smelling garment cannot possibly have spent weeks or months in a compressed bale in a warehouse or shipping container; therefore, it is the more wrinkled and musty clothing that is likely to be "new" from America, while the fresh-pressed and clean-smelling clothing is more likely to be "old"—that is, worn or presorted in Africa.

Mitumba dealers told me repeatedly that 90 percent of a bale's value comes from 10 percent of the items. For every GAP shirt in perfect condition that might fetch $3.00 there will be a dozen pieces that will be hard to unload even at 50 cents. Once the few jewels have been skimmed, the bale's market value drops dramatically. As a result, successfully plying the mitumba trade is about keeping track of jewels. A bale consisting only of suburban activities will be a losing proposition for Geofrey. If the sports teams, GAPs, and Nike snowflakes have been pilfered, the Fun Run and family vacation T-shirts that are left will not allow him to cover his costs. In Dar Es Salaam, just as in Brooklyn, the business is all about snowflakes.

When Geofrey gets the chance to skim for jewels himself he takes it. Many importers order clothing in larger bales, say 500 or even up to 1,500 pounds, which are too large for a single dealer to purchase. In these cases, the importer or wholesaler hosts a party of sorts, to which Geofrey and his peers will try to cadge an invitation. Sometimes, the dealers will pay 1,000 to 2,000 schillings ($10 to $20) to be invited. There are refreshments and a competitive camaraderie leading up to the highlight of the party: the breaking open of the bale. The bale breaking is a highlight because only if mitumba dealers can see the breaking with their own eyes can they be sure that the jewels have not been skimmed, and in a large bale from the United States, the chances of valuable jewels are high. The mood is festive and raucous because of the surprise to come: You just never know what the Americans will throw away, and to be invited to the party to get first crack at the jewels can mean a windfall for the week.

The wholesaler breaks the bale and the melee begins. A 1,000-pound bale might contain up to 3,000 articles of clothing, and almost every bale will contain surprises. The dealers begin a competitive rummaging and quickly pull out the jewels. Multiple miniauctions for the jewels take place simultaneously: The spotless Nike attracts offers of $1.00, which quickly rise to $1.50 and then $2.00. The baby overalls with the tags still attached draw bids of 50 cents, then 75, and finally $1.25. A special find is to uncover a group of identical items—six matching yellow sweaters, say, or a dozen blue twill shirts—the matching clothing has a ready and profitable market as uniforms for businesses.

The mini-auctions at the bale-breaking parties are close to a perfectly competitive market. There are many buyers; there is perfect information; there is, as an economist might say, excellent price discovery. And there is good fun. The element of surprise keeps it a fun market as well as a functioning one, and the party is a treasure hunt as well as a market. The hunt for treasure does not stop with the clothing but extends to the pockets, as Americans throw away not just perfectly good clothing but perfectly good money as well. U.S. dollars, no less.

The most valuable jewels will never make it to the crowded Manzese market. Instead, the top-of-the-line jewels hang from trees in the commercial area near the harbor, close to Dar Es Salaam's only office tower, its handful of banks, and its second-floor walkup stock exchange. These jewels—a perfect suit, say, or a like-new prom dress—hang like solitaires from the trees on the main boulevard, away from the pedestrian hubbub of the Manzese. A trader lucky enough to nab such a jewel will hire a helper to sit under the tree and guard the jewel until it is purchased, or until nightfall, whichever comes first.

The middle and upper classes often do not enter the crowds at the Manzese market, though they too are dressed in mitumba. Just as a wealthier family might have help to shop for food, many Tanzanians also have relationships with mitumba dealers who know their size and style preferences, and keep a watch for just the right suit or dress shirt. Such personal shoppers make house and office calls when just the right jewels turn up in the bales.

When Geofrey Milonge emerges from the competitive market as a buyer he almost immediately joins another perfectly competitive market as a seller. There are hundreds of stalls and thousands of T-shirts in the

Manzese market, and the consumers have nothing if not choices. At the other end of the spectrum from the jewels are the dregs, the clothing that is hard to unload at any price. Most mitumba dealers have a card table or two in the middle of their stall that is piled high with clearance items that haven't sold. While the vendors' better offerings will neatly line the stall on hangers, the dregs are simply piled up, mitumba's answer to the clearance table at Wal-Mart.

Most stalls have a worker with a microphone who drones on in a mesmerizing chant to entice shoppers to stop. As evening approaches, the competition intensifies because the shopkeepers would much rather unload a few more garments than pack them until the next day. The voices from the microphones form a cacophony that gets louder and louder as the afternoon wears on. The stall owners like Geofrey Milonge are especially loathe to pack up the clearance table items as darkness approaches. The Swahili chants ring out as the prices for items on the clearance table drop like a sharp curve along with the sun. By the end of the day the clothing on the clearance table that sold for a dime at noon might go for two for a penny.

For Geofrey Milonge, the day ends in a seller's competition as intense as the buyer's competition with which he started the morning. If he rests in the morning the competition will snag the jewels, and if he rests in the evening the competition will snag his customers. The markets at the center of Geofrey's livelihood are more flexible—and closer to a "real" market—than anything the T-shirt has experienced before. With no barriers between himself and the market, Geofrey must adjust his selling prices by men's or women's, by size, by color, by weather, and by time of day and time of month, and he must adjust his buying prices at the bale-breaking party, by trying to predict who will happen by that morning, what they will want, and what they will pay.

Ed Stubin and Geofrey Milonge describe this global industry with remarkably similar stories. In both cases, survival depends upon their skill in spotting the jewels among the snowflakes and knowing their value in the market. Both men stress that they depend upon personal relationships with suppliers and personal knowledge about their customers. On both sides of the Atlantic, the snowflake imperative keeps the businesses small and nimble, in close touch with suppliers and customers. Once you stop paying attention, or take your eye off the T-shirt river, or off your customer, you're finished.

Here, at the end of the T-shirt's life, is a global industry where it pays to be the little guy, where the power equation is flipped upside down away from the multinational corporations. Indeed, the grandfather and founder of the used clothing business in Tanzania was victim of his own success. His far-flung empire, though built on profits from the used clothing trade, became much too big to keep track of snowflakes.

Too Big for Used Britches

Mohammed Enterprises Tanzania Limited (METL) is today one of the largest private companies in Tanzania, a conglomerate involved in manufacturing, agriculture, and trade. METL manufactures soap, sweeteners, cooking oil, textiles, clothing, and bicycles, and it owns 31,000 hectares of farmland producing sisal, cashews, and dairy products. METL is also a major trading house selling sesame seeds to Japan, pigeon peas to India, cocoa to the United States, and beeswax to Europe. METL seems to operate as a completely Westernized company today, committed to market awareness, customer focus, and corporate responsibility. Even METL's rise is a Western-sounding story.

As the family story goes, Gulam Dewji, METL's chairman, got his start in the 1960s by arbitraging onions in rural Tanzania. He drove a rickety truck across the crumbling non-roads, finding villages that had extra onions and connecting them with villages that had too much squash. He had a sense of market trends and impeccable timing, and he gradually added trucks and employees. In another place and time Gulam Dewji might have run a hedge fund, but in 1960s Tanzania, Gulam used his market timing talents on onions. Gulam remembers that the villagers, while poor, usually had enough to eat. They did not, however, have clothing, at least not to speak of. In rural Tanzania at the time, adults were mostly in rags and children were mostly naked.

Currency controls meant that hard currency was rarely available to import clothing, and mismanagement meant that the local textile industry was poorly equipped to supply the local market. There was special official scorn—and an outright ban—on mitumba. Though it was illegal to import used clothing, much made it through the porous borders with Mozambique and Kenya. But it was a furtive and haphazard trade, an underbelly business that was lubricated by bribes to border guards in the middle of the night.

In 1985, Julius Nyerere stepped down and the mitumba trade was legalized. Gulam immediately saw the business opportunity presented by the liberalization. From his decades of traveling through the rural areas he knew that people wanted decent clothing. It was not a matter of emulating Westerners, it was instead a matter of pride: Tanzanians had no desire to look like Americans; they wanted to look like well-dressed Tanzanians. Gulam went to America and began to meet with used clothing exporters.

During the next 10 years, METL's mitumba business grew rapidly and Gulam was soon importing 4,000 tons of used clothing per month into the port at Dar Es Salaam. Mitumba quickly reached not only the cities but far into the rural areas as well. A network of traders plied the backcountry as Gulam had once done with onions, and mitumba markets soon sprang up in every town.

Gulam purchased the clothing from American dealers in huge bales weighing up to 2,000 pounds apiece. Compared to the intricate sorting and mining processes that characterize the business today, the process was loose at best. Often the clothing had been sorted into just three categories: Category A contained only clothing that was in like-new condition; Category B clothing was in fairly good shape, a bit faded, perhaps, or missing a button; and Category C contained garments that were torn or stained. The bales were delivered to METL's cavernous warehouse, where they were broken up and sorted again and readied for market.

Just as Ed Stubin had once found it easier—most of the clothing he sorted was saleable at a profit—Gulam, too, found the early days to be the good old days. People in Tanzania had had so few choices and so little income that they welcomed almost everything from America. A bit of wear made little difference, especially in the countryside, as the clothing was usually a step up from the rags for the adults or the nakedness for the children. Gulam could sell almost everything that arrived in the bales from America, usually at a profit.

At the beginning, there were still many self-reliance ideologues who believed that the practice of wearing the white world's castoffs was shameful. Gradually, however, the ideologues toned down and began to dress in mitumba as well. Indeed, as Karen Hansen found in Zambia, the availability of mitumba was put forth as evidence of progress in the village. ("There is even mitumba now," residents would say, so as to point to the improved quality of life.[8])

But with widespread acceptance also came the maturing of the market and the erosion of Gulam's first-mover advantages. METL was growing and diversifying into other businesses, and the agility required to keep up with the mitumba trade was difficult to maintain. There were few barriers to entry, and it seemed that almost everyone had a friend of a friend in the United States or Europe who could begin to send over bales of clothing, so hundreds of nimble entrepreneurs emerged to buy and sell mitumba. The mitumba trade was an intensely personal business, built relationship by relationship as had happened with Gulam and his American suppliers. The relationships were needed to keep unhappy surprises in the bales to a minimum and happy surprises frequent enough to engender continued loyalty but not so frequent as to erase the black ink. The delicate balance required by the snowflake business required constant attention—attention that Gulam wanted to focus on other parts of METL's activities. Most important, however, was the fact that customers were getting pickier. Not only had the market for Category C clothing all but disappeared, customers now wanted certain styles and certain colors at certain times. Without the time or attention to keep his ear to the ground in the marketplace, Gulam found it difficult to compete with the small entrepreneurs who spent their energies staying on top of consumer preferences. Gradually, Gulam ceded his mitumba business to smaller traders. You need to be small to do this, Gulam told me.

Partly because of his success in the mitumba trade, small was what he wasn't. But for the entrepreneurs to follow him, there were opportunities, and chances for little guys to participate in a global market.

Friend or Foe to Africa?

In both the richest and poorest countries of the world, critics of the used clothing trade are not hard to find. More than 30 countries effectively ban the import of used clothing, either through outright prohibitions (e.g., Botswana, Malawi) or impenetrable bureaucratic walls (e.g., Ethiopia, Morocco).[9] Even when imports are allowed, the barriers are often daunting, even by African standards. Tariffs can be prohibitive, and some countries require convoluted health certifications as well. The use by many African countries of preshipment inspection (PSI) companies—essentially privately run Customs authorities—has led to charges of overvaluation, corruption, and simple ineptitude.

The barriers to the mitumba trade have in large measure been erected by the groans of the local textile industry, which echo those of Americans threatened by Chinese T-shirts in 2004 or British threatened by Indian cottons in 1720. The industry's groaning obituaries and ominous employment trends are of course more poignant in Africa than in North Carolina, but the essential message of doom and gloom is the same. In Kenya, more than 87 textile factories closed between 1990 and 1998, and similar tales of industrial demise emanate from Zambia, Uganda, and Tanzania.[10] About 30,000 jobs in Zambia's textile industry have been lost in recent years, approximately the same number that have been lost during the same period in North Carolina.[11] In at least one case, a large fire was set in a mitumba market, allegedly by textile workers threatened by the trade.[12]

The fascinating twist, of course, is that while North Carolina has lost its textile industry to low-wage workers from China, the African textile industry has lost to the high-wage workers of America, who live in a land of such plenty that clothing is given away for free. How, indeed, can anyone, even China, compete with free? What's worse, critics charge, is that the swells of mitumba not only shrink employment in the textile factories, they also keep Africa from putting its foot on the development ladder offered by textile manufacturing—a ladder, as we have seen, that has lifted China, the United States, Japan, and countless other countries into the industrial age.

There is little evidence, however, that the African textile industries— at least in many countries—would be flourishing but for mitumba. The African press is riddled with derisive comments about the quality and price of locally made products, and with references to poor management and the failure of the local textile corporations to serve their customers. The

Tanzanian textile industry, ironically, seems to have withered long before the flood of mitumba, and now is recovering even in the face of swells of used clothing imports. While protected from these used clothing imports—and indeed while protected from virtually all textile and apparel imports—output per worker as well as capacity utilization in the Tanzanian textile industry fell by approximately 40 percent.[13] Furthermore, as numerous cases show, producing for export rather than domestic production is the more effective industrial development ladder, and mitumba presents no threat at all to African export markets.

As for employment, while mitumba may destroy some jobs, it very clearly creates others. A drive along busy Moragora Road shows a level of economic activity unmatched anywhere else in the city and hundreds, perhaps thousands, of people who are very clearly working. The traders, importers, sorters, and launderers who people the mitumba trade show an astonishing variety of skills, and the tailors, in particular, are a marvel of the employment created by mitumba. Not only do the tailors adapt Americans' clothing to the thinner African figures, they create blouses and shirts to match "new" suits, and they turn curtains into dresses, socks into bathmats, and skirts into tablecloths and tablecloths into skirts. Though empirical estimates of the job destruction/creation patterns are impossible to come by, Gulam Dewji is convinced that the mitumba trade has created many more jobs than it has destroyed. In his peak years, Gulam Dewji had more than 100 people employed in sorting, grading, and distributing used clothing, more than had ever been employed in most Tanzanian textile mills.

The moribund textile industry in East Africa is testament not so much to mitumba but to the handicaps faced by African manufacturing in general, which are in turn similar to the handicaps faced by the African cotton farmers. While some of the blame must be borne by rich country policies such as subsidies and trade barriers, textile factories are in trouble in Africa for the same reasons that factories of any kind are in trouble in Africa: corruption, political risk, low education levels, insecure property rights, macroeconomic instability, and ineffective commercial codes—in a phrase, bad governance.[14] To use Thomas Friedman's technology analogy, Africa has a better operating system than it used to (capitalism vs. socialism), and its hardware (roads, ports, communications) is improving. But much of Africa lacks the software (effective police and courts, enforceable rights and laws, transparent regulatory frameworks) necessary for factories to operate successfully.[15]

If the plight of the textile industry is testament to bad governance, the vigorous mitumba trade is testament to the entrepreneurial energy and resourcefulness of the African people. A decade or so ago it was common for observers to draw a line between the "formal" and "informal" sectors of African economies, and to assume that the development of the formal was to be encouraged and the informal discouraged. Yet today, at least some countries realize that it is the informal sector that should be encouraged; this, after all, is the part of the economy that is working. Further, some experts have pointed out that so many types of activities are now lumped under the heading "informal" that the category has lost much meaning, and our Westernized perspective has led us to label as "informal" most organizational forms that do not look American.

While it is clearly desirable for African countries to develop the institutions to support organized and formal economic activities, we should also laud the fact that the mitumba trade and other similar activities have provided a step out of the village as well as a step up the economic ladder for people who did not have factory alternatives. While Western business students study entrepreneurship, Geofrey Milonge lives it, and the entrepreneurial training ground provided by the mitumba trade can only bode well for the future of all types of economic activity in Africa. It is a generalization, though not an absurd one, to say that the informal economy in Africa works better than the formal economy, and to suppress the part of Africa that is working seems to be a counterproductive prescription.

In fact, even as the mitumba trade has been liberalized, the state of Tanzania's formal textile and apparel sector has improved considerably. In 2002, Tanzania gained duty-free access for its apparel exports to the United States when it qualified for textile benefits under the African Growth and Opportunity Act (AGOA). Though success in the quota-free world is by no means assured, the signs are encouraging, and Gulam Dewji believes that Tanzania can hold its own against China in a few niche markets. Cotton apparel exports to the United States from Tanzania increased seven-fold from 2002 to 2003, and year-to-date figures as of April 2004 suggest an additional 76 percent increase for 2004.[16] Several mitumba dealers in Dar Es Salaam told me proudly that, for the first time, clothing produced in Africa is now showing up in mitumba bales from America. Gulam Dewji and his sons are bullish on Tanzania's textile industry: with profits from the mitumba trade they have purchased and refurbished several textile factories with an eye on the immense American market, and at its mill on the northern coast of Tanzania, METL is producing T-shirts for export to America.

Promise for the African industry, then, lies not in closing the doors to American used clothing but in opening the doors to the American market. AGOA, though riddled with provisions authored by the U.S. textile industry, is a step in the right direction.

Many critics of the mitumba trade suggest darkly that if Americans only knew what they wrought by throwing away their clothing, fewer people would be lined up outside the Salvation Army trucks. News accounts invariably imply that the donors who drop off their clothing have no idea that the clothing will likely be sold to "middlemen" who will earn a "huge" profit from the donor's largesse. Of course, with so many sinister insinuations in the news, perhaps the secret is now out. But what is unclear is what the critics would have done with the donated clothing instead.

Some have argued that clothing donated for charitable purposes should simply be donated to Africans. The difficulty with this prescription is that it has proven impossible to suppress the mitumba trade even when commercial imports are banned. Donated clothing quickly makes its way to mitumba markets, though the trade becomes more illicit and hidden. Researchers in Sweden cite evidence from several countries that suggests donated clothing is unlikely to reach those who have a true physical need for clothing but instead is rapidly sent into the markets.[17] Researchers have also found that clothing intended for refugees in Asia efficiently enters the market. Clothing given away in this manner will still enrich a middleman, but it will be an illegal one.[18] And whether we like it or not, charities are no match for markets when it comes to giving people the clothing that they need or want. Trailer loads and ship loads of clothing are often donated following natural disasters such as hurricanes, but without people like Ed Stubin and Geofrey Milonge to match clothing with customers, most of these donations rot in warehouses. Charities are ill-equipped to provide the sorting, grading, and distribution functions so ably provided by Ed and Geofrey, and so most disaster relief organizations nearly beg the well-intentioned not to send clothing to disaster areas.[19]

Banning mitumba imports, as, for example, South Africa has done, simply leads people to find ways around the barriers. Just as the British could not be forced into woolen underwear once they had tried cotton, denying mitumba to people who have tasted access to cheap and fashionable clothing is next to impossible. In countries where used clothing imports are banned, smuggling along porous borders is rampant, and used clothing is often found hidden in shipping containers. Banning the trade only drives it underground to enrich crooked border guards rather than legitimate businesspeople.

As for the huge profits, it is often said that huge markups are de rigueur, exploiting both the charity and the African customer. Critics point, for example, to the men's khakis that sell for $5.00 in the mitumba market but were purchased for perhaps 7 cents from the charity. Even a cursory look at the economics of the industry, however, seems to rule out the possibility of huge and easy profits. Ed Stubin estimates that the majority of the goods flowing into his business are sold at a loss, because the selling prices for clothing destined to become wiping rags and fiber (between 1 and 5 cents per pound) are significantly lower than the price paid to purchase the material (between 5 and 7 cents per pound). For Ed Stubin, for example, the "huge markups" on clothing destined for Africa must cover the losses he incurs on fiber and rags as well as his 80-person payroll, factory operating expenses, not to mention, for Tanzania, a 25 percent tariff. The fact that a "huge profit" is made on the pair of perfect khakis obscures the reality of just how unusual this snowflake is both for Geofrey Milonge and for Ed Stubin.

Media accounts of the used clothing trade also seem to have a magnetic attraction to the word "shadowy." After spending time with the industry's players, however, I wonder whether it is judgmental observers rather than shadowy behavior—whatever that is—on the part of the players that is the more interesting phenomenon. The used clothing dealers I encountered were from varied backgrounds and ethnicities, and had in common nothing more shadowy than the quick wits and market awareness needed by gazelles who wake up to race every morning.

The notion that global trade is about powerful corporations peopled with well-tailored Waspish vice presidents is belied by the reality of the used clothing exporters, who are from Brooklyn, Brownsville, Pakistan, and India, in short, from Main Street rather than K Street or Wall Street. Far from "shadowy," they represent a heartening parable about economic democracy: It is a positive, not a negative, that people from across the American experience can form the backbone of a successful global industry, and can play and win in a global game of faster better cheaper, and do so without the walls that protect their peers in many other industries.

The democratizing influence of the mitumba trade extends to Africa as well. As Quinn has argued, the policies adopted by most Sub-Saharan African countries following independence resulted in a concentration of political and economic power that has few parallels in modern history.[20] As is true for much of the cotton agriculture industry in Africa, state ownership and control excluded and impoverished those at the bottom of the power structure. The policies allegedly implemented to lift the masses—especially state ownership—instead funneled money and power to the top, where it was dispersed as largesse through a web of patronage and corruption.[21] State ownership of the textile industry by an unelected government enriched the few and excluded the many, and Geofrey Milonge and his present-day colleagues in the Manzese market had little participation—either political or economic—in such a system. The mitumba trade, however, is run by the masses rather than the elite, and is governed by relationships among importers, customers, drivers, menders, and dealers rather than by what many observers have titled the "kleptocracies" still common in much of Africa. Mitumba has not only allowed ordinary people to dress well, it has let them into the club as well. Excluded from the elite clubs and without effective software to govern formal markets, African entrepreneurs rely on the relationships, trust, and social networks that have been created by the mitumba trade. Thanks to mitumba, Geofrey Milonge and his entrepreneurial peers are players now, and are finding their own way around Africa's challenges.

A final critique of the mitumba trade is the humiliation argument. How, critics charge, can Africa hold its head high while wearing clothing that has been cast off at least three times? While in Tanzania, I heard about ideologues who protested the humiliation wrought by Tanzanians wearing the white world's castoffs, but I did not meet any of them. Gulam Dewji and his sons told me that their numbers were dwindling rapidly, as most of the old ideologues were now clothed in mitumba as well; 300 years ago, even the English woolen workers eventually preferred cotton underwear. Gulam and his sons never had any patience for the humiliation argument. They pointed out, over and over again, that humiliation comes not from mitumba, but from having no clothes to wear.

There is something missing from both the critiques and the compliments of the mitumba industry in Tanzania: Whatever the economic costs and benefits of the trade, it is clearly true as well that mitumba is fun. I found that taxi drivers, shopkeepers, and high school students—far from being embarrassed—delight in talking about mitumba. The challenge and reward of shrewd shopping are as significant in Tanzania as they are in suburban America. Just as a sharply dressed soccer mom might drop her voice and whisper, "Can you believe it? I got it for $5.99 at Wal-Mart," Tanzanians delight in their fashionable mitumba finds. Over and over again, Tanzanians pointed out their natty clothing to me, and then dropped their voices, smiled, and said, "*Mitumba.*" Shopping for mitumba is a fun and rewarding pastime in Tanzania for the same reasons that Americans enjoy trips to the mall. Yet the Manzese market in Dar Es Salaam is more interesting, and much more full of surprises, than any suburban shopping mall. While Americans have a relatively good idea what will be on display at the GAP, or at Sears, the mitumba shopper is not so much on a shopping trip as a treasure hunt: You just never know what the Americans will throw away next.

As Karen Hansen noted in her study of the used clothing trade in Zambia, the appeal of mitumba is not in emulating Westerners but is instead in the desire to be smartly turned out. Zambians, Hansen argues, make the West's clothing their own, and the ensembles they put together from shopping in mitumba markets reflect Zambian, not Western, cultural norms.[22] And while some would argue that mitumba fills basic clothing needs in much of Africa, Hansen finds that it is wants rather than needs that are satisfied by mitumba. An afternoon spent browsing the mitumba markets to piece together the perfect outfit is not about protection from the elements, or about trying to look American. It is, rather, about the fun and reward of being a smartly dressed and astute shopper.

Finally, it is hard to imagine a global industry with a more compelling environmental story to tell, and the used clothing trade stands to benefit considerably from increased attention to environmental issues. Without polluting chemicals or processes, the industry recycles 93 percent of the textiles it receives, which are already considered a waste product.[23] Today, most of the material comes from charities, but in the future, textile recycling may develop in the same manner as it has for glass, paper, and aluminum. The average American throws away about 68 pounds of clothing and textiles per year, and while a few communities have textile recycling programs, about 85 percent of this waste goes to landfills today, where it occupies about 4 percent of landfill space.[24] Almost all participants in the industry agree that the untapped potential is vast, as textile recycling can bring municipalities approximately $80 to $150 per ton and more than pay for its costs.

Bernie Brill has a vision. Within a few years he would like to see textile bins next to the glass recycling bins, or, better yet, bins at the entrance to the suburban shopping malls. He would like to make it easier on the moms lined up in the parking lot in Bethesda, Maryland. They should be able to pull up the new Lexus and drop off the old T-shirts at the same place they buy their new ones, making suburban Saturdays just a bit less busy. It would be good for the moms, good for the environment, good for Africa, and good for business.

Tanzania—indeed much of eastern Africa—has seen dramatic regime change over the past two decades as policies have shifted to market liberalization. In many cases, the policies have been less than voluntary, as many countries have had to adopt "Washington consensus" policies of liberalization in exchange for IMF and World Bank lending. Critics of the new policies feared that liberalization would lead to declines in already low standards of living, reduce the level of public services, and cause declines in farmer incomes. Unprepared and ill-equipped to compete in world markets, Tanzania, critics feared, would be pummeled by market forces that would leave the least well-off in even worse straits. On the other side, the World Bank advanced the now-familiar argument that liberalization offered the best hope for Africa's poor.[25]

Tony Waters set out to settle the debate for himself.[26] Carefully researching conditions in a small rural village in western Tanzania both before economic liberalization (in 1985) and after (1995 to 1996), Waters found that neither the alarmists' nor the optimists' predictions had come to pass. Things were not much better, and not much worse, in the tiny village. Even with the radical regime change, Waters found that life in rural Tanzania was about the same. The people of Shunga village are still ruled more by the earth's rhythms than by the regime in Washington, or for that matter, the regime in Dar Es Salaam. The houses looked the same, as did the school, the shops, and the roads. People seemed neither richer nor poorer, better off nor worse off. What happened in Washington and Dar Es Salaam did not seem to make much difference at all in rural Tanzania, and the more Waters searched for change the more things looked the same. Waters concluded that at least in this small remote village, nothing had really changed.

But there was one thing Waters noticed, almost as an afterthought: People were better dressed. This may seem a small thing to us, but because it is the only thing, it is important to the people in Shunga. Thanks to world trade, and thanks to Gulam, Ed, and Geofrey—who race like gazelles every day through the global marketplace—life was just a little better in a remote corner of one of the world's poorest countries.

Don't Look Now, But China Is behind You

While relations among U.S. used clothing dealers are intensely competitive, the industry as a whole would seem to occupy a secure place in the global industrial landscape. Rich Americans buy more and more clothing each year and therefore unload more and more as well. The falling price of new clothing—particularly from China—will only accelerate this trend. In addition, the growing penchant for recycling will likely divert increasing amounts of clothing from the waste stream. Together, then, continued rampant consumerism as well as changing waste disposal practices would seem to assure a growing supply of American used clothing for the global market.

Growing demand appears to be a safe prediction as well. Trade barriers to used clothing continue to fall, thanks both to SMART's efforts and to the general trend toward import liberalization in most countries. Perhaps more important, the poorer countries continue to have high rates of population growth, as well as a growing attraction to fashionable clothing.

There is a natural economic success story here, a simple market dynamic that portends well for the future. At the end of the T-shirt's life, there is a refreshingly simple story of a winning business for America, a story built on a clean market logic rather than a web of political intrigue. While the U.S. textile and apparel industry is kept alive only by unnatural acts of life support in Washington, and U.S. cotton producers compete through politics, here is another business, mostly unheard of and largely ignored, whose promise lies in the simple matter of a compelling economic logic.

At the end of my T-shirt's life, it is refreshing, too, to see a real market in action, to see prices that move with the location of a collection bin or the time of day, where anyone with a bale is allowed to play. Such flexibility is the result of the faster better cheaper race that Stubin and Milonge engage in every day from opposite ends of the world, where everyone must keep their eyes on the markets and attend to numerous fluid relationships with customers, suppliers, and competitors. The used clothing trade is a dance of the gazelles with no protection from the lions. It is a marvel to watch.

Thankfully, here finally is a business that at least should be safe from low-wage competitors, especially from China. It is not a big industry or a sexy industry, but it is a secure spot, if not always for the Stubins, at least for America. China has only a limited tradition of charitable giving, and incomes are still far too low to allow for large volumes of castoffs. The comparative advantage of U.S. clothing recyclers lies in America's wealth and consumerism, both characteristics with staying power for the foreseeable future, both characteristics in which China is far behind.

But sometimes Ed Stubin thinks about a different market logic. It is not that he is really worried, but he sees a China threat somewhere on the horizon.

The first leg of a T-shirt's journey from Brooklyn to Africa begins with a truck ride to the port of New Jersey. It costs Trans-Americas about $400 to send 50,000 pounds of clothing on the 10-mile ride. The ride to Africa costs another $2,500, a journey of a month and a half with a stop in Europe. Container shipping is yet another industry ruled by clean market forces. When the supply of empty cargo ships at a given port swells, the price to load the container and send it on its way falls. America's rampant consumerism has implications not just for the supply of used clothing available to world markets, but for shipping costs as well.

Thanks to our penchant for consumption, in 2003 the U.S. merchandise trade deficit swelled to $532 billion, and in October 2004, the United States announced the largest monthly trade deficit in its history. The billions spent on French wines, Chinese clothing, and German cars not only was unreciprocated, it also left hundreds of cargo ships at U.S. ports begging for something to ship back. At the broadest level, the merchandise trade deficit in the United States means that shipping stuff into America costs much more than shipping it out.

The price of shipping from America, however, reflects not just America's trade deficit, but also the demand for cargo ships elsewhere. Therefore, in cases where a country has a large imbalance with the United States, shipping costs will be unbalanced as well. The U.S. trade deficit with China was $124 billion in 2003, with imports from China approximately five times greater than exports to China from the United States. This means that shippers are keen to get ships from New Jersey back to the ports of Shanghai and Guangzhou in order to deliver more goods to America, but there are relatively few goods waiting to board the ships. In order to get ships back to China, the shipping companies in 2004 were dropping their prices to desperate levels: a 50,000-pound container of clothing could be shipped from New Jersey to China for approximately $400, about the same amount as it costs to send a truck from Brooklyn to the New Jersey port.

Given the shipping pricing trends that result from the U.S. trade deficit, Ed Stubin sees how at least some of the U.S. clothing recycling industry could shift to China. The Chinese could buy in bulk from the charities, ship to China for next to nothing, and do the sorting right there in the export processing zones; the clothing would never even have to leave the port. The workers would make $1.00 per hour instead of $10.00, and all of the other costs would be a fraction of America's, too. The total shipping costs from the United States to Africa, even with the extra leg added onto the trip, could be lower than they are now. What's more, as the American manufacturing base dwindles, America needs a lot fewer wiping rags and much less shoddy, while demand for both is growing in China. China would have easy access to the South Asian markets of India and Pakistan as well, where demand for shoddy is growing.

If cotton can travel from Texas to China to become a T-shirt, and then travel all the way back to the United States to be worn a first time and then to Africa to be worn a second time, then certainly a return trip to China would not be a major detour. Ed Stubin is not a cotton farmer or a textile mill owner, so it doesn't even occur to him to look to Washington to build a wall, not that anyone would listen anyway.

The logic and the math play through Ed Stubin's mind sometimes. He thinks about everything he and his family have built here on the East River, how Morton settled here as an immigrant, and how the business raised three generations of Stubins. The family and its history sit right here on the water, half a square block of solid and permanent-looking red brick with a stunning view of Manhattan. To Ed Stubin, and especially to his son Eric, it seems like it has been here forever.

Ed Stubin is a gazelle with no walls to keep out the lions, so he doesn't have much time to think about all this. But Stubin understands markets, and he respects them. He also understands that even though he is one of the industry's bigger players, he is actually very small. Stubin is confident that his family will continue to successfully navigate the markets, just as they have for more than 60 years. He is confident that they will continue to adapt and survive—thrive, even—in the global race of faster better cheaper. But Stubin feels the market winds blowing against the side of the big brick building on the East River. It is a strong and unpredictable wind, and it is coming all the way from China.

CONCLUSION

M y T-shirt's story is really just an extended anecdote, and so is unable to confirm or discredit a theory, or to settle definitively a debate between opposing views on trade or globalization. My T-shirt's story also cannot be generalized to broad sweeps about globalization. The industries, the point in time, the product, and the countries are each unique. Yet the story of even this very simple product can illuminate, if not settle, a number of ongoing debates.

During the past five years, the backlash against trade liberalization that began in street protests has evolved into more mainstream reservations about global trade on the part of citizens the world over. This evolution was abundantly clear in the 2004 congressional and national elections, as candidates were forced to explain to an uneasy public their positions on trade agreements, the China threat, outsourcing, labor standards, and a host of related issues, and it was even clear at the 2004 Olympics as a broad coalition of activist groups protested against multinational apparel companies and the alleged sweatshop conditions under which the athletes' sportswear was produced.[1] As the business establishment and most economists continue to laud the effects of free trade and competitive markets, a wide array of other groups fear the effects of unrelenting market forces, especially upon workers. Yet the debate over the promise versus the perils of competitive markets is at least somewhat displaced in the case of my T-shirt: Whatever the positive or negative effects of competitive markets, in my T-shirt's journey around the world it actually encountered very few free markets.

My T-shirt was born in Texas because of a long tradition of public policy that has protected farmers from a variety of risks including price risks, labor market risks, credit risks, and weather risks. While American growers have and continue to display remarkable creativity and adaptability in both the technical and business sides of cotton agriculture, these tendencies are bolstered by the economic, educational, and political infrastructure of the United States, which fosters effective public-private partnerships that facilitate the growers' innovation and progress.

The rules of the game that govern global production of T-shirts are the result of the efforts of generations of activists, who continue to push back against the markets and rewrite both labor law and accepted corporate practice. My T-shirt was made in China under the state-engineered hukou system that constrains labor mobility and limits the flexibility of labor markets. And while globalization activists' favorite targets are large U.S.-based multinational firms, most of the companies in my T-shirt's life story were relatively small family firms (Sherry Manufacturing, Shanghai Brightness, Trans-Americas, the Reinsch farm) rather than large multinationals, and the two biggest companies in my T-shirt's life story (Shanghai Knitwear and the Shanghai Number 36 Cotton Mill) were owned by the Chinese government.

My T-shirt's journey from China to the United States is engineered today by a web of highly political constraints on markets, in which both rich and poor country producers seek political protection from markets, and especially from the China threat. The China threat, in turn, because of the political protections for industry (state ownership, the hukou system, subsidies, and a managed currency), is really a political threat rather than a market threat.

As we have seen, it is only at the retail level, and after it is tossed into a Salvation Army bin, that my T-shirt's life is a story about markets rather than politics. It is political reactions to markets, political protection from markets, and political involvement in markets, rather than competition in markets, that are at the center of my T-shirt's life story. To either glorify or vilify the markets is to dangerously oversimplify the world of trade. To paraphrase James Carville, "It's the politics, stupid."

We might view all of these protective political maneuvers as an "artificial" interference with the market mechanism. Indeed, it has become fashionable to equate the market mechanism with biological processes such as survival of the fittest, in which nature is best left alone. But while interference may be less than optimal as economic policy, it is surely not unnatural; in fact the reverse is true. What could be more natural than seeking protection from a world of Darwinian survival?

My T-shirt's story, then, is not a tale of Adam Smith's market forces, but is instead a tale of Karl Polanyi's double movement, in which market forces on the one hand meet demands for protection on the other. This call for protection is not just from textile workers or cotton farmers, but from citizens everywhere who feel a growing unease about international trade even as incomes rise. In some cases the political protections make things worse for the poor (U.S. cotton subsidies), while in other cases, they make things better (minimum labor standards). In all cases, however, they are central to the story.

Neither trade nor theorizing about trade began with Adam Smith. There was trade in textiles and clothing, and debates surrounding this trade, long before there were economists. For centuries, trade was a subject of moral and religious debate, rather than a subject for economic analysis. Indeed, in perusing the early Christians' debates over trade, I am struck by the complete absence of economic discussion.[2] While economists often despair that *noneconomic* factors influence debates over trade policy, with a long historical view we see that it has only been relatively recently that *economic* factors entered into trade discussions, let alone became central. That moral discourse continues to pervade debates about trade should not be surprising.

My T-shirt reveals that the moral and political discussions are critical today if the double movement is to have widespread blessings. Some players in my T-shirt's life story—Nelson Reinsch, North Carolina textile workers—have some protections. A few—Ed Stubin and Geofrey Milonge—are either winning or at least afloat by competing in the markets. Neither side of the double movement, however, has reached millions. Most African cotton farmers, for instance, are granted neither political protections nor market opportunities nor access to technical or even basic literacy. In China, while most sweatshop workers are happy to have escaped the farm, these young women are second-class citizens in a country where even first-class citizens lack political voice. It is not the cruelty of market forces that has doomed millions of African farmers and Asian sweatshop workers. It is instead exclusion from opportunities found in market competition, political participation, or both.

This exclusion occurs both at the hands of developing country governments who either retain the spoils from the markets (African governments) or fail in various ways to give their citizens voice (Chinese government), or at the hands of rich country governments that continue to maintain a shameful double standard in trade policy (U.S. government). Fortunately, positive change is afoot. Cutting agricultural subsidies, democratization, and giving poor countries a place at the table at trade negotiations are all steps in the right direction.

Since completing my travels, I have come to believe in a moral case for trade that is even more compelling to me than the economic case. After observing two world wars, former Secretary of State Cordell Hull wrote in his memoirs that he had come to believe that trade was an instrument of peace:

> I saw that you could not separate the idea of commerce from the idea of war and peace. You could not have serious war anywhere in the world and expect commerce to go on as before. . . . And [I saw that] wars were often caused by economic rivalry. . . . I thereupon came to believe that . . . if we could increase commercial exchanges among nations over lowered trade and tariff barriers and remove international obstacles to trade, we would go a long way toward eliminating war itself.[3]

As I followed my T-shirt around the globe, each person introduced me to the next and then the next until I had a chain of friends that stretched all the way around the world: Nelson and Ruth Reinsch, Gary Sandler, Patrick and Jennifer Xu, Mohammed and Gulam Dewji, Geofrey Milonge, Auggie Tantillo, Ed Stubin, Su Qin and Tao Yong Fang. How can I type this list of names without agreeing with Cordell Hull? The Texans, Chinese, Jews, Sicilians, Tanzanians, Muslims, Christians, whites, blacks, and browns who passed my T-shirt around the global economy get along just fine. Actually, much, much better than fine, thank you very much. All of these people, and millions more like them, are bound together by trade in cotton, yarn, fabric, and T-shirts. I believe that each of them, as they touch the next one, is doing their part to keep the peace.

So, what do I say to the young woman on the steps at Georgetown University who was so concerned about the evils of the race to the bottom, so concerned about where and how her T-shirt was produced? I would tell her to appreciate what markets and trade have accomplished for all of the sisters in time who have been liberated by life in a sweatshop, and that she should be careful about dooming anyone to life on the farm. I would tell her that the poor suffer more from exclusion from politics than from the perils of the market, and that if she has activist energy left over it should be focused on including people in politics rather than shielding them from markets. And I would tell her about the shoulders she stands on, about her own sisters and brothers in time and the noble family tree of activists, and the difference they have made in a day's life at work all over the world. I would tell her that in just five short years, I have seen the difference her own generation has made, and that someday people will stand on her shoulders too. I would tell her that Nike, Adidas, and GAP need her to keep watching, and so do Wal-Mart and the Chinese government. I would tell her that Yuan Zhi needs her, and that future generations of sweatshop workers and cotton farmers need her as well. I would tell her to look both ways, but to march on.

ACKNOWLEDGMENTS

My first thanks are to the people in this story. In my travels around the world I have been blessed by hospitality, kindness, and insights from people on three continents who have welcomed me into their homes and businesses, and patiently explained things to me. As a tenured professor at an American university, my livelihood is as immune as it is possible to get from the gale-force winds of global economic and political change, so I humbly concede that to live this story is a far greater challenge than to write it. My respect for my many new friends who get up every day to face these challenges is immense. My thanks and admiration are especially due to Nelson and Ruth Reinsch, Gary Sandler, Su Qin, Tao Yong Fang, Patrick Xu, Mohammed and Gulam Dewji, Geofrey Milonge, Auggie Tantillo, and Ed Stubin.

Georgetown University has been my second home for more than 20 years, and I have benefited from innumerable conversations with my students and colleagues. Special thanks are due to our student activists, who first sparked the idea for this book, and who have changed my mind more than once. Their energy and engagement are inspirational, even when we disagree, and I am tremendously proud of them and the difference that they continue to make in the course that globalization takes. Many of the ideas in this book were discussed at meetings of the university's Licensing Oversight Committee, which has been chaired successively by Jim Donahue, Michael Garanzini, and Dan Porterfield.

A number of capable research assistants and administrative assistants have helped me in the course of this research. Thanks are due to Brooke Barber, Lan Feng, Russell Jame, Renee Jiang, Dana Omahen, Ann Pitchayanonnetr, and Emma Thompson. Thanks too to Jennifer Boettcher of the Lauinger Library at Georgetown.

My students and faculty colleagues on the fall 2003 voyage of Semester at Sea also deserve thanks for our many conversations and shared

216

experiences that helped me to sharpen the ideas in this book. Semester at Sea also made possible additional field research in China and Tanzania.

I have interviewed many dozens of people in the course of my research, and I hope that their mention in the notes throughout the book can serve as thanks for now. In addition to the many interviewees mentioned throughout the book, many other friends and colleagues went beyond the call in reading, critiquing, and discussing parts of the manuscript. Thanks especially to Bernie Brill, Ev Ehrlich, John Glavin, Greg Hitz, Johny Johansson, Lamar Reinsch, John Quinn, and Ron Sorini. And Jock Nash's electronic updates on textile trade policy were invaluable.

My agent, Tom Power, deserves thanks for his enthusiasm, as does the team at Wiley, especially Emily Conway and Richard Narramore, and Danielle Lake of North Market Street Graphics.

I am lucky enough to have two of the best friends and literary critics in the world in Elaine Romanelli and Annette Shelby, both also colleagues at Georgetown, who have been listening, reading, and talking with me about this book for years, and who have been supporting me in untold other ways as well. And I would like to thank my brother, Michael Rivoli, for his strength, kindness, and patience.

Finally, I would like to thank my children, Denny and Annalisa, for growing up into such terrific people, and for their patience, confidence, and good humor throughout this project. But most of all I wish to thank Dennis Quinn: wonder-dad, editor, cheerleader, graph-maker and wonderful husband—for everything, great and small.

NOTES

Preface

1. Bhagwati, *In Defense of Globalization*, ix.
2. For recent treatments of globalization, see Bhagwati, *In Defense of Globalization*; as well as Wolf, *Why Globalization Works*; Micklethwait and Wooldridge, *A Future Perfect*; Friedman, *The Lexus and the Olive Tree*; Tonelson, *The Race to the Bottom*; and Greider, *One World, Ready or Not.*
3. Polanyi, *The Great Transformation.*
4. Dougherty, *Who's Afraid of Adam Smith?* 6.

Chapter 1

1. See Glade et al., "The Cotton Industry in the United States"; Eisa et al., *Cotton Production Prospects*; Gillham et al., *Cotton Production Prospects*; as well as data reported at http://www.usda.gov/nass/pubs/agr04/acro04.htm.
2. Porter, *The Competitive Advantage of Nations*, 15.
3. Williams, "Talks Unravel Over Cotton."
4. De Jonquières and Williams, "Top WTO Nations Hail Deal on Doha."

Chapter 2

1. Quoted in Dodge, *Cotton: The Plant That Would be King*, 40–41.
2. Data are from Bruchey, *Cotton and the Growth of the American Economy*, which also contains an in-depth discussion of the U.S. cotton industry during this period.
3. Earle, "The Price of Precocity: Technical Choice and Ecological Constraint in the Cotton South, 1840–1890."
4. Wright, *The Political Economy of the Cotton South.*
5. Callender, "The Early Transportation and Banking Enterprises of the States in Relation to the Growth of Corporations," 118.
6. Wright, *The Political Economy of the Cotton South*, 28, 52.
7. Breeden, *Advice Among Masters: The Ideal in Slave Management in the Old South*, contains a number of rich sources on the planters' management of slave labor.
8. DeBow, reproduced in Bruchey, *Cotton and the Growth of the American Economy*, 84.
9. Whitney's letters are compiled in Hammond, "Correspondence of Eli Whitney Relative to the Invention of the Cotton Gin."

10. Bruchey, *Cotton and the Growth of the American Economy*, Tables 1a and 1c.
11. Landes, *The Wealth and Poverty of Nations*, 157.
12. Ibid.
13. Ibid., 342.
14. Ibid.
15. Ibid., 336.
16. Ibid., 342.
17. Andrews (1853), reproduced in Bruchey, 71. Other western European colonies, of course, also relied on slave labor. Production on plantations in the Caribbean and South America was devoted especially to sugar and rubber.
18. Hammond, Speech Before the U.S. Senate, 1858. *Congressional Globe*, March 4, 1859, p. 959.
19. Ibid.
20. A recent study of this topic is Schmidt, *Free to Work*. See also the discussion in Daniel, *Breaking the Land*.
21. In *The Cotton Plantation South*, Aiken discusses the implication of crop lien laws during this period.
22. Johnson, Embree, and Alexander, *The Collapse of Cotton Tenancy*, 25.
23. Rosengarten, *All God's Dangers*, 106.
24. Johnson, Embree, and Alexander, *The Collapse of Cotton Tenancy*, 12.
25. See Daniel, *Breaking the Land*, Chapter 1, for a discussion of the government's attempt to manage the boll weevil and the disparate effects on rich and poor farmers.
26. Street, *The New Revolution in the Cotton Economy*, 38.
27. Rosengarten, *All God's Dangers*, 144.
28. Ibid., 223.
29. Foley, *The White Scourge*, 120.
30. Aiken, *The Cotton Plantation South*, 109.
31. Material on the Taft Ranch is from Foley (1996 and 1997).

Chapter 3

1. In addition to the secondary sources cited, the material in this chapter is from personal interviews conducted in Lubbock, Washington, Hong Kong, and Shanghai during 1999 to 2004. Interviewees include Nelson, Ruth, and Lamar Reinsch; John Johnson, Lonnie Winters, and Jack Kenwright of the Plains Cotton Cooperative Association; Don Harper and Ron Harkey of the Farmers Cooperative Compress; Randy Kennedy and Barbara Burleson of the Citizens Shallowater Cooperative Gin; Hunter Colby and Stephen MacDonald of the USDA; Manfred Tsai of Nobletex Holdings; and Yan Hong, an independent consultant. Telephone interviews were conducted with Dave Kinard of the National Cottonseed Producer's Association, Gail Kring of the Plains Cooperative Oil Mill, Terry Townsend of the International Cotton Advisory Committee, and Ed Price of the USDA.
2. Day, "The Economics of Technological Change and the Demise of the Share-

cropper." Other classic studies on the mechanization of cotton production include Sayre, "Cotton Mechanization Since World War II," and Street, *The New Revolution in the Cotton Economy.*

3. Rosengarten, *All God's Dangers,* 466.
4. Quoted in Grove, "The Mexican Farm Labor Program," 309.
5. Foley, "Mexicans, Mechanization, and the Growth of Corporate Cotton Culture," 285, 295.
6. Grove, "The Mexican Farm Labor Program," 307.
7. Ibid., 312–313.
8. Daniel, *Breaking the Land,* 94–95.
9. Rosengarten, *All God's Dangers.*
10. Ibid., 492.
11. Dewan, "Black Farmers' Refrain: Where's All Our Money?"
12. Gwin, "Looking Back: No Cotton Picking for Me, Thanks."
13. In *Cotton's Renaissance,* Jacobson and Smith provide a careful study of marketing innovation in the industry.
14. Anthony and Mayfield, *Cotton Ginners Handbook,* 6.
15. For a survey of USDA involvement in this research see Finlay, "The Industrial Utilization of Farm Products and By-Products: The USDA Regional Research Laboratories."
16. Wrenn, *Cinderella of the New South,* xvi.
17. Lichtenstein, *Field to Fabric,* 33.
18. Hayes, "Aquaculture Gets Hooked on Oilmeals," 1.
19. Ibid.
20. Buckley, "Starting at the Bottom," 2B.
21. www.deltabusinessjournal.com/archives/7-99 accessed 1/25/04.
22. www.farmerscompress.com accessed 1/6/2004.
23. This discussion of the cotton farmers' foray into the textile industry is based on Lichtenstein, *Field to Fabric.*
24. www.pcca.com/publications/newsreleases accessed 12/6/03.
25. Rosengarten, *All God's Dangers,* 190.
26. Lichtenstein, *Field to Fabric,* 38.
27. USDA (1996) contains a description of HVI cotton testing processes.
28. Oxfam, *Cultivating Poverty,* discussed throughout.
29. Agricultural Outlook reported in *Cultivating Poverty,* 33; Hart, "Agricultural Situation Spotlight," Figure 1.
30. This description of the 2002 Farm Bill is necessarily simplified. In particular, I abstract from the "base acreage/base yield" complexities, which link the farmers' direct payment and the countercyclical payment to their historical cotton acreage and yields, rather than to current production. Farmers may receive these payments even if their land is not planted in cotton, or even if it is not planted at all. Subsidies therefore technically depend upon historical acreage and yields rather than current acreage and yields. Also, the "loan rate" is adjusted for cotton quality. For a detailed description, see Westcott, Young, and Price, *The 2002 Farm Act.*

31. Townsend, *Subsidies Beyond 2006*, 2.
32. The difference between the U.S. cotton price and the average world price in 2004 was approximately 10 cents, or 30 percent of the world price (www .cotton.org/econ/prices/).
33. See Farm Subsidy Database at http://www.ewg.org/farm/step2cotton.php.
34. Environmental Working Group Farm Subsidy database at http://www.ewg.org/ .farm/progdetail.php?fips=48219&progcode=cotton.
35. FAOSTAT, cited in Oxfam, *Cultivating Poverty*, 9.
36. ICAC 2001, cited in Oxfam, *Cultivating Poverty*, 11.
37. Oxfam, *Cultivating Poverty*, 2.
38. Under pressure from the WTO and other cotton-producing countries, the United States plans to continue to "decouple" production from subsidies so that subsidies do not lead to higher production. However, because of the specialized assets associated with cotton production, subsidies—even when decoupled from production—often encourage higher cotton production.
39. Econometric studies of the effects of cotton subsidies include Pan, *The Impact of U.S. Cotton Programs;* Poonyth et al., *The Impact of Domestic and Trade Policies on the World Cotton Market;* Sumner, *A Quantitative Simulation Analysis of the Impacts of U.S. Cotton Subsidies on Cotton Prices and Quantities;* and Tokarick, *Measuring the Impact of Distortions in Agricultural Trade in Partial and General Equilibrium.*
40. See the sources cited in Eisa et al., *Cotton Production Prospects*, 26. On the challenges facing African cotton farmers, see Carr, *Improving Cash Crops in Africa.*
41. Eisa et al., *Cotton Production Prospects*, 28.
42. Karp, "Deadly Crop," 1A.

Chapter 4

1. In addition to the secondary sources cited, this account is based on interviews and factory visits in China in March 2000, March 2003, July 2003, and March 2004. Interviewees include Patrick Xu, Hong Yan, Tao Yong Fang, Su Qin, Li Guo Ping, and He Yuan Zhi.
2. See Economic Research Service, "Briefing Room: Cotton Trade," July 19, 2002.
3. World Trade Atlas, accessed 8/4/2004.
4. See Honig, *Sisters and Strangers*, Table 1, 24.
5. The classic account of the Chinese labor movement during this period is Chesneaux, *The Chinese Labor Movement.*
6. Honig, *Sisters and Strangers*, 10.
7. Quoted in Ling, *In Search of Old Shanghai*, 93.
8. Honig, *Sisters and Strangers*, 1.
9. World Trade Atlas, accessed 12/20/03.
10. www.nlcnet.org/china accessed 3/7/01.
11. Author's calculations from UN Comtrade data, based on SITC code 84 (apparel).
12. National Labor Committee (1998) p. 1; www.nlc.net.org/China accessed 6/21/00.

Chapter 5

1. For comparative indicators of development, see Pomeranz, *The Great Divergence.*
2. See Blue, "China and Western Social Thought in the Modern Period."
3. Chao and Chao, *The Development of Cotton Textile Production in China,* 28.
4. Quoted in Dodge, *Cotton: The Plant That Would be King,* 21.
5. Ibid.
6. Deane, *The First Industrial Revolution,* 92.
7. Ibid., 87.
8. A recent discussion of labor policies in early British textile factories is in Rose, *Firms, Networks and Business Values.*
9. Pinchbeck, *Women Workers and the Industrial Revolution,* 188.
10. Ibid., 190.
11. Ibid., 194.
12. Ibid., 190.
13. Robson, *The Cotton Industry in Britain,* Table A2, 334; Bazely (1854) cited in Farnie, *The English Cotton Industry and the World Market.*
14. Dalzell, *Enterprising Elites,* 5.
15. Ibid., 5.
16. Ibid.
17. Rose, *Firms, Networks, and Business Values,* 41.
18. http://www.psnh.com/AboutPSNH/EnergyPark/Amoskeg.asp, accessed 1/27/04. See Hareven and Langenbach, *Amoskeag: Life and Work in an American Factory City,* for oral histories from former Amoskeag workers.
19. Rose, *Firms, Networks, and Business Values,* 198.
20. Cited in Ware, *The Early New England Cotton Manufacture,* 249.
21. Ibid., 250, 252.
22. Ibid., 252.
23. Ibid., 251.
24. See Josephson, *The Golden Threads,* for an early treatment of the social controls on New England mill girls. Additional insight may be gleaned from the letters collected in Dublin, *Farm to Factory.*
25. Josephson, *The Golden Threads,* 23.
26. Hareven and Langenbach, *Amoskeag,* 20.
27. Kane, *Textiles in Transition,* presents a careful study of the movement of the U.S. cotton textile industry from New England to the South.
28. For analyses of wage differentials between Northern and Southern mills, see Wright, "Cheap Labor and Southern Textiles," and Kane, *Textiles in Transition.*
29. Holleran, "Child Labor and Exploitation in Turn-of-the-Century Cotton Mills."
30. Saxonhouse and Wright, "Two Forms of Cheap Labor in Textile History."
31. Hearden, *Independence and Empire,* 125.
32. Ibid., 102–103.
33. U.S. Department of State, cited in Hearden, 66.
34. Ibid., 129.
35. Hearden, 128–129.

36. Ibid., 129.
37. Michl, cited in Rose, *Firms, Networks and Business Values*, 204.
38. Copeland, *The Cotton Manufacturing Industry of the United States*, 40–41.
39. Ibid.
40. Byerly, *Hard Times Cotton Mill Girls*, 45.
41. Ibid., 3.
42. Robson, *The Cotton Industry in Britain*, 4.
43. Destler, Fukui, and Sato, *Textile Wrangle*, 29.
44. McNamara, *Textiles and Industrial Transition*, 36–37.
45. Chokki, "Labor Management in the Cotton Spinning Industry."
46. Moser, *The Cotton Textile Industry of Far Eastern Countries*, 13.
47. Tsurumi, *Factory Girls*, 107.
48. Ibid., note 1, 121.
49. Cited in Chokki, "Labor Management," 8.
50. Moser, *The Cotton Textile Industry of Far Eastern Countries*, 16.
51. See Chokki, 160; and Tsurumi, Chapter 8.
52. For accounts of working conditions in early Japanese textile factories see Tsurumi (1990).
53. Superb analyses of the geographic movement of the textile and apparel industries in search of lower costs are in Anderson, *New Silk Roads*.
54. Beazer, *The Commercial Future of Hong Kong*, 61, 67.
55. Berger and Lester, *Made by Hong Kong*, 142.
56. Song, *The Rise of the Korean Economy*, 105; Scott, "Foreign Trade," 337.
57. Scott, "Foreign Trade," 360.

Chapter 6

1. For a complete treatment of China's hukou system, see Solinger, *Contesting Citizenship in Urban China*.
2. Foreign Broadcast Information Services, cited in Solinger, 217.
3. Human Rights in China, *Institutionalized Exclusion*.
4. See http://www.aflcio.org/issuespolitics/globaleconomy/china_petition.cfm
5. Wang and Zuo, "Inside China's Cities: Institutional Barriers and Opportunities for Urban Migrants."
6. Ibid., 277.
7. Ibid., 278.
8. "Off to the City," *The Economist*.
9. Woodman, "China's Dirty Clean Up."
10. Ibid.
11. Knight, Song, and Huaibin, "Chinese Rural Migrants."
12. "Off to the City," *The Economist*.
13. Kuhn, "Migrants: A High Price to Pay for a Job," 30.
14. Ibid., 30.
15. Ibid., 32.
16. Knight, Song, and Huaibin, "Chinese Rural Migrants," 92.

17. Ibid., 91–92.
18. For a survey of China labor issues, see Chan, *China's Workers Under Assault.*
19. Pinchbeck, *Women Workers and the Industrial Revolution,* 17.
20. Byerly, *Hard Times Cotton Mill Girls,* 64–65.
21. Lee, *Gender and the South China Miracle,* 78.
22. Ibid., 78.
23. Honig, *Creating Chinese Ethnicity,* 62–63.
24. Hall et al., *Like a Family,* 66.
25. Minchin (1977) studies the integration of the Southern textile industry in depth.
26. Hall et al., *Like a Family,* 157.
27. Byerly, *Hard Times Cotton Mill Girls,* 141.
28. Ibid., 94.
29. Kristof and WuDunn, *Thunder from the East,* 128.
30. Josephson, *The Golden Threads,* 64.
31. Lee, *Gender and the South China Miracle.*
32. Ibid., 5–9.
33. Ibid., 134–135.
34. Ibid., 130.
35. For Korea, see Kim, *Class Struggle or Family Struggle?* For Taiwan, see Kung, *Factory Women in Taiwan.*
36. Josephson, *The Golden Threads,* 92.
37. Frowne (1902), quoted in Stein, *Out of the Sweatshop.*
38. Hessler, "Letter from China."
39. Hume (1748), quoted in Anderson, *New Silk Roads,* xvix.
40. Schlosser, "Urban Life," 22.
41. Pressley, "The South's New-Car Smell," A1.
42. See discussions in Varley, *The Sweatshop Quandary,* and Pollin et al., *Global Apparel Production.*
43. Hutchins and Harrison, *History of Factory Legislation* provides a full account of early British factory legislation.
44. Engels, *The Condition of the Working Class.* 170.
45. Ibid., 173.
46. Byerly, *Hard Times Cotton Mill Girls,* 85.
47. Tsurumi, *Factory Girls,* 44, 168.
48. Hutchins and Harrison, *History of Factory Legislation,* 248.
49. Losciale, "Rules May Ease Aches."
50. McCracken, "The Lives They Lived."
51. U.S. Department of Labor, *Wages, Benefits, Poverty Line.*
52. Spar and Burns, "Hitting the Wall," 5.
53. Featherstone, *Students Against Sweatshops,* chronicles the development of the student-led anti-sweatshop movement in the United States.
54. See, for example, Rosoff, "Beyond Codes of Conduct." A number of case studies of U.S. corporations' current practices are in Hartman, et al., *Rising Above Sweatshops.*

55. See Fong, "A Chinese Puzzle"; and Goodman, "In China's Cities, a Turn From Factories."

56. See Moran, *Beyond Sweatshops*, for a survey.

57. Dougherty, *Who's Afraid of Adam Smith?* See especially Chapter 3.

Chapter 7

1. Chapters 7 to 9 rely on interviews during 2001 to 2004 in Washington, Alexander City, Alabama, and Shanghai with Erik Autor, Phyllis Bonanno, Christopher Champion, Jennifer Hillman, Julia Hughes, John Jackson, Cass Johnson, Donna Lee McGee, Michael Levy, Carlos Moore, James Moore, Paul O'Day, Michael Ryan, Ronald Sorini, Auggie Tantillo, Earl Whipple, Patrick Xu, and Tom Young. Telephone discussions were held with Jack Albertine, Ross Arnold, Michael Hubbard, Jeff Martin, and David Trumbull.

2. Underhill, *Industrial Crisis*, 4.

3. Joint Textile Industry letter on China to President Bush at www.atmi.org accessed July 20, 2003. The letter was signed by American Textile Manufacturers Institute, American Manufacturing Trade Action Coalition, National Textile Association, American Yarn Spinners Association, American Fiber Manufacturers Association, National Cotton Council, American Sheep Industry Association, American Textile Machinery Association, Carpet and Rug Institute, Association of Georgia's Textile, Carpet & Consumer Products Manufacturers, Hosiery Association, Industrial Fabrics Association International, North Carolina Manufacturers Association, and Textile Distributors Association.

4. Joint Press Release, Amtac et al., June 9, 2004.

5. For an account of the pre-election safeguard campaign, see Blustein, "Textile Makers Fight for Limits." The status of China safeguard petitions is reported at http://www.otexa.ita.doc.

6. World Trade Atlas, accessed June 3, 2004, for HTS categories 61 (knit apparel) and 62 (woven apparel).

7. See http://www.ustr.gov/regions/whemisphere/camerica/regional.shtml.

8. As of 2003, only 19 of the 48 countries in the Sub-Saharan Africa region had been granted apparel benefits by the United States. Textile and apparel trade provisions of these agreements are at http://otexa.ita.doc.gov/Trade_Act_2000.htm#.

9. USITC *Harmonized Tariff Schedule of the United States* (2003) (Rev 1). This abstracts from a further complexity, because if the T-shirt is all white without a collar or pocket, then it falls under the "underwear" category.

10. http://www.customs.gov/xp/cgov/import/textiles_and_quotas/archived/2003_year_rpt/.

11. Dickerson, *Textiles and Apparel in the Global Economy*, 399.

12. Friman, *Patchwork Protectionism*.

13. Includes employment in NCAIS categories 313 (textile mills), 314 (textile product mills), and 316 (apparel). See http//www.bls.gov for employment data by industry.

14. Friman, "Rocks, Hard Places, and the New Protectionism," 691.
15. On the effects of geographic concentration on political influence in trade policy, see Schiller, "Trade Politics in the American Congress," or Metcalfe and Goodwin, "An Empirical Analysis of the Determinants of Trade Policy Protection."
16. Aggarwal, *Liberal Protectionism*, 164.
17. The Reagan letter is excerpted in Brandis, *The Making of Textile Trade Policy*, 56.
18. Conti, *Reconciling Free Trade*, xiv.
19. See Conti for an analysis of presidential rhetoric related to trade.
20. Quoted in Rosen, *Making Sweatshops*, 82.
21. Quoted in Rothgeb, *U.S. Trade Policy*, 102.
22. Aggarwal, *Liberal Protectionism*, 53
23. Ikenson, *Threadbare Excuses*, 9.
24. Cline, *The Future of World Trade in Textiles*, 163.
25. Vinson's letter is excerpted in Brandis, *The Making of Textile Trade Policy*, 25.
26. Aggarwal, *Liberal Protectionism*, 111.
27. Ibid., 69.
28. Nixon, Public Papers, 944–946.
29. Brandis, *The Making of Textile Trade Policy*, 46.
30. Cline, *The Future of World Trade in Textiles*, 150; GATT principles prohibit quantitative restraints, or quotas, as well as market access that discriminate across countries.
31. Cline, *The Future of World Trade in Textiles*, 163.
32. Quotas and bilateral agreements are at http://otexa.ita.doc.gov/
33. SMEs are shown in http://otexa.ita.doc.gov/correlations
34. Ikenson, *Threadbare Excuses*, 10.
35. Dickerson, *Textiles and Apparel in the Global Economy*, 365.
36. Quoted in Rothgeb, *U.S. Trade Policy*, 21.
37. Quoted in Destler, *American Trade Politics*, 5.
38. Quoted in Conti, *Reconciling Free Trade*, 22.
39. Dickerson, *Textiles and Apparel in the Global Economy*, 366.
40. Cline, *The Future of World Trade in Textiles*, 213.
41. In *Making Sweatshops*, Rosen provides a complete treatment of the political rise of the retail industry on the subject of trade.
42. Schott and Buurman, *The Uruguay Round*, 5.
43. The baseline import figures were derived from 1990 imports. Product lists for each tranche of the phase-out are at http://otexa.ita.doc.gov/#IMPORTQUOTAS.
44. USITC, *The Economic Effects of Significant U.S. Import Restraints*, 61.
45. Dickerson, *Textiles and Apparel in the Global Economy*, 378.

Chapter 8

1. Based on employment and output data for NCAIS 313, 314, and 315. See http://data.bls.gov/servlet/SurveyOutput/Servlet.

2. "The Misery of Manufacturing," *The Economist*, September 27, 2003, 61.

3. Disentangling the import effect on employment from the productivity effect is of course complex. The USITC estimates that the demise of the quota system will have relatively small employment effects in the United States, ranging from 1 percent in textile products to 6 percent in apparel. See USITC, *The Economic Effects of Significant U.S. Import Restraints, Fourth Update*, Table 3-5.

4. Spiegelman and McGuckin, *China's Experience*. The authors found that China lost 1.8 million jobs in the textile sector during the 1995 to 2002 period, while the United States lost 202,000. During the same period, Chinese labor productivity rose by over 300 percent.

5. USITC, *Economic Effects of Significant Export Restraints, Second Update*, 1999, 29.

6. Hufbauer and Elliott, *Measuring the Costs of Protection*, 13.

7. USITC, *Economic Effects of Significant Export Restraints, Fourth Update*, 2004. The study's worst-case estimate for job losses due to the elimination of quotas is (in 2002) 40,040 jobs, while its lowest estimate for economywide costs is $7 billion. See p. 71 and Tables 3-1 and 3-5.

8. Schott and Buurman, *The Uruguay Round*, 59.

9. This account is based on Tanzer, "The Great Quota Hustle."

10. De Jonquières, "Clothes on the Line."

11. In July 2004, Kenyan authorities set ablaze 16 containers of clothing from China that was destined to be transshipped through Nairobi. Ali, "Clothes Worth Sh960m from China Set Ablaze."

12. Tanzer, "The Great Quota Hustle," 124.

13. My estimate is based on the quota prices reported by the Hong Kong Trade and Development Council at http://tdc-link.tdc.org.hk/quota/China/china.asp on July 7, 2004, and the quota allocation to China for 2004 at http://www.customs.gov/xp/cgov/import/textiles_and_quotas/textile_status_rpt/.

14. Irwin, *Against the Tide*, 3.

15. Ibid.

16. Quoted in Irwin, *Against the Tide*, 1.

17. See Aaronson, *Trade and the American Dream*, as well as *Taking Trade to the Streets* by the same author, for full accounts of research related to public opinion on trade.

18. See Irwin, *Against the Tide*, for a discussion of early views on trade.

19. For a description of a variety of anti–Wal-Mart sentiments, see Walmartwatch.org. *The Los Angeles Times* was awarded a 2004 Pulitzer for its coverage of Wal-Mart's business practices and their effects.

20. See the discussion in Irwin, *Free Trade Under Fire*, 103–104. The evidence suggests that laid-off textile and apparel workers have poorer reemployment than laid-off workers in other industries.

21. Thomas, *Mercantilism and the East India Trade*, 49.

22. Ibid., 44.

23. Quoted in Lemire, *Fashion's Favourite*, 16.

24. Thomas, *Mercantilism and the East India Trade*, 50.

25. Ibid., 47.

26. Ibid., 62.
27. Quoted in Lemire, *Fashion's Favourite*, 25.
28. Ibid., 24n.
29. Thomas, *Mercantilism and the East India Trade*, 62.
30. Lemire, *Fashion's Favourite*, 31.
31. Also allowed under the various acts were the domestically produced "fustians," which combined linen and cotton.
32. Quoted in Lemire, *Fashion's Favourite*, 32.
33. See Lemire for colorful accounts of the "calicoe protests."
34. For details of the ban, see Lemire, Chapter 3.

Chapter 9

1. This account is based on accounts from www.insidetrade.com during September 2001 to February 2002 and from personal discussions with Ronald Sorini of Sandler, Travis, and Rosenberg, Erik Autor of the National Retail Federation, and Cass Johnson of ATMI during spring 2002. See also Blustein, "A Pakistani Setback."
2. Import quotas, as well as fill rates, may be found at www.customs.ustreas.gov/quotas/.
3. Ramey, "Wal-Mart Gets Political," and www.opensecrets.org.
4. Ibid.
5. See Gresser, "Who Gets Hit?" and "It's Expensive Being Poor."
6. De Jonquières, "Clothes on the Line."
7. Calculations are based on square meter equivalents and measure the change from 2000 to 2003. See http://www.ita.otexa.doc for trade data by category.
8. I have based these calculations on 2001 to 2003 trade data for the categories that were fully released from quota in 2002. See http://otexa.ita.doc.gov/scripts/tqsum2.exe.
9. De Jonquières, "Clothes on the Line."
10. For studies on the likely market share effects of the quota phase-out, see USITC, *Textiles and Apparel*, and Nordas, *The Global Textile and Clothing Industry*. See also Malone, "Low-Wage Nations Import Share to Surge."
11. Malone, "Low Wage Nations Import Share to Surge."
12. Nordas, *The Global Textile and Clothing Industry*, Chapter IV.
13. Magnusson, "Where Free Trade Hurts."
14. Nathan Associates, *Changes in Global Trade Rules*, 6.
15. Bussey, "China to Collar Textiles?"
16. Just-Style.com, "Cambodia: Garment Sector Will Survive After Quotas."
17. Pollin, Burns, and Heintz, *Global Apparel Production and Sweatshop Labor*.
18. See http://www.fairtextiletrade.org/istanbul/declaration.html accessed 7/1/2004.
19. See http://www.iccr.org/issues/css/featured.php accessed 10/6/2004.
20. For updates on the textile and apparel trade regime, see www.georgetown.msb.edu/faculty/rivolip.

Chapter 10

1. This chapter relies on interviews in the spring and summer of 2004 with Ed Stubin, Sunny Stubin, and Eric Stubin of Trans-Americas Trading Company in Brooklyn, New York, and with members attending the meeting of the Secondary Materials and Recycled Textiles (SMART) Association in Miami, Florida, in April 2004, especially Florrie Usatch, Jerry Usatch, Lynne Warshaw, Bob Woycke, and Sandy Woycke. I have also benefited from discussions with Anna Flaaten, trade specialist at the U.S. Department of Commerce, and Bernard Brill, Executive Vice-President of SMART.
2. http://dataweb.usitc.gov, accessed 6/4/2004.
3. World Trade Atlas accessed 6/4/2004.
4. Estimates vary widely regarding the number of firms engaged in the business. I asked government officials, association officials, and businesspeople how many firms were active in the industry and was told repeatedly that "nobody knows," though most guessed several thousand. The 3,000 figure is from Brill, "Textiles."
5. *Fort Lauderdale Sun Sentinal*, 1997. "Tokyo Seized by Jeans Fever." Actually, I found that used jeans sell for up to $100 just a few blocks from my Georgetown office, at a shop called "Deja Blue."
6. World Trade Atlas, accessed 6/10/2004. Technically, Canada imports more American used clothing than does Japan, but virtually all of this is then sorted and baled for subsequent re-export.
7. Zinman, "Vintage T-Shirts," *The Washington Post*, Sunday Source.
8. Lucy Norris has studied the export of shoddy from the West to India, as well as the used clothing trade in India. For fascinating accounts of both, see "Creative Entrepreneurs" and "Cloth That Lies."

Chapter 11

1. In addition to the sources cited herein, this section draws from discussions in Dar Es Salaam, Tanzania, in October 2003 with Mohammed Dewji, Gulam Dewji, and Mehdi Rehmtulah of Mohammed Enterprises Limited, as well as discussions with a number of used clothing merchants, especially Geofrey Milonge. I have also benefited from discussions with officials at the Tanzanian embassy in Washington, especially Said Ngosha Magonya.
2. See Reed, *Economic Change*, 47.
3. Coulson, *Tanzania: A Political Economy*, contains an assessment of Tanzania's post-independence economic policies.
4. See The World Bank, *World Development Report*, for comparative data relating to economic and social development.
5. Danielson and Skoog, "From Stagnation to Growth," 149.
6. http://dataweb.usitc.gov accessed 6/10/2004.
7. Hansen, *Salaula*. Hansen refers to *salaula* (the term for used clothing from the Zambian Bemba language) rather than *mitumba* (from Swahili).
8. Ibid., 90.

9. The count of countries that ban or effectively ban used clothing is not fixed. My estimate of 30 is based on data provided by SMART, and from discussions with Anna Flaaten of the U.S. Department of Commerce.

10. See Barasa, "Cheap Imports Killing Kenya's Textile Industry"; Dougherty, "Trade Theory vs. Used Clothes in Africa."

11. Jeter, "The Dumping Ground."

12. Panafrican News Agency, "Millions Go Up in Smoke as Fire Guts Huge Market."

13. World Bank, *A World Bank Country Study: Tanzania at the Turn of the Century*, 76–78.

14. "A Survey of Sub-Saharan Africa," *The Economist*.

15. See Fafchamps, *Market Institutions*, for a comprehensive study.

16. http://otexa.ita.doc.gov/msrcty accessed 6/14/2004.

17. Wicks and Bigsten, *Used Clothes as Development Aid*.

18. Norris, "Cloth That Lies."

19. See, for example, http://ww.ucc.org/disaster accessed 9/3/2004.

20. Quinn, *The Road Oft Traveled*.

21. Danielson and Skoog, "From Stagnation to Growth," discusses the case of Tanzania in this context.

22. Hansen, *Salaula*, 196.

23. The MassRecycler, "One of the World's Oldest Recycling Industries."

24. See Platt, *Weaving Textile Reuse into Waste Reduction*, or Council for Textile Recycling, "Don't Overlook Textiles!"

25. The debate over the efficacy of World Bank programs in Africa is an extensive one. For an African perspective, see the papers collected in Mkandawire and Soludo, *African Voices on Structural Adjustment*.

26. Waters, "Beyond Structural Adjustment."

Conclusion

1. "No Sweat," *The Economist*.

2. For a review of this literature, see Irwin, *Against the Tide*.

3. Quoted in Rothgeb, *U.S. Trade Policy*, 17.

BIBLIOGRAPHY

Aaronson, Susan A., with forewords by William V. Roth, Jr. and Robert T. Matsui. *Trade and the American Dream: A Social History of Postwar Trade Policy.* Lexington, KY: University Press of Kentucky, 2004.

Aaronson, Susan A., with forewords by Pat Choate and I.M. Destler. *Taking Trade to the Streets: The Lost History of Public Efforts to Shape Globalization.* Ann Arbor, MI: University of Michigan Press, 2004.

Aggarwal, Vinod K. *Liberal Protectionism: The International Politics of Organized Textile Trade.* Berkeley: University of California Press, 1985.

Aiken, Charles S. *The Cotton Plantation South: Since the Civil War.* Baltimore, MD: Johns Hopkins University Press, 1998.

Ali, Abdulsamad. "Clothes Worth Sh960m from China Set Ablaze." *The Nation (Nairobi)* (July 17, 2004).

Anderson, Kym, ed. *New Silk Roads: East Asia and World Textile Markets.* Cambridge: Cambridge University Press, 1992.

Anthony, W.S., and William D. Mayfield, eds. *Cotton Ginners Handbook.* Washington, DC: U.S. Department of Agriculture, 1994.

Bakken, Børge, ed. *Migration in China.* Copenhagen: NIAS, 1998.

Barasa, Lucas. "Cheap Imports Killing Kenya's Textile Industry." *The Nation (Nairobi)* (November 24, 1998).

Beazer, William F. *The Commercial Future of Hong Kong.* New York: Praeger Publishers, 1978.

Berger, Suzanne, and Richard K. Lester, eds. *Made by Hong Kong.* Hong Kong: Oxford University Press, 1997.

Bhagwati, Jagdish N. *In Defense of Globalization.* New York: Oxford University Press, 2004.

Blewett, M.H. *Surviving Hard Times: The Working People of Lowell.* Lowell, MA: Lowell Museum, 1982.

———. *The Last Generation: Work and Life in the Textile Mills of Lowell Massachusetts, 1910–1960.* Amherst, MA: University of Massachusetts Press, 1990.

Blue, Gregory. "China and Western Social Thought in the Modern Period." In *China and Historical Capitalism: Genealogies of Sinological Knowledge,* edited by Timothy Brook and Gregory Blue. Cambridge: Cambridge University Press, 1999.

Blustein, Paul. "A Pakistani Setback." *The Washington Post* (December 26, 2001): A01.

———. "Textile Makers Fight for Limits; With Caps Expiring, U.S. Industry Fears Glut of Chinese Imports." *The Washington Post* (October 13, 2004): E01.

Brandis, R. Buford. *The Making of Textile Trade Policy, 1935–1981.* Washington, DC: American Textile Manufacturers Institute, 1982.

Brattain, M. "Making Friends and Enemies: Textile Workers and Political Action in Post-World War II Georgia." *The Journal of Southern History* 63, no. 1 (February 1997): 91–138.

Breeden, James O., ed. *Advice Among Masters: The Ideal in Slave Management in the Old South.* Westport, CT: Greenwood Press, 1980.

Brill, Bernard. "Textiles." In *The McGraw-Hill Recycling Handbook,* edited by Herbert F. Lund, 17.1–17.12. New York: McGraw Hill, 2001.

Bruchey, Stuart. *Cotton and the Growth of the American Economy: 1790–1860.* New York: Harcourt, Brace, 1967.

Buckley, J. Taylor. "Starting at the Bottom: Plucky Entrepreneurs Roll Out Cotton Toilet Tissue." *USA Today* (August 14, 1998): 2B.

Bussey, Jane. "China to Collar Textiles?" *The Miami Herald,* July 22, 2004, C1.

Byerly, Victoria. *Hard Times Cotton Mill Girls: Personal Histories of Womanhood and Poverty in the South.* Ithaca, NY: ILR Press, 1986.

Callender, Guy S. "The Early Transportation and Banking Enterprises of the States in Relation to the Growth of Corporations." *Quarterly Journal of Economics* 17 (1903): 114–131.

Carr, Stephen J. *Improving Cash Crops in Africa: Factors Influencing the Productivity of Cotton, Coffee, and Tea Grown by Smallholders.* World Bank Technical Paper No. 216. Washington, DC: World Bank, 1993.

Chan, Anita. *China's Workers Under Assault: The Exploitation of Labor in a Globalizing Economy (Asia and the Pacific).* Armonk and London: M.E. Sharpe, 2001.

Chao, Kang, and Jessica C.Y. Chao. *The Development of Cotton Textile Production in China.* n.p.: Harvard University, East Asian Research Center, 1977.

Chesneaux, Jean. *The Chinese Labor Movement 1919–1927.* Stanford, CA: Stanford University Press, 1968.

Chokki, Toshiaki. "Labor Management in the Cotton Spinning Industry." In *Japanese Economic History 1600–1960: The Textile Industry and the Rise of the Japanese Economy,* edited by Michael Smitka. New York: Garland Publishing, 1998.

Christy, David. *Cotton Is King.* Reprinted in *Cotton Is King and Pro-Slavery Arguments,* edited by E.N. Elliott. Augusta, GA: Pritchard, Abbott & Zoomis, 1860.

Cline, William R. *The Future of World Trade in Textiles and Apparel.* (Rev. ed.) Washington, DC: Institute for International Economics, 1990.

Cobb, Thomas R. *An Inquiry into the Law of Negro Slavery in the United States of America.* New York: Arno Press and the New York Times, 1858, reprinted 1968.

Coclanis, P.A. "Introduction: African Americans in Southern Agriculture, 1877–1945." *Agricultural History* 72, no. 2 (Spring 1998): 135–139.

Cohen-Lack, Nancy. "A Struggle for Sovereignty: National Consolidation, Emancipation, and Free Labor in Texas, 1865." *The Journal of Southern History* 63, no. 1 (February 1992): 57–98.

Conkin, P.K. "Hot Humid and Sad." *The Journal of Southern History* 64, no. 1 (February 1998): 3–22.

Conti, Delia B. *Reconciling Free Trade, Fair Trade, and Interdependence: The Rhetoric of Presidential Economic Leadership.* Westport, CT: Praeger, 1998.

Cook, Sarah, and Margaret Maurer-Fazio, eds. *The Workers' State Meets the Market: Labour in China's Transition.* London: Frank Cass, 1999.

Copeland, Melvin Thomas. *The Cotton Manufacturing Industry of the United States.* New York: Augustus M. Kelly, 1966.

Coulson, Andrew. *Tanzania: A Political Economy.* Oxford: Clarendon Press, 1982.

Council for Textile Recycling. *Don't Overlook Textiles!* (1997).

Dalzell, Robert F., Jr. *Enterprising Elites: The Boston Associates and the World They Made.* NY: W.W. Norton, 1987.

Daniel, Pete. "The Transformation of the Rural South 1930 to the Present." *Agricultural History* 55, no. 3 (July 1981): 231–248.

———. *Breaking the Land: The Transformation of Cotton, Tobacco, and Rice Cultures Since 1880.* Urbana and Chicago: University of Illinois Press, 1985.

———. "Rhythm of the Land." *Agricultural History* 68, no. 4 (Fall 1994): 1–22.

Daniels, C. "Gresham's Laws: Labor Management on an Early-Eighteenth-Century Chesapeake Plantation." *The Journal of Southern History* 62, no. 2 (May 1996): 205–238.

Danielson, Anders, and Gun Eriksson Skoog. "From Stagnation to Growth in Tanzania: Breaking the Vicious Circle of High Aid and Bad Governance?" In *From Crisis to Growth in Africa?*, edited by Mats Lundahl. London: Routledge, 2001.

Day, Richard H. "The Economics of Technological Change and the Demise of the Sharecropper." *The American Economic Review* 57, no. 3 (June 1967): 427–449.

Dean, Judith M. "The Effects of the U.S. MFA on Small Exporters." *The Review of Economics and Statistics* 72, no. 1 (February 1990): 63–69.

———. "Market Disruption and the Incidence of VERs Under the MFA." *The Review of Economics and Statistics* 77, no. 2 (May 1995): 383–388.

Deane, Phyllis. *The First Industrial Revolution.* 2nd ed. Cambridge: Cambridge University Press, 1979.

DeBow, J.D.B., ed. *A Mississippi Planter, in Industrial Resources of the Southern and Western States.* 3 volumes. Washington, DC: DeBow, 1852.

De Jonquieres, Guy. "Clothes on the Line." *Financial Times* (July 19, 2004): 13.

De Jonquieres, Guy, and Frances Williams. "Top WTO Nations Hail Deal on Doha." *Financial Times* (August 2, 2004): 1.

De Melo, Jaime, and David Tarr. "Welfare Costs of U.S. Quotas in Textiles, Steel and Autos." *The Review of Economics and Statistics* (1990): 489–497.

Destler, I.M. *American Trade Politics.* 3rd ed. Washington, DC: Institute for International Economics, 1995.

Destler, I.M., Haruhiro Fukui, and Hideo Sato. *Textile Wrangle: Conflict in Japanese-American Relations, 1969–1971.* Ithaca, NY: Cornell University Press, 1979.

Dewan, Shaila, "Black Farmers' Refrain: Where's All Our Money?" *New York Times* (August 1, 2004).

Dickerson, Kitty, *Textiles and Apparel in the Global Economy.* 3rd ed. Upper Saddle River, NJ: Merrill, Prentice-Hall, 1999.

Dodge, Bertha S. *Cotton: The Plant That Would Be King.* Austin, TX: University of Texas Press, 1984.

Dodson, Charles. "Financial and Structural Characteristics of U.S. Commercial Cotton Farms, 1991–1992." *Economic Research Service*, no. 715.

Donaldson, G.F., and J.P. McInerney. "Changing Machinery Technology and Agricultural Adjustment." *American Journal of Agricultural Economics* 55, no. 5 (December 1973): 829–839.

Dougherty, Carter. "Trade Theory vs. Used Clothes in Africa." *New York Times* (June 3, 2004): Col. 3, p. 1.

Dougherty, Peter J. *Who's Afraid of Adam Smith?: How the Market Got Its Soul.* Hoboken, NJ: John Wiley & Sons, 2002.

Dublin, T. *Women at Work: The Transformation of Work and Community in Lowell, Massachusetts, 1826–1860.* New York: Columbia University Press, 1979.

———. *Farm to Factory: Women's Letters, 1830–1860.* 2nd ed. New York: Columbia University Press, 1993.

———. *Transforming Women's Work: New England Lives in the Industrial Revolution.* Ithaca, NY: Cornell University Press, 1994.

Dupre, Daniel. "Ambivalent Capitalists on the Cotton Frontier: Settlement and Development in the Tennessee Valley of Alabama." *The Journal of Southern History* 56, no. 2 (May 1990): 215–240.

Earle, Carville. "The Price of Precocity: Technical Choice and Ecological Constraint in the Cotton South, 1840–1890." *Agricultural History* 66, no. 3 (Summer 1992): 25–60.

Eckes, Alfred E., Jr. *Opening America's Market: U.S. Foreign Trade Policy Since 1776.* Chapel Hill, NC: University of North Carolina Press, 1995.

Economic Research Service. "Briefing Room: Cotton Trade," July 19, 2002.

Eisa, Hamdy M., et al. *Cotton Production Prospects for the Decade to 2005: A Global Overview.* World Bank Technical Paper No. 231. Washington, DC: World Bank, 1994.

Eisler, B. *The Lowell Offering.* Philadelphia, PA: J.B. Lippincott Company, 1977.

Engels, Friedrich. *The Condition of the Working Class in England,* Translated and edited by W.O. Henderson and W.H. Chaloner. New York: Macmillan, 1958.

Fafchamps, Marcel. *Market Institutions in Sub-Saharan Africa: Theory and Evidence.* Cambridge: MIT Press, 2004.

Farnie, D.A. *The English Cotton Industry and the World Market 1815–1896.* Oxford: Clarendon Press, 1979.

Featherstone, Liza, and United Students Against Sweatshops. *Students Against Sweatshops.* London: Verso, 2002.

Ferleger, L. "Sharecropping Contracts in the Late Nineteenth-Century South." *Agricultural History* 67, no. 3 (Summer 1993): 31–46.

Finlay, Mark R. "The Industrial Utilization of Farm Products and By-Products: The USDA Regional Research Laboratories." *Agricultural History* 64, no. 2 (Spring 1990): 41–53.

Foley, Neil. "Mexicans, Mechanization, and the Growth of Corporate Cotton Culture in South Texas: The Taft Ranch, 1900–1930." *The Journal of Southern History* 62, no. 2 (May 1996): 275–302.

———. *The White Scourge: Mexicans, Blacks, and Poor Whites in Texas Cotton Culture.* Berkeley and Los Angeles, CA: University of California Press, 1997.

Fong, Mei. "A Chinese Puzzle," *The Wall Street Journal,* August 16, 2004, B1.

Friedman, Thomas. *The Lexus and the Olive Tree: Understanding Globalization.* New York: Anchor, 2000.

Friman, H. Richard. "Rocks, Hard Places, and the New Protectionism: Textile Trade Policy Choices in the United States and Japan." *International Organization* 42, no. 4 (Autumn 1988): 689–723.

———. *Patchwork Protectionism: Textile Trade Policy in the United States, Japan, and West Germany.* Ithaca: Cornell University Press, 1990.

Fulton, M. "The Future of Canadian Agricultural Cooperatives: A Property Rights Approach." *American Journal of Agricultural Economics* 77 (December 1995): 1144–1152.

Galenson, Walter, ed. *Economic Growth and Structural Change in Taiwan: The Postwar Experience of the Republic of China.* Ithaca: Cornell University Press, 1979.

Gardner, B.L. "The Federal Government in Farm Commodity Markets: Recent Reform Efforts in a Long-Term Context." *Agricultural History* 70, no. 2 (Spring 1996): 177–195.

"Garment Sector Will Survive After Quotas," just-style.com (June 22, 2004).

Garside, A.H. *Cotton Goes to Market: A Graphic Description of a Great Industry.* New York: Frederick A. Stokes Company, 1935.

Gillham, Fred E.M., et al. *Cotton Production Prospects for the Next Decade.* World Bank Technical Paper No. 287. Washington, DC: World Bank, 1995.

Glade, Edward H., Jr., Mae Dean Johnson, and Leslie A. Meyer. "U.S. Cotton Distribution Patterns, 1993/94." *Economic Research Service/USDA,* No. 940.

Glade, Edward H., Jr., Leslie A. Meyer, and Stephen MacDonald. "Cotton: Background for 1995 Farm Legislation." *Agricultural Economic Report,* No. 706 (April 1995): 1–30.

Glade, Edward H., Jr., Leslie A. Meyer, and Harold Stults. "The Cotton Industry in the United States." *Economic Research Service/USDA,* No. 739.

Goodman, Peter S. "In China's Cities, a Turn From Factories; Labor Pool Shifts as Urban Workers Seek Better Lives," *The Washington Post,* September 25, 2004, A1.

Greider, William. *One World, Ready or Not: The Manic Logic of Global Capitalism.* New York: Simon & Schuster, 1997.

Gresser, Edward. "It's Expensive Being Poor." *The Far Eastern Economic Review* (June 10, 2004).

———. "Who Gets Hit?" Progressive Policy Institute, June 11, 2003. http://www.ppionline.org/ppi_ci.cfm?knlgAreaID=108&subsecID=900010&contentID=251757.

Grim, V. "The Politics of Inclusion: Black Farmers and the Quest for Agribusiness Participation, 1945–1990s." *Agricultural History* 69, no. 2 (Spring 1995): 257–271.

Grove, Wayne A. "The Mexican Farm Labor Program, 1942–1964: Government-Administered Labor Market Insurance for Farmers." *Agricultural History* 70, no. 2 (Spring 1996): 302–320.

Gwin, Adrian. "Looking Back: No Cotton Picking for Me, Thanks." *Charleston Daily Mail* (January 9, 1999): 6A.

Hall, Jacquelyn Dowd, et al. *Like a Family: The Making of a Southern Cotton Mill World.* New York: W.W. Norton & Company, 1987.

Hammond, James Henry. "On the Admission of Kansas," Speech before the U.S. Senate, March 4, 1858. *Congressional Globe:* 959.

Hammond, Matthew B. "Correspondence of Eli Whitney Relative to the Invention of the Cotton Gin." *American Historical Review* 3, no. 1 (October 1897).

Hanlan, J.P. *The Working Population of Manchester, New Hampshire, 1840–1886*. Ann Arbor, MI: UMI Research Press, 1981.

Hansen, Karen Tranberg. *Salaula: The World of Secondhand Clothing and Zambia*. Chicago and London: University of Chicago Press, 2000.

Hareven, T.K. *Family Time and Industrial Time: The Relationship Between the Family and Work in a New England Industrial Community*. New York: Cambridge University Press, 1982.

Hareven, Tamara K., and Randolph Langenbach. *Amoskeag: Life and Work in an American Factory-City*. Hanover: University Press of New England, 1978.

Hart, Chad E. "Agricultural Situation Spotlight: How the Brazil-U.S. Cotton Dispute Could Affect Iowa's Agriculture." *Iowa Ag Review* 10, no. 3 (Summer 2004).

Hartman, Laura P., Dennis G. Arnold, and Richard E. Wokutch, eds. *Rising Above Sweatshops*. Westport, CT: Praeger, 2003.

Hayes, Keri. "Aquaculture Gets Hooked on Oilmeals." *Bluebook Update Online Archive*.

Hayter, Delmar. "Expanding the Cotton Kingdom." *Agricultural History* 62, no. 2 (1988): 225–233.

Hearden, Patrick J. *Independence and Empire: The New South's Cotton Mill Campaign 1865–1901*. DeKalb, IL: Northern Illinois University Press, 1982.

Hessler, Peter. "Letter from China: Boomtown Girl, Finding a New Life in the Golden City." *The New Yorker* (May 28, 2001): 108–119.

Hirst, F.W. *From Adam Smith to Philip Snowden: A History of Free Trade in Great Britain*. New York: Adelphi Company, 1925.

Holleran, Philip M. "Child Labor and Exploitation in Turn-of-the-Century Cotton Mills." *Explorations in Economic History* 30 (1993): 485–500.

Honig, Emily. *Sisters and Strangers: Women in the Shanghai Cotton Mills 1919–1949*. Stanford, CA: Stanford University Press, 1986.

————. *Creating Chinese Ethnicity: Subei People in Shanghai 1850–1980*. New Haven: Yale University Press, 1992.

"How To Make Africa Smile: A Survey of Sub-Saharan Africa." *The Economist* (January 17, 2004): 3–16.

Hufbauer, Gary Clyde, and Kimberly Ann Elliott. *Measuring the Costs of Protection in the United States*. Washington, DC: Institute for International Economics, 1994.

"Human Rights in China." *Institutionalized Exclusion: The Tenuous Legal Status of Internal Migrants in China's Major Cities*. Report by HRIC (November 6, 2002).

Hutchins, B.L., and A. Harrison. *A History of Factory Legislation*. New York: Burt Franklin, 1903.

Ikenson, Dan. *Threadbare Excuses: The Textile Industry's Campaign to Preserve Import Restraints*. Trade Policy Analysis No. 25. Washington, DC: CATO Institute, Center for Trade Policy Studies, 2003.

Iredale, Robyn, Naran Bilik, and Fei Guo, eds. *China's Minorities on the Move: Selected Case Studies*. New York: M.E. Sharpe, 2003.

Irwin, Douglas A. *Against the Tide: An Intellectual History of Free Trade*. Princeton, N.J.: Princeton University Press, 1996.

————. *Free Trade Under Fire*. Princeton, NJ: Princeton University Press, 2002.

Jacobson, Timothy Curtis, and George David Smith. *Cotton's Renaissance: A Study in Market Innovation*. Cambridge: Cambridge University Press, 2001.

Jeter, Jon. "The Dumping Ground: As Zambia Courts Western Markets, Used Goods Arrive at a Heavy Price," *The Washington Post*, April 22, 2002, A1.

Johnson, Charles S., Edwin R. Embree, and W.W. Alexander. *The Collapse of Cotton Tenancy*. Chapel Hill, NC: University of North Carolina Press, 1935.

Johnson, G.L. "A Forward Look at Agricultural Policy Analysis (Based on 1945–1995 Experiences)." *Agricultural History* 70, no. 2 (Spring 1996): 153–176.

Josephson, H. *The Golden Threads: New England's Mill Girls and Magnates*. NY: Duell, Sloan and Pearce, 1949.

Josling, Timothy. *Agricultural Trade Policy: Completing the Reform*. Washington, DC: Institute for International Economics, 1998.

Just-style.com. "Cambodia: Garment Sector Will Survive After Quotas," June 22, 2004. http://www.just-style.com/news_detail.asp accessed August 10, 2004.

Kane, N.F. *Textiles in Transition: Technology, Wages, and Industry Relocation in the U.S. Textile Industry, 1880–1930*. Westport, CT: Greenwood Press, 1988.

Karp, Jonathan. "Deadly Crop: Difficult Times Drive India's Cotton Farmers to Desperate Action." *Wall Street Journal* (February 18, 1998): 1A.

Kim, Seung-Kyung. *Class Struggle or Family Struggle? The Lives of Women Factory Workers in South Korea*. New York: Cambridge University Press, 1997.

Knight, John, Lina Song, and Jia Huaibin. "Chinese Rural Migrants in Urban Enterprises: Three Perspectives." In *The Workers' State Meets the Market: Labour in China's Transition*, edited by Sarah Cook and Margaret Maurer Fazio. London: Frank Cass, 1999.

Krishna, K.M., and L.H. Tan. *Rags and Riches: Implementing Apparel Quotas Under the Multi-Fibre Arrangement*. Ann Arbor, MI: University of Michigan Press, 1998.

Kristof, Nicholas D., and Sheryl WuDunn. *Thunder from the East: Portrait of a Rising Asia*. New York: Alfred A. Knopf, 2000.

Kuhn, Anthony. "Migrants: A High Price to Pay for a Job." *Far Eastern Economic Review* (January 22, 2004): 30–32.

Kung, Lydia. *Factory Women in Taiwan*. New York: Columbia University Press, 1994.

Landes, D.S. *The Wealth and Poverty of Nations: Why Some Are So Rich and Some So Poor*. New York: W. W. Norton, 1998.

Lang, Mahlon G. "The Future of Agricultural Cooperatives in Canada and the United States: Discussion." *American Journal of Agricultural Economics* 77, no. 5 (December 1995): 1162–1165.

Lee, Ching Kwan. *Gender and the South China Miracle: Two Worlds of Factory Women*. Berkeley: University of California Press, 1998.

Lemire, Beverly. *Fashion's Favourite: The Cotton Trade and the Consumer in Britain, 1660–1800*. New York: Oxford University Press, 1991.

Lichtenstein, J. *Field to Fabric: The Story of American Cotton Growers*. Lubbock, TX: Texas Tech University Press, 1990.

Ling, Pan. *In Search of Old Shanghai*. Hong Kong, 1982.

Losciale, Alessandra. "Rules May Ease Aches of Workers: Employers Protest Ergonomic Standard." *The Denver Post* (January 2, 2001): Business Sec., p. C-01.

Lynch, John. *Toward an Orderly Market: An Intensive Study of Japan's Voluntary Quota in Cotton Textile Exports*. Tokyo: Sophia University, 1968.

Magnusson, Paul, et al. "Where Free Trade Hurts: Thirty Million Jobs Could Disappear with the End of Apparel Quotas." *Business Week Online* (December 15, 2003).

Malone, Scott. "Low-Wage Nations Import Share to Surge." *Women's Wear Daily* (June 3, 2004): 1.

Marcus, A.I. "The Wisdom of the Body Politic: The Changing Nature of Publicly Sponsored American Agricultural Research Since the 1830s." *Agricultural History* 62, no. 2 (1988): 4–26.

McCracken, Elizabeth. "The Lives They Lived: Rose Freedman, B. 1893: Out of the Fire." *New York Times* (December 30, 2001): Sec. 6, Col. 1, p. 19.

McNamara, Dennis L. *Textiles and Industrial Transition in Japan.* Ithaca: Cornell University Press, 1995.

Metcalfe, Mark R., and Barry K. Goodwin. "An Empirical Analysis of the Determinants of Trade Policy Protection in the U.S. Manufacturing Sector." *Journal of Policy Modeling* 21, no. 2 (March 1999): 153–165.

Micklethwait, John, and Adrian Wooldridge. *A Future Perfect: The Challenge and Promise of Globalization.* New York: Random House, 2003.

"Millions Go Up in Smoke as Fire Guts Huge Market." *Panafrican News Agency (PANA) Daily Newswire* (September 6, 2000).

Minchin, Timothy J. *What Do We Need a Union For?* Chapel Hill: University of North Carolina Press, 1977.

"The Misery of Manufacturing." *The Economist* (September 27, 2003): 61–62.

Mitchell, R. B. *International Historical Statistics: The Americas, 1750–1993.* London: Macmillan Reference, 1998.

Mkandawire, Thandika, and Adebayo Olukoshi, eds. *Between Liberalisation and Oppression: The Politics of Structural Adjustment in Africa.* Dakar, Senegal: CODESRIA, 1995.

Mkandawire, Thandika, and Charles C. Soludo, eds. *African Voices on Structural Adjustment: A Companion to Our Continent, Our Future.* Trenton, NJ: Africa World Press, 2003.

"Mobility in China: Off to the City." *The Economist* (September 1, 2001): 36.

Moore, John H. "Two Cotton Kingdoms." *Agricultural History* 60, no. 4 (Fall 1986): 1–16.

————. *The Emergence of the Cotton Kingdom in the Old Southwest: Mississippi, 1770–1860.* Baton Rouge, LA: Louisiana State University Press, 1988.

Moran, Theodore H. *Beyond Sweatshops: Foreign Direct Investment and Globalization in Developing Countries.* Washington, DC: Brookings Institution Press, 2002.

Moser, Charles K. *The Cotton Textile Industry of Far Eastern Countries.* Boston: Pepperell Manufacturing Company, 1930.

Nathan Associates. *Changes in Global Trade Rules for Textiles and Apparel: Implications for Developing Countries,* November 20, 2002.

National Labor Committee. *Behind the Label "Made in China,"* Executive Summary, 1, 1998.

Nordas, H.K. *The Global Textile and Clothing Industry Post the Agreement on Textiles and Clothing* (WTO Working Paper ERSD). Geneva, Switzerland: World Trade Organization, 2004.

Norris, Lucy. "Cloth That Lies: The Secrets of Recycling in India." In *Clothing as Material Culture,* edited by S. Küchler and D. Miller. Oxford: Berg, 2004.

————. "Creative Entrepreneurs: The Recycling of Second-Hand Indian Clothing." In *Old Clothes, New Looks: Second Hand Fashion*, edited by A. Palmer and H. Clark. Oxford: Berg, 2004.

"No Sweat; Sportswear." *The Economist* (August 21, 2004).

Novak, James L., Greg Traxler, Max Runge, and Charles Mitchell, Jr. "The Effect of Mechanical Harvesting Technology on Southern Piedmont Cotton Production, 1896–1991." *Agricultural History* 69, no. 2 (Spring 1995): 349–367.

"Off to the City" *The Economist* (September 1, 2001): 36.

Olmstead, Alan L., Bruce F. Johnston, and Brian G. Sims. "Forward to the Past: The Diffusion of Animal-Powered Tillage Equipment on Small Farms in Mexico." *Agricultural History* 60, no. 1 (Winter 1986): 62–72.

"One of the World's Oldest Recycling Industries." *The Massrecycler* 8, no 4 (September/October): 1.

Oxfam. *Cultivating Poverty: The Impact of US Cotton Subsidies on Africa* (Oxfam Briefing Paper No. 30). Oxfam International, 2002.

Pan, Suwen, et al. *The Impact of U.S. Cotton Programs on the World Market: An Analysis of Brazilian and West and Central African WTO Petitions*. Lubbock, TX: Texas Tech University, 2004.

Park, Young-Il, and Kym Anderson. "The Rise and Demise of Textiles and Clothing in Economic Development: The Case of Japan." *Economic Development and Cultural Change* 39, no. 3 (April 1991): 531–548.

Pinchbeck, Ivy. *Women Workers and the Industrial Revolution, 1750–1850*. London: Virago, 1969.

Platt, Brenda. *Weaving Textile Reuse into Waste Reduction*. Washington, DC: Institute for Local Self-Reliance, 1997.

Polanyi, Karl, with foreword by Robert M. MacIver. *The Great Transformation*. Boston: Beacon Press, 1944.

Pollin, Robert, Justine Burns, and James Heintz. *Global Apparel Production and Sweatshop Labor: Can Raising Retail Prices Finance Living Wages?* (PERI Working Paper Series No. 19, Rev., April 2002). Amherst, MA: University of Massachusetts Amherst, Political Economy Research Institute, 2002.

Pomeranz, Kenneth. *The Great Divergence: China, Europe and the Making of the Modern World Economy*. Princeton, NJ: Princeton University Press, 2000.

Poonyth, Daneswar, et al. *The Impact of Domestic and Trade Policies on the World Cotton Market* (FAO Commodities and Trade Policy Research Working Paper No. 8, April 2004). FAO, Commodities and Trade Division, 2004.

Porter, Michael E. *The Competitive Advantage of Nations*. New York: The Free Press, 1990.

Pressley, Sue Anne. "The South's New-Car Smell: As Auto Plants Replace Region's Textile Mills, an Economy and a Way of Life Undergo Changes." *The Washington Post* (May 11, 2001): A22.

Progressive Policy Institute. *Who Gets Hit? A Summary of Tariff Policy in 2002* (June 11, 2003).

Quinn, John James. *The Road Oft Traveled: Development Policies and Majority State Ownership of Industry in Africa*. Westport, CT: Praeger, 2002.

Ramey, Joanna. "Wal-Mart Gets Political," *Women's Wear Daily*, August 2, 2004.

Reed, David. *Economic Change, Governance and Natural Resource Wealth: The Political Economy of Change in Southern Africa*. London: Earthscan, 2001.

Reidy, Joseph P. *From Slavery to Agrarian Capitalism in the Cotton Plantation South: Central Georgia, 1800–1880*. Chapel Hill, NC: University of North Carolina Press, 1992.

Richards, H.I. *Cotton and the AAA*. Menasha, WI: George Banta Publishing, 1936.

Robson, R. *The Cotton Industry in Britain*. London: Macmillan, 1957.

Rose, Mary B. *Firms, Networks and Business Values: The British and American Cotton Industries Since 1750*. Cambridge: Cambridge University Press, 2000.

Rosen, Ellen Israel. *Bitter Choices: Blue-Collar Women in and out of Work*. Chicago: University of Chicago Press, 1987.

———. *Making Sweatshops: The Globalization of the U.S. Apparel Industry*. Berkeley: University of California Press, 2002.

Rosengarten, T. *All God's Dangers: The Life of Nate Shaw*. New York: Alfred A. Knopf, 1974.

Rosoff, Robert J. "Beyond Codes of Conduct: Addressing Labor Rights Problems in China." *The China Business Review Online* (March-April 2004).

Rostow, W.W. *The Process of Economic Growth*. 2nd ed. New York: The Norton Library, 1962.

———. *How It All Began: Origins of the Modern Economy*. New York: McGraw-Hill, 1975.

Rothgeb, John M., Jr. *U.S. Trade Policy: Balancing Economic Dreams and Political Realities*. Washington, DC: CQ Press, 2001.

Rothstein, Morton. "The New South and the International Economy." *Agricultural History* 57, no. 4 (October 1983): 385–402.

Rozelle, Scott, J. Edward Taylor, and Alan DeBrauw. "Migration, Remittances, and Agricultural Productivity in China." *American Economic Review* 89, no. 2 (May 1999): 287–291.

Saxonhouse, Gary, and Gavin Wright. "Two Forms of Cheap Labor in Textile History." In *Japanese Economic History 1600–1960: The Textile Industry and the Rise of the Japanese Economy*, edited by Michael Smitka. New York: Garland Publishing, 1998.

Sayre, Charles R. "Cotton Mechanization Since World War II." *Agricultural History* 53, no. 1 (January 1979): 105–124.

Schiller, Wendy J. "Trade Politics in the American Congress: A Study of the Interaction of Political Geography and Interest Group Behavior." *Political Geography* 18, no. 7 (September 1999): 769–789.

Schlosser, Eric. "Urban Life: Saturday Night at the Hacienda, How Manchester, England Transformed Itself from a Bleak Industrial-Age Relic into a Postindustrial Entertainment Zone." *Atlantic Monthly* 282, no. 4 (October 1998): 22.

Schmidt, James D. *Free to Work: Labor Law, Emancipation, and Reconstruction, 1815–1880*. Athens, GA: University of Georgia Press, 1998.

Schott, Jeffrey J., and Johanna W. Buurman. *The Uruguay Round: An Assessment*. Washington, DC: Institute for International Economics, 1994.

Scott, Maurice. "Foreign Trade." In *Economic Growth and Structural Change in Taiwan: The Postwar Experience of the Republic of China*. Ithaca: Cornell University Press, 1979.

Shui, S., John C. Beghin, and Michael Wohlgenant. "The Impact of Technical Change, Scale Effects, and Forward Ordering on U.S. Fiber Demands." *American Journal of Agricultural Economics* 75, no. 3 (August 1993): 632–641.

Smedes, Susan D. *Memorials of a Southern Planter.* Baltimore, MD: Cushing and Bailey, 1887.

Smitka, Michael, ed. *Japanese Economic History 1600–1960: The Textile Industry and the Rise of the Japanese Economy.* New York: Garland Publishing, 1998.

Snyder, R.E. *Cotton Crisis.* Chapel Hill, NC: University of North Carolina Press, 1984.

Solinger, Dorothy J. *Contesting Citizenship in Urban China: Peasant Migrants, the State, and the Logic of the Market.* Berkeley, CA: University of California Press, 1999.

Song, Byung-Nak. *The Rise of the Korean Economy,* 2nd ed. Hong Kong: Oxford University Press, 1997.

Spar, Debora, and Jennifer Burns. "Hitting the Wall: Nike and International Labor Practices," Harvard Business School Press, Case 9-700-047. 2000, rev 2002.

Spiegelman, Matthew, and Robert H. McGuckin III. *China's Experience with Productivity and Jobs* (Report No. R-1352-04-RR). (June 2004).

Stein, Leon, ed. *Out of the Sweatshop: The Struggle for Industrial Democracy.* New York: Quadrangle/New York Time Books, 1977.

Street, James H. *The New Revolution in the Cotton Economy: Mechanization and Its Consequences.* Chapel Hill, NC: University of North Carolina Press, 1957.

Sumner, Daniel A. *A Quantitative Simulation Analysis of the Impacts of U.S. Cotton Subsidies on Cotton Prices and Quantities* (Prepared for WTO Dispute Panel). Davis, CA: University of California Agricultural Issues Center.

"A Survey of Sub-Saharan Africa," *The Economist* (January 17, 2004).

Tanzer, Andrew. "The Great Quota Hustle." *Forbes* (March 6, 2000): 119–125.

Thomas, H. *The Slave Trade: The Story of the Atlantic Slave Trade, 1440–1870.* New York: Simon & Schuster, 1997.

Thomas, Parakunnel Joseph. *Mercantilism and the East India Trade.* New York: A.M. Kelley, 1965.

Tokarick, Stephen. *Measuring the Impact of Distortions in Agricultural Trade in Partial and General Equilibrium.* Washington, DC: IMF, 2003.

"Tokyo Seized by Jeans Fever." *Fort Lauderdale Sun Sentinal* (July 27, 1997).

Tonelson, Alan. *The Race to the Bottom: Why a Worldwide Worker Surplus and Uncontrolled Free Trade Are Sinking American Living Standards.* CO: Westview Press, 2000.

Townsend, Terry. *Subsidies Beyond 2006.* Paper Presented to The Liverpool Cotton Association, Liverpool (October 2, 2003).

Trela, Irene, and John Whalley. "Global Effects of Developed Country Trade Restrictions on Textiles and Apparel." *The Economic Journal* 100 (December 1990): 1190–1205.

Tsurumi, E. Patricia. *Factory Girls: Women in the Thread Mills of Meiji Japan.* New Jersey: Princeton University Press, 1990.

Tucker, B.M. *Samuel Slater and the Origins of the American Textile Industry, 1790–1860.* Ithaca, NY: Cornell University Press, 1984.

Underhill, Geoffrey R.D. *Industrial Crisis and the Open Economy: Politics, Global Trade and the Textile Industry in the Advanced Economies.* New York: St. Martin's Press, 1998.

U.S. Department of Agriculture. *The Cotton Industry in the United States* (July 1996). Agricultural Economic Report No. 739. Washington, DC: USDA, 1996.

U.S. Department of Labor. *Wages, Benefits, Poverty Line, and Meeting Workers' Needs in the Apparel and Footwear Industries of Selected Countries.* Washington, DC: U.S. Department of Labor, ILAB, 2000.

U.S. International Trade Commission. www.dataweb.usitc.gov.

U.S. International Trade Commission. *The Economic Effects of Significant U.S. Import Restraints* (2nd update 1999). Investigation No. 332-325, Publication 3201. Washington, DC: USITC, 1999.

————. *Textiles and Apparel: Assessment of the Competitiveness of Certain Foreign Suppliers to the U.S. Market* (Vol. 1). Investigation No. 332-448, Publication No. 3671. Washington, DC: USITC, 2004.

————. *The Economic Effects of Significant U.S. Import Restraints* (4th update 2004). Investigation No. 332-325, Publication 3701. Washington, DC: USITC, June 2004.

Varley, Pamela, ed. *The Sweatshop Quandary: Corporate Responsibility on the Global Frontier.* Washington, DC: IRRS, 1998.

"Vintage T-Shirts: Could Yours Be Worth Big Bucks?" *The Washington Post* (October 17, 2004).

Wang, Feng, and Xuejin Zuo. "Inside China's Cities: Institutional Barriers and Opportunities for Urban Migrants." *American Economic Review* 89, no. 2 (May 1999): 276–280.

Ware, C.F. *The Early New England Cotton Manufacture: A Study in Industrial Beginnings.* Boston: Houghton Mifflin, 1931.

Waters, Tony. "Beyond Structural Adjustment: State and Market in a Rural Tanzania Village." *African Studies Review* 40, no. 2 (September 1997): 59–89.

Westcott, Paul C., C. Edwin Young, and J. Michael Price. *The 2002 Farm Act: Provisions and Implications for Commodity Markets* (Electronic rep. from the ERS). Agricultural Information Bulletin No. 778, USDA, Economic Research Service, November 2002.

Whayne, J.M. "Black Farmers and the Agricultural Cooperative Extension Service: The Alabama Experience, 1945–1965." *Agricultural History* 72, no. 3 (Summer 1998): 523–551.

Whigham, T. "Paraguay and the World Cotton Market: The "Crisis" of the 1860s." *Agricultural History* 68, no. 3 (Summer 1994): 1–15.

Wicks, Rick, and Arne Bigsten. *Used Clothes as Development Aid: The Political Economy of Rags* (Rep. of a Study for Sida—The Swedish International Development Cooperation Agency). Göteborg, Sweden: Göteborg University, Department of Economics, 1996.

Williams, Frances. "Talks Unravel over Cotton." *Financial Times* (September 16, 2003): 21.

Willoughby, Lynn. *Fair to Middlin': The Antebellum Cotton Trade of the Apalachicola/Chattahoochee River Valley.* Tuscaloosa, AL: University of Alabama Press, 1993.

Woeste, Victoria Saker. *The Farmer's Benevolent Trust: Law and Agricultural Cooperation in Industrial America, 1865–1945.* Chapel Hill, NC: University of North Carolina Press, 1998.

Wolf, Martin. *Why Globalization Works.* New Haven: Yale University Press, 2004.

Woodman, H.D. *King Cotton & His Retainers: Financing & Marketing the Cotton Crop of the South, 1800–1925.* Lexington, KY: University of Kentucky Press, 1968.

Woodman, Sophia. "China's Dirty Clean Up." *New York Review* (May 11, 2000): 50–52.

Woodruff, N.E. "Mississippi Delta Planters and Debates over Mechanization, Labor and Civil Rights in the 1940s." *The Journal of Southern History* 60, no. 2 (May 1994): 263–284.

World Bank. *A World Bank Country Study: Tanzania at the Turn of the Century—Background Papers and Statistics.* Washington, DC: Government of Tanzania and the World Bank, 2002.

———. *World Development Report.* Washington, DC: World Bank, 2003.

Wrenn, L.B. *Cinderella of the New South: A History of the Cottonseed Industry, 1855–1955.* Knoxville, TN: University of Tennessee Press, 1995.

Wright, Gavin. *The Political Economy of the Cotton South: Households, Markets, and Wealth in the Nineteenth Century.* New York: W. W. Norton, 1978.

———. "Cheap Labor and Southern Textiles, 1880–1930." *The Quarterly Journal of Economics* (November 1981): 605–629.

Zhao, Yaohui. "Leaving the Countryside: Rural-to-Urban Migration Decisions in China." *American Economic Review* 89, no. 2 (May 1999): 281–286.

Zinman, Greg. "Vintage T-Shirts; Could Yours Be Worth Big Bucks?" *The Washington Post* (October 17, 2004): M06.

INDEX

Cotton industry:
  in Africa, 7, 35, 36, 51, 54–55
  in American South, 8, 10–22, 27, 29, 33, 36, 53
  business practices in, 40
  in China, xvii, 17–19, 45, 48, 56, 65–70
  government subsidies for, 6, 8, 32–34
  imports/exports in, 50, 51, 52, 142
  in India, 17, 18, 153
  mechanization in, 27–30, 31, 35–38
  production process in, 66
  rise of, 9–10
  in Southeast Asia, 36
  in Texas, xvii, 22–27, 36–38, 41, 43, 45–49
  U.S. as leader in, 4–8, 11, 18–19, 51, 52, 72
  yields in, 4, 30
Cotton plant:
  characteristics of, 8
  growing of, 11–12
  harvesting of, 12, 29, 31
  maximizing use of, 41–45
  quality of, 47–48
  varieties of, 15
Cotton prices:
  under Farm Bill (2002), 49–50
  global, 51–52
  in 1930s, 32–33
  setting, 46–47
  technological innovation and, 75
  in West Africa, 55
Cottonseed, 15, 42–44
Cottonseed flour, 44
Cottonseed oil, 25, 43, 45
Cotton stripper, 36–38
Coulson, Andrew, 189n.
Crawford, Texas, 49
Crop Disaster Program, 50
Crop insurance, 51, 56
Crop lien laws, 21
Cultivating Poverty (Oxfam report), 5
Cultural Revolution (China), 64, 85
Custody and Repatriation laws (China), 89

DAGRIS Corporation, 55
Dar Es Salaam, Tanzania, 173, 190, 191, 194, 197
Dalzell, Robert F., Jr., ix, 78n
Daniel, Pete, 21n, 22n, 33n
Danielson, Anders, 189, 204n
Dawood, Abdul, 158
Day, Richard H., 27–28
Dayton Hudson, 136
Deane, Phyllis, 75n.

DeBow, J.D.B., 14n
De Jonquieres, Guy, 6n, 145n, 165n, 166n
DeMint, Jim, 158, 163–164
Democratization, 106, 204, 214
Destler, I.M., 83n, 134
Developing countries. *See also specific countries*
  economic growth of, 151–152, 167–168, 201
  fashion in, 208
  import quotas and, 165
  industrialization in, 152
  tariffs and, 164–165
Dewan, Shaila, 34n
Dewji, Gulam, 196, 197, 198, 200, 202, 205
Dickerson, Kitty G., 122n, 133n, 134n, 138n
Discrimination:
  in government farm programs, 34
  in textile mills, 92–93
Dodge, Bertha S., 9n, 74n
Dougherty, Peter, xi, 107
Dougherty, Carter, 199n
Douglas, Billie, 92
Dublin, T., 80n
Dupre, Daniel.

Earle, Carville, 12n
East India Company, 153
Economic growth:
  demise of mills and, 98, 100
  of developing countries, 151–152, 167–168, 201
  free trade and, 129, 149
  textiles role in, 76, 82
  working conditions and, 106–107
Economist, 89n, 141n, 200n, 211n
Edwards, John, 139–140
Eisa, Hamdy M., 4n, 54n, 56n
Eisenhower, Dwight, 124, 127
Elections, U.S. (2004), viii, 162, 211
Elliott, Kimberly Ann ,144
Employment:
  demise of, in textile industry, 98, 99, 112–113, 123, 139–142, 150, 199
  in Muslim countries, 172
  in retail industry, 124
  in Tanzanian mitumba industry, 200
  trade policy and, 144, 148, 162, 167–168
Engels, Friedrich, 103
Entrepreneurship:
  in Africa, 201, 204
  in Britain, 9, 155
  in China, 95, 145

Shanghai Number 36 Cotton Yarn Factory,
     65–68, 86, 105, 212
Sharecropping:
   government subsidies effect on, 33
   legacy of, 53
   rise of, 20–23
   textile industry and, 82
Sherry Manufacturing, xiii–xv, 111, 118, 212
Short Term Arrangement on Cotton Textiles
     (STA), 128
Skoog, Gun Eriksson, 189, 204n
Slavery. See also Plantations
   demise of, 20
   legacy of, 53
   in U.S. cotton industry, 8, 11, 13–14, 19
Smith, Adam, x, 213
Smith, George David 40n
Smuggling, of used clothing, 203
Snowflake factor, in clothing recycling, 178,
     182, 192, 193, 195
Social activism:
   anti-globalization, vii–viii, 70, 100–102, 145,
     169, 211, 212
   for improved working conditions, 101–107
Socialism:
   in African continent, 200–201
   in Tanzania, 189, 190
Solinger, Dorothy J., 87n
Soludo, Charles C., 207n
Song, Byung-Nak, 85n
Song, Lena, 89n, 90n
Sorini, Ron, 159
Spar, Debora, 106n
Spiegelman, Matthew, 142n
Spinning, of cotton, 74–75
Spinning jenny, 75
Sri Lanka, 148, 165, 167
State ownership:
   in Africa, 204
   in China, 67, 69
Street, James H., 22n
Stubin, Ed, 179, 180, 184–187, 191, 195, 203,
     209, 210, 213
Stubin, Eric, 179, 210
Stubin, Morton, 179, 210
Stubin, Sunny, 179, 181, 182
Stults, Harold, 4n.
Sumner, Daniel A., 52n
Su Qin, 69–70
Sweatshops:
   in China, 14, 68, 71–72, 213

competing with, 115
protections against, 169–170
protests against, xii, 211
as rural escape route, 90–97
in Taiwan and Korea, 84
T-shirt production in, 14
working conditions in, viii, 101–107

Taft, Charles, 23
Taft Ranch, 24
Taiwan, 84–85, 95, 128
TAL Apparel, 99
Tantillo, Auggie, 112–115, 117–120, 124–126,
     132–135, 150, 162, 166, 172
Tanzania:
   poverty in, 188–189
   recycled clothing industry in, 190–205, 207,
     208–209
   regime change in, 206–207
Tanzer, Andrew, 145, 146n
Tao Yong Fang, 59, 66, 67
Target, 159, 162
Tariffs:
   on apparel imports, 120, 130, 159, 160, 163
   Central American exports and, 169
   effect on developing countries, 164–165
   Kennedy's cuts in, 128, 137
   Muslim countries and, 171
   on recycled clothing imports, 199, 203
Taussig, Frank, 149
TELCOT, 48
Tenant farming. See Sharecropping
Tenenbaum, Inez, 163, 164
Texas, cotton industry in, xvii, 22–27, 36–38,
     41, 43, 45–49
Texas Tech University, 25, 26
Textile industry:
   in Britain, 9–10, 17–18, 75–78
   child labor in, 74, 76, 80, 81, 83, 102, 103
   in China, 62, 63, 69–72, 74, 89–90, 166–171,
     212
   cotton imports and, 50
   employment in, 140–142, 150, 199
   as global, 62, 84, 112, 115, 123
   import quotas in (see Import quotas)
   in Japan, 83–84
   modern economy and, 76, 99–100
   in Pakistan, 159–160
   political power of, 135, 161–164
   recycling in (see Clothing, recycled)
   in Tanzania, 196, 199–202